Dictionary of Educational Acronyms, Abbreviations, and Initialisms

Second Edition

Compiled and Edited by James C. Palmer
and Anita Y. Colby

ERIC Clearinghouse for Junior Colleges

ORYX PRESS
1985

The rare Arabian Oryx is believed to have inspired the myth of the unicorn. This desert antelope became virtually extinct in the early 1960s. At that time several groups of international conservationists arranged to have 9 animals sent to the Phoenix Zoo to be the nucleus of a captive breeding herd. Today the Oryx population is over 400 and herds have been returned to reserves in Israel, Jordan, and Oman.

Copyright © 1985 by
The Oryx Press
2214 North Central at Encanto
Phoenix, Arizona 85004-1483

Published simultaneously in Canada

Printed and Bound in the United States of America

Library of Congress Cataloging in Publication Data

Palmer, James C.
    Dictionary of educational acronyms, abbreviations,
and initialisms.

    1. Education—Acronyms.   2. Education—Abbreviations.
I. Colby, Anita Y.   II. ERIC Clearinghouse for Junior
Colleges.   III. Title.
LB15.P35   1985   370′.3′21   84-42814
ISBN 0-89774-165-X

Contents

Introduction

Since the publication of the first edition of the *Dictionary of Educational Acronyms, Abbreviations, and Initialisms*, thousands of documents, journal articles, and monographs have been added to the education literature. This second edition of the *Dictionary* provides an updated listing of acronyms and other short forms found in this new body of literature.

The majority of entries in this revised listing were gleaned from a review of the 1983 and 1984 editions of *Resources in Education*, as well as from a review of the 1983 and 1984 editions of 150 journals in the field of education. Care was taken to select journals representing a variety of educational topics, including the scope areas of the 16 ERIC (Educational Resources Information Center) Clearinghouses:

> ERIC Clearinghouse on Adult, Career, and Vocational Education
> ERIC Clearinghouse on Counseling and Personnel Services
> ERIC Clearinghouse on Educational Management
> ERIC Clearinghouse on Elementary and Early Childhood Education
> ERIC Clearinghouse on Handicapped and Gifted Children
> ERIC Clearinghouse on Higher Education
> ERIC Clearinghouse on Information Resources
> ERIC Clearinghouse for Junior Colleges
> ERIC Clearinghouse on Languages and Linguistics
> ERIC Clearinghouse on Reading and Communication Skills
> ERIC Clearinghouse on Rural Education and Small Schools
> ERIC Clearinghouse for Science, Mathematics and Environmental Education
> ERIC Clearinghouse for Social Studies/Social Science Education
> ERIC Clearinghouse on Teacher Education
> ERIC Clearinghouse on Tests, Measurement, and Evaluation
> ERIC Clearinghouse on Urban Education

Other sources include newsletters published by educational organizations and associations, the ERIC *Source Code Directory*, and acronyms listed for educational associations in the 18th edition of the *Encyclopedia of Associations* (Detroit: Gale, 1983). In all, the revised list includes 4,011 acronyms and other short forms that are part of the current education vocabulary. Of these, 1,995 did not appear in the first edition of the *Dictionary*. Users may wish to retain their copies of the first edition as a reference source for acronyms used in the education literature prior to 1983.

The *Dictionary* is arranged in two sections. In the first it is arranged alphabetically by acronym, and for identical acronyms, alphabetically by unabbreviated form. In the second entries are arranged alphabetically by their unabbreviated forms. The reverse list is published as a convenience to users; it should not serve as an authority list for these acronyms.

In most cases, each entry provides only the acronym and the terminology it represents. Occasionally, the entry will include a modifier in parentheses. The modifier usually indicates a geographic place or identifies a parent organization. For example:

OLPR   Office for Library Personnel Resources
         (American Library Association)
PASS   Portable Assisted Study Sequence Program
         (California)

Usually, the *Dictionary* provides only the unabbreviated form of the acronym and no additional clarification. Some entries begin with ''Not an acronym.'' This indicates to the user that a term which appears to be an acronym is, rather, the form of a name used to identify a program, agency, or software package. For example:

ORION   Not an acronym: On-line catalog at the University of California, Los Angeles
PREST   Not an acronym: A computer-based reading and study skills curriculum developed for Navy recruits

The user should also be aware that many abbreviated forms are not composed of the initial letters of the compound terms they represent. For example:

EA   ERIC Clearinghouse on Educational
            Management

Thus, some of the abbreviations listed may appear to be unrelated to the terminology they represent. Despite this lack of visual relation, however, such abbreviations are commonly used in the educational literature.

In using the *Dictionary,* two limitations should be kept in mind. First, the *Dictionary* is not an authority list. Acronyms are listed as they are used and explained in the literature. Unless there was an obvious need to verify the accuracy, no further authority work was completed. Second, the *Dictionary* is not exhaustive. Acronyms and abbreviations continue to proliferate, and no listing of short forms is ever complete. The user will undoubtedly encounter acronyms not listed on these pages, but we hope that the *Dictionary* will be useful in most cases.

We wish to extend special thanks to Ron Kelley and Catherine Palmer for assistance in typing the manuscript. Any errors or omissions are, of course, our responsibility.

James C. Palmer
Postgraduate Researcher

Anita Y. Colby
Documents Coordinator

PART I

Acronyms, Abbreviations, and Initialisms

AA	Associate in Arts
AAA	American Academy of Advertising
AAA	American Arbitration Association
AAA	Areawide Agencyon Aging
AAA	Associate in Applied Arts
AAACE	American Association for Adult and Continuing Education
AAAE	Alliance of Associations for the Advancement of Education
AAAE	American Association of Academic Editors
AAAE	Association of Arts Administration Educators
AAAL	American Association for Applied Linguistics
AAAS	American Association for the Advancement of Science
AAASS	American Association for the Advancement of Slavic Studies
AAB	Associate in Arts in Business
AABC	American Association of Bible Colleges
AABT	Association for Advancement of Behavior Therapy
AAC	Afro-Asian Center
AAC	Association of American Colleges
AACD	American Association for Counseling and Development
AACE	Alaska Association for Computers in Education
AACE	American Association for Career Education
AACJC	American Association of Community and Junior Colleges
AACN	American Association of Colleges of Nursing
AACR	Anglo-American Cataloging Rules
AACRAO	American Association of Collegiate Registrars and Admissions Officers
AACS	American Association for Chinese Studies
AACS	American Association of Christian Schools
AACSB	American Assembly of Collegiate Schools of Business
AACTE	American Association of Colleges for Teacher Education
AADE	American Association of Diabetes Educators
AAE	Alliance for Arts Education
AAES	American Association of Evangelical Students
AAESA	American Association of Educational Service Agencies
AAESPH	American Association for the Education of Severely/Profoundly Handicapped
AAGC	American Association for Gifted Children
AAHC	Association of Academic Health Centers
AAHE	American Association for Higher Education
AAHE	American Association of Housing Educators
AAHE	Association for the Advancement of Health Education
AAHPERD	American Alliance for Health, Physical Education, Recreation and Dance
AAHSLD	Association of Academic Health Sciences Library Directors
AAI	Adjusted Agreement Index
AAI	Adolescent Abuse Inventory
AAIA	Association on American Indian Affairs
AAIE	Association for the Advancement of International Education
AALE	Associate in Arts in Law Enforcement
AALL	American Association of Law Libraries
AALR	American Association for Leisure and Recreation
AALS	Association of American Law Schools
AAMC	Association of American Medical Colleges
AAMD	American Association on Mental Deficiency
AAN	Associate in Applied Nursing
AAP	Affirmative Action Plan
AAP	Association of American Publishers
AAPE	American Academy of Physical Education
AAPICU	American Association of Presidents of Independent Colleges and Universities
AAPS	American Association of Phonetic Sciences
AAPSS	American Academy of Political and Social Science
AAPT	American Association of Physics Teachers
AAPY	American Association of Professors of Yiddish
AARTS	Association of Advanced Rabbinical and Talmudic Schools
AAS	American Astronomical Society
AAS	Associate in Applied Science
AAS	Association for Asian Studies
AASA	American Association of School Administrators
AASC	American Association of Specialized Colleges
AASCU	American Association of State Colleges and Universities
AASE	American Association of Special Educators
AASECT	American Association of Sex Educators, Counselors, and Therapists
AASG	American Association of Students of German
AASL	American Association of School Librarians
AASLH	American Association for State and Local History
AASL NPSS	AASL Non-Public Schools Section
AASL SS	AASL Supervisors Section

AASPA	American Association of School Personnel Administrators
AAT	Achievement Anxiety Test
AAT	Auditory Attending Task
AATA	American Association of Teachers of Arabic
AATE	American Association of Teachers of Esperanto
AATEA	American Association of Teacher Educators in Agriculture
AATF	American Association of Teachers of French
AATG	American Association of Teachers of German
AATI	American Association of Teachers of Italian
AATS	American Academy of Teachers of Singing
AATSEEL	American Association of Teachers of Slavic and East European Languages
AATSP	American Association of Teachers of Spanish and Portuguese
AAU	Association of American Universities
AAU	Association of Atlantic Universities (Canada)
AAUA	American Association of University Administrators
AAUBO	Association of Atlantic University Business Officers (Canada)
AAUP	American Association of University Professors
AAUP	Association of American University Presses
AAUPI	American Association of University Professors of Italian
AAUS	American Association of University Students
AAUW	American Association of University Women
AAUWEF	American Association of University Women Educational Foundation
AAVIM	American Association for Vocational Instructional Materials
AAVMC	Association of American Veterinary Medical Colleges
AAWB	American Association of Workers for the Blind
AAWCJC	American Association of Women in Community and Junior Colleges
A.B.	Artium Baccalaureus
ABA	American Bar Association
ABACUS	Arizona Basic Assessment and Curriculum Utilization System
ABC	A Better Chance
ABC	Approaches to Behavior Change Inventory
ABCA	American Business Communication Association
ABCE	Adult Basic and Continuing Education
ABCT	Alabama Basic Competency Tests
ABD	All But Dissertation

ABE	Adult Basic Education
ABET	Accreditation Board for Engineering and Technology
ABFSE	American Board of Funeral Service Education
ABIC	Adaptive Behavior Inventory for Children
ABLA	American Business Law Association
ABLE	Adult Basic Learning Examination
ABOPS	Association of Business Officers of Preparatory Schools
ABS	Adaptive Behavior Scales
ABSEL	Association for Business Simulation and Experiential Learning
ABS-PS	Adaptive Behavior Scale—Public School Version
ABWH	Association of Black Women Historians
ABWHE	Association of Black Women in Higher Education
ACA	Association for Communication Administration
ACAAC	American College Admissions Advisory Center
ACAD	American Conference of Academic Deans
ACB	Airman Classification Battery
ACBC	Achenbach Child Behavior Checklist
ACBE	Association for Community-Based Education
ACBIS	Academic Collective Bargaining Information Service
ACCC	Association of Canadian Community Colleges
ACCCEL	Assessing the Cognitive Consequences of Computer Environments for Learning Project
ACCE	American Council for Construction Education
ACCE	American Council on Cosmetology Education
ACCH	Association for the Care of Children's Health
ACCT	Association of Community College Trustees
ACCTA	Association of Counseling Center Training Agents
ACCU	Association of Catholic Colleges and Universities
ACCW	New York Association of Child Care Workers
ACDM	Association of Chairmen of Departments of Mechanics
ACE	American Council on Education
ACE	Association Canadienne d'Éducation
ACE	Association of Collegiate Entrepreneurs
ACE	Association of Cooperative Educators
ACEHSA	Accrediting Commission on Education for Health Services Administration
ACEI	Association for Childhood Education International

ACEJ	American Council on Education for Journalism
ACEJMC	Accrediting Council on Education in Journalism and Mass Communication
ACES	Army Continuing Education System
ACES	Association for Counselor Education and Supervision
ACESIA	American Council for Elementary School Industrial Arts
ACFP	Association Canadienne de la Formation Professionelle
ACGME	Accreditation Council for Graduate Medical Education
ACHE	Action Committee for Higher Education
ACHE	Association for Continuing Higher Education
ACIAS	American Council of Industrial Arts Supervisors
ACIASAO	American Council of Industrial Arts State Association Officers
ACIATE	American Council on Industrial Arts Teacher Education
ACIS	American Council on International Sports
ACL	Adjective Check List
ACL	American Classical League
ACL	Association for Computational Linguistics
ACLA	American Comparative Literature Association
ACLD	Association for Children and Adults with Learning Disabilities
ACLS	American Council of Learned Societies
ACM	American College of Musicians
ACM	Associated Colleges of the Midwest
ACM	Association for Computing Machinery
AC/MRDD	Accreditation Council for Services for Mentally Retarded and other Developmentally Disabled Persons
ACOG	American College of Obstetricians and Gynecologists
ACP	Associated Collegiate Press
ACPA	American Catholic Personnel Association
ACPA	American College Personnel Association
ACPAR	Association Council for Policy Analysis and Research
ACPE	Association for Continuing Professional Education
ACRA	American Collegiate Retailing Association
ACRES	American Council on Rural Special Education
ACRL	Association of College and Research Libraries
ACRL AAS	ACRL Asian and African Section
ACRL ANSS	ACRL Anthroplogy and Sociology Section
ACRL ARTS	ACRL Arts Section
ACRL BIS	ACRL Bibliographic Instruction Section
ACRL CJCLS	ACRL Community and Junior College Libraries Section

ACRL EBSS	ACRL Education and Behavioral Sciences Section
ACRL LPSS	ACRL Law and Political Science Section
ACRL RBMS	ACRL Rare Books and Manuscripts Section
ACRL SEES	ACRL Slavic and East European Section
ACRL STS	ACRL Science and Technology Section
ACRL ULS	ACRL University Libraries Section
ACRL WESS	ACRL Western European Specialists Section
ACRS	Abbreviated Conners Parent/Teacher Rating Scale
ACS	American Chemical Society
ACS	Association of Caribbean Studies
ACSA	Asociation of Collegiate Schools of Architecture
ACSC	Accrediting Commission for Specialized Colleges
ACSC	American Council on Schools and Colleges
ACSI	Association of Christian Schools International
ACSL	American Computer Science League
ACSN	Appalachian Community Service Network
ACSP	Association of Collegiate Schools of Planning
ACSUS	Association for Canadian Studies in the United States
ACT	American College Test
ACT	American College Testing Program
ACTA	Association Canadienne de Technologie Advancée
ACTFL	American Council on the Teaching of Foreign Languages
ACTP	American College Testing Program
ACTR	American Council of Teachers of Russian
ACTS	Auditory Comprehension Test for Sentences
ACUA	Association of College and University Auditors
ACUCAA	Association of College, University, and Community Arts Administrators
ACUHO-I	Association of College and University Housing Officers—International
ACU-I	Association of College Unions—International
ACUPAE	American Council for University Planning and Academic Excellence
ACURA	Association for the Coordination of University Religious Affairs
ACUTA	Association of College and University Telecommunications Administrators
ACYF	Administration for Children, Youth, and Families
ADA	Average Daily Attendance
ADCIS	Association for the Development of Computer-based Instructional Systems
ADD	Attention Deficit Disorders
ADE	Association of Departments of English

ADERI	American Disability Evaluation Research Institute
ADFL	Association of Departments of Foreign Languages
ADM	Average Daily Membership
ADN	Associate Degree Nursing
ADPSO	Association of Data Processing Service Organizations
ADS	American Dialect Society
ADT	Wepman Auditory Discrimination Test
ADTSEA	American Driver and Traffic Safety Education Association
AEA	American Economic Association
AEA	American Education Association
AEA	Arts, Education and Americans, Inc.
AEA	Augustinian Educational Association
AECCP	Alaska Early Childhood Certification Process
AECT	Association for Educational Communications and Technology
AED	Academy for Educational Development
AEDC	American Economic Development Council
AEDS	Association for Educational Data Systems
AEE	Alliance for Environmental Education
AEE	Association for Experiential Education
AEEP	Association for Environmental Engineering Professors
AEF	Aerospace Education Foundation
AEF	Armenian Educational Foundation
AEFA	American Education Finance Association
AEI	Acclimizatization Experiences Institute
AEJMC	Association for Education in Journalism and Mass Communication
AEL	Appalachian Educational Laboratory
AERA	American Educational Research Association
AESA	American Educational Studies Association
AESIS	Australian Earth Sciences Information System
AESP	Appalachian Educational Satellite Project
AETS	Association for the Education of Teachers in Science
AEVH	Association for Education of the Visually Handicapped
AFAIU	American Friends of the Alliance Israelite Universelle
AFB	American Foundation for the Blind
AFDC	Aid to Families with Dependent Children
AFHPSP	Armed Forces Health Professional Scholarship Program
AFHU	American Friends of the Hebrew University
A-FILE	Adolescent-Family Inventory of Life Events and Changes
AFIPS	American Federation of Information Processing Societies
AFL-CIO	American Federation of Labor—Congress of Industrial Occupations
AFNA	American Foundation for Negro Affairs
AFRAT	Air Force Reading Abilities Test
AFS	American Field Service
AFSA	American Federation of School Administrators
AFSCME	American Federation of State, County and Municipal Employees
AFT	American Federation of Teachers
AFT-TCRE	American Federation of Teachers— Teacher Center Resource Exchange
AGAT	Ability Grouped Active Teaching
AGB	Association of Governing Boards of Universities and Colleges
AGHE	Association for Gerontology in Higher Education
AGI	American Geological Institute
AGLS	Association for General and Liberal Studies
AGLSP	Association of Graduate Liberal Studies Programs
AGRICOLA	Agricultural Online Access (U.S. Department of Agriculture)
AGS	Association of Graduate Schools
AH	American Humanics
AHA	American Historical Association
AHA	American Hominological Association
AHE	Association for Humanistic Education
AHEA	American Hungarian Educators' Association
AHEC	Area Health Education Centers (California)
AHJCP	Association of Hillel/Jewish Campus Professionals
AHSGE	Alabama High School Graduation Examination
AHSSPPE	Association on Handicapped Student Services Programs in Postsecondary Education
AIAA	American Industrial Arts Association
AIASA	American Industrial Arts Student Association
AIAW	Association for Intercollegiate Athletics for Women
AIB	Academy of International Business
AIBS	American Institute of Biological Sciences
AICA	Alliance of Independent Colleges of Art
AICCT	Association for the Improvement of Community College Teaching
AICE	American Institute for Character Education
AIChE	American Institute of Chemical Engineers
AICM	Association of Independent Colleges of Music
AICS	Association of Independent Colleges and Schools
AICU	Association of International Colleges and Universities
AID	Accepting Individual Differences Curriculum

AIDA	American Indian Development Association
AIDP	Advanced Institutional Development Program
AIDS	American Institute for Decision Sciences
AIESEC	Association Internationale des Étudiants en Sciences Économiques et Commerciales
AIESI	Association Internationale des Écoles des Sciences de l'Information
AIGE	Association for Individually Guided Education
AIHE	Association for Innovation in Higher Education
AIIS	American Institute of Indian Studies
AILA	Association Internationale de Linguistique Appliquée
AILACTE	Association of Independent Liberal Arts Colleges for Teacher Education
AILSA	American Indian Law Students Association
AIM	Associated Information Managers
AIM/ARM	Abstracts of Instructional and Research Materials in Vocational and Technical Education
AIMAV	Association Internationale pour la Recherche et la Diffusion des Méthodes Audio-Visuelles et Structo-Globales
AIMS	American Institute of Musical Studies
AIMS	Association of Independent Maryland Schools
AIMS	Automated Instructional Materials Service
AIPE	American Institute for Professional Education
AIPT	Association for International Practical Training
AIR	American Institutes for Research in the Behavioral Sciences
AIR	Association for Institutional Research
AIRIA	Adult Inventory of Reading Interests and Attitudes
AIS	Academy of Independent Scholars
AIS	American Indian Scholarships
AIS	American Indian Studies
AIS	Artists In the Schools Program
AISP	Association of Information Systems Professionals
AIT	Agency for Instructional Television
AIT	Assessment of Instructional Terms
AITCT	Alabama Initial Teacher Certification Test
AJCU	Association of Jesuit Colleges and Universities
AJL	Association of Jewish Libraries
ALA	Adult Learning Association
ALA	American Library Association
ALANET	Not an acronym: Name of the Electronic Mail and Information Network of the American Library Association
ALARM	Assessment of Language And Reading Maturity Test
ALAS	Auxiliary Loans to Assist Students
ALCF	Association of Lutheran College Faculties
ALEA	American Lutheran Education Association
ALEM	Adaptive Learning Environments Model
ALIS	Automated Library Information System
ALISE	Association for Library and Information Science Education
ALMA	Association of Labor Mediation Agencies
ALP	Academic Library Program
ALPBP	Assessment of Language Proficiency of Bilingual Persons Project
ALSA	American Legal Studies Association
ALSA	Area Library Service Authority
ALSC	Association for Library Service to Children (American Library Association)
ALSP	Adkins Life Skills Program
ALSS	Association of Lutheran Secondary Schools
ALT	Academic Learning Time
ALTA	American Library Trustee Association
AM	Academy of Management
A.M.	Artium Magister
AMA	American Management Association
AMAE	Association of Mexican American Educators
AMATYC	American Mathematical Association of Two-Year Colleges
AMC	Association of Mercy Colleges
AMCEE	Association for Media-based Continuing Education for Engineers, Inc.
AMCS	Association of Military Colleges and Schools of the U.S.
AMEG	Association for Measurement and Evaluation in Guidance
AMES	Actualization of Mainstream Experience Skills Project (Iowa)
AMHCA	American Mental Health Counselor Association (American Personnel and Guidance Association)
AMI	Association for Multi-Image
AMIDEAST	American Mideast Educational and Training Services, Inc.
AMOAS	Administrative Management by Objectives Appraisal System
AMS	Academy of Marketing Science
AMS	Administrative Management Society
AMS	American Mathematical Society
AMS	American Montessori Society
AMTEP	Automobile Mechanic Training Evaluation Project (Southern Association of Colleges and Schools)
ANA	American Nurses' Association
ANARAP	Administration for Native Americans Research Analysis Project
ANCOVA	Analysis of Covariance
ANEF	American-Nepal Education Foundation
ANOVA	Analysis Of Variance

ANPEO	Assembly of National Postsecondary Educational Organizations
ANSI	American National Standards Institute
ANS-IE	Nowicki-Strickland Internal-External Control Scale for Adults
ANSS	American Nature Study Society
AoA	Administration on Aging
AOE	Association of Overseas Educators
AOJT	Association of Orthodox Jewish Teachers
AOPE	Associated Organizations for Professionals in Education
AOS	Acceptance of Others Scale
AP	Advanced Placement
APA	American Philological Association
APA	American Philosophical Association
APA	American Psychiatric Association
APA	American Psychological Association
APC	Assessment Policy Committee (National Assessment of Educational Progress)
APCISS	Alumi Presidents' Council of Independent Secondary Schools
APCU	Association of Presbyterian Colleges and Universities
APCYA	A Presidential Classroom for Young Americans
APE	Administrator Performance Evaluation
APEID	Asian Program of Educational Innovation for Development
APEM	Association for Professional Education for Ministry
APEP	Academic Program Evaluation Project
APGA	American Personnel and Guidance Association
APHA	American Public Health Association
API	Affective Perception Inventory
API	American Press Institute
APL	Adult Performance Level
APLIC	Association for Population/Family Planning Libraries and Information Centers, International
APLS	Association for Politics and the Life Sciences
APM	Advanced Progressive Matrices
APP	Annual Program Plan
APPA	Association of Physical Plant Administrators of Universities and Colleges
APPLES	Asian and Pacific Professional Language and Education Services
APQ	Autonomic Perception Questionnaire
APRRE	Association of Professors and Researchers in Religious Education
APS	Academy of Political Science
APSA	American Political Science Association
APT	Appalachia Preschool Test
APT	Applied Performance Tests
APT	Assessments of Performance in Teaching (South Carolina)
AR	Academic Ranking
AR	Auditory Reception

ARAPCS	Association for Research, Administration, Professional Councils and Societies
ARC	American Reading Council
ARC	Association of Retarded Citizens
ARCA	American Rehabilitation Counseling Association (American Personnel and Guidance Association)
ARF	American Reading Forum
ARIA	American Risk and Insurance Association
ARIMA	Auto Regressive Integrated Moving Average Model
ARL	Association of Research Libraries
ARLIS/NA	Art Library Society of North America
ARMA	Association of Records Managers and Administrators
ARMSI	Alaska Resources for the Moderately/Severely Impaired
ARO	Army Research Office
ARP	Advisory Role Play
ARPA	Advanced Research Projects Agency
ARPANET	Advanced Research Projects Agency Network
ARPDP	Association of Rehabiliation Programs in Data Processing
ARROE	American Registry of Research and Research-Related Organizations
ARTFL	American and French Research on the Treasury of the French Language Project
ARTS	Arts Recognition and Talent Search
ARTTC	Alaska Rural Teacher Training Corps
ARVIC	Association for Religious and Value Issues In Counseling
ASA	African Studies Association
ASA	American Schools Association
ASA	American Sociological Association
ASA	American Student Association
ASA	American Studies Association
ASAHP	American Society of Allied Health Professions
ASBCS	Association of Southern Baptist Colleges and Schools
ASBDA	American School Band Directors' Association
ASBO	Association of School Business Officials of the United States and Canada
ASC	Assembly of State Conferences (American Association of University Professors)
ASC	Associated Schools of Construction
ASCA	American School Counselor Association
ASC/AIA	Association of Student Chapters, American Institute of Architects
ASCCC	Academic Senate for California Community Colleges
ASCD	Association for Supervision and Curriculum Development
ASCI	Art Self-Concept Inventory

ASCII   American Standard Code for Information Interchange
ASCLA   Association of Specialized and Cooperative Library Agencies
ASCS   Academic Self-Concept Scale
ASCUS   Association for School, College, and University Staffing
ASE   Adult Secondary Education
ASE   American Society of Educators
ASEE   American Society for Engineering Education
ASEE   American Society for Environmental Education
ASEH   American Society for Environmental History
ASEI   American Sports Education Institute
ASEP   Automotive Service Education Program (General Motors)
ASET   Academy of Security Educators and Trainees
ASFSA   American School Food Service Association
ASGW   Association for Specialists in Group Work
ASHA   American School Health Association
ASHA   American Speech-Language-Hearing Association
ASHE   Association for the Study of Higher Education
ASID   American Society of Interior Designers
ASIDIC Association of Information and Dissemination Centers
ASIS   American Society for Information Science
ASJMC   Association of Schools of Journalism and Mass Communication
ASJSA   American Society of Journalism School Administrators
ASLHA   American Speech-Language-Hearing Association
ASLNY   Art Students' League of New York
ASMT   American Society of Medical Technology
ASOR   American Schools of Oriental Research
ASOS   A Study Of Schooling
ASPAC   Cultural and Social Center for the Asian and Pacific Region (South Korea)
ASSJ   Association for the Sociological Study of Jewry
ASSR   American Society for the Study of Religion
ASTA   American String Teachers Association
ASTD   American Society for Training and Development
ASTIIT American Society for Technion—Israel Institute of Technology
ASUC   American Society of University Composers
ASVAB   Armed Services Vocational Aptitude Battery
ATA   Academic Travel Abroad

A&TBCB Architectural and Transportation Barriers Compliance Board
ATBQ   Attitudes Toward Blindness Questionnaire
ATC   Athletic Training Council
ATCI   Attitudes Toward College Inventory
ATDP   Attitudes Toward Disabled Persons Questionnaire
ATE   Association of Teacher Educators
ATEA   American Technical Education Association
ATEC   Aviation Technician Education Council
ATERS   Attitudes Toward Educational Research Scale
ATESL   Association of Teachers of English as a Second Language
ATFI   Attitudes Toward Feminist Issues Scales
ATGSB   Admission Test for Graduate Study in Business
ATHI   Attitudes Toward Handicapped Individuals Scale
ATI   Aptitude Treatment Interaction
ATI   Articulation Test of Intelligibility
ATJ   Association of Teachers of Japanese
ATLA   American Theological Library Association
ATMS   Attitudes Toward Mainstreaming Scale
ATP   Admissions Testing Program
ATPM   Association of Teachers of Preventive Medicine
ATS   American Technical Society
ATS   Association of Theological Schools
ATSR   Attitudes Toward Sex Roles Instrument
ATTW   Association of Teachers of Technical Writing
AUBER   Association for University Business and Economic Research
AUC   Apple University Consortium
AUCC   Association of Universities and Colleges of Canada
AUHS   Adapted Uzgiris-Hunt Scales
AUPHA   Association of University Programs in Health Administration
AUSUDIAP Association of U.S. University Directors of International Agricultural Programs
AUU   Association of Urban Universities
AV   Audio-Visual
AVEPDA American Vocational Education Personnel Development Association
AVERA   American Vocational Education Research Association
AVKO   Audio, Visual, Kinesthetic, and Oral
AVKOERF AVKO Educational Research Foundation
AVS   Area Vocational Schools
AVSL   Association of Visual Science Librarians
AVTA   Automatic Vocal Transaction Analyzer
AVTI   Area Vocational and Technical Institute
AWARE   Assisting Women to Advance through Resources and Encouragement Project
AWCI   Affective Work Competencies Inventory
AWE   Association for World Education

AWLNET	Area Wide Library Network (California)
AWS	Attitudes Toward Women Scale
AWU	Association for World University
AYA	American Yoga Association
B.A.	Bachelor of Arts
BABEL	Bay Area Bilingual Education League (California)
BAEF	British American Educational Foundation
BAI	Bell Adjustment Inventory
B.A.in Ed.	Bachelor of Arts in Education
BALLOTS	Bibliographic Automation of Large Library Operations using a Timesharing System
BAN	Best Asymptotically Normal
BARS	Behaviorally Anchored Rating Scales
B.A.S.	Bachelor of Arts in Science
BAS	Bibliographic Access System
BAS	British Ability Scales
BASA	Behavioral Assessment of Speech Anxiety
BASIC	Beginner's All-Purpose Symbolic Instruction Code
BASIS	Basic Achievement Skills Individual Screener
BASIS	Battelle Automated Search Information System
BAT	Behavioral Assertiveness Test
BAT	Bureau of Apprenticeship and Training (U.S. Department of Labor)
BATR	Beginning Assessment Test of Reading
B.B.A.	Bachelor of Business Administration
BBB	Building Better Boards for Community Organizations Project (American Association of Community and Junior Colleges)
BCAC	Biology Classroom Activity Checklist
BCALA	Black Librarians Caucus (American Library Association)
BCC	Border College Consortium
BCR	Bibliographic Center for Research
BCTF	British Columbia Teachers' Federation
B.D.	Bachelor of Divinity
BD	Behavior Disorder or Behaviorally Disordered
B.D.A.	Bachelor of Domestic Arts
BDAE	Boston Diagnostic Aphasia Examination
BDHI	Buss Durkee Hostility Inventory
BDI	Beck Depression Inventory
B.E.	Bachelor of Engineering
BE	Bilingual Education
BE	Black English
BEA	Bilingual Education Act of 1968
BEA	Broadcast Education Association
BEAM	Business Education Association of Maine
BEBA	Bilingual Education Bibliographic Abstracts
BECBSG	Big Eight Council on Black Student Government
BECSAS	Barclay Early Childhood Skill Assessment Center

B.Ed.	Bachelor of Education
B.E.E.	Bachelor of Electrical Engineering
BEM	Behavior Engineering Model
BEOG	Basic Education Opportunity Grants
BEP	Basic Education Program
BERA	Business Education Research of America
BEST	Basic Educational Skills through Technology Project (U.S. Department of Education)
BEST	Better Educational Services through Testing Project (Kansas)
BETA	Bilingual Evaluation Technical Assistance Project
B.F.A.	Bachelor of Fine Arts
BHEF	Business-Higher Education Forum
BI	Brain Injured
BIA	Braille Institute of America
BIA	Bureau of Indian Affairs (U.S. Department of the Interior)
BIBCON	Bibliographic Records Conversion
BIBLIOS	Book Inventory Building and Library Oriented System
BICCC	Business Industry Community College Coalition
BICS	Basic Interpersonal Communicative Skills
BID	Bellevue Index of Depression
BINL	Bilingual Inventory of Natural Languages
BIOSIS	Biosciences Information Service
BIP	Bakersfield Individualized Process
BL	British Library
BLRI	Barrett-Lennard Relationship Inventory
BLS	Bureau of Labor Statistics (U.S. Department of Labor)
BLSA	Black Law Student Association
BLST	Bankson Language Screening Test
B.M.	Bachelor of Music
B.M.E.	Bachelor of Music Education
B.Mus.Ed.	Bachelor of Music Education
BOCES	Board of Cooperative Educational Services
BOLT	Bahia Oral Language Test
BOOTS	Basic Organizing/Optimizing Training Schedules (U.S. Navy)
BPC	Behavior Problem Checklist
BRAIN	Baruch Retrieval of Automated Information for Negotiations
BRI	Basic Reading Inventory
BRISC	Brighton Reading and Individualized Skills Continuum
BRP	Behavior Rating Profile
BRPT	Behavioral Role-Playing Test
BRS	Bibliographic Retrieval Service
B.S.	Bachelor of Science
BSA	Bibliographic Society of America
BSAP	Basic Skills Assessment Program (South Carolina)
B.S.C.E.	Bachelor of Science in Civil Engineering
B.S.Ch.E.	Bachelor of Science in Chemical Engineering
BSCS	Biological Sciences Curriculum Study

B.S.E. Bachelor of Science in Engineering
B.S.Ed. Bachelor of Science in Education
B.S.E.E. Bachelor of Science in Electrical Engineering
BSID Bayley Scales of Infant Development
BSLS Basic Skills Learning System
BSM Bilingual Syntax Measure
B.S.M.E. Bachelor of Science in Mechanical Engineering
B.S.Med.Tech. Bachelor of Science in Medical Technology
B.S.N. Bachelor of Science in Nursing
B.S.Phar. Bachelor of Science in Pharmacy
BSRI Bem Sex Role Inventory
BSSE Beliefs about Science and Science Education Scale
BSUF British Schools and Universities Foundation
BT Broader Term
BTANYS Business Teachers Association of New York State
BTBC Boehm Test of Basic Concepts
BTES Beginning Teacher Evaluation Study
BTI Boston Theological Institute
BUF Black United Front
BURSAR Not an acronym: Name of a software program that monitors funds generated through extracurricular activities

CA Chemical Abstracts
CA Chronological Age
CAA College Art Association of America
CAAE Canadian Association for Adult Education
CAAT Colleges of Applied Arts and Technology (Ontario)
CAB Comprehensive Ability Battery
CACI Catholic Alumni Clubs, International
CACREP Council for Accreditation of Counseling and Related Educational Programs
CAD Computer-Aided Design
CADAM Computer-Graphics Augmented Design and Manufacturing System
CADMS Costing and Data Management System (National Center for Higher Education Management Systems)
CAD PI Computer Assisted Diagnostic and Prescription Instruction
CADRE Collegial Association for the Development and Renewal of Educators
CAE Certificate in Adult Education
CAE Computer-Aided Engineering
CAE Council on Anthropology and Education
CAEF Chinese-American Educational Foundation
CAEL Cooperative Assessment of Experiential Learning Project
CAEL Council for the Advancement of Experiential Learning

CAEO Coalition of Adult Education Organizations
CAEP Connecticut Assessment of Educational Progress
CAFIAS Cheffers' Adaptation of Flanders' Interaction Analysis System
CAG Computer-Assisted Guidance
CAHEA Committee on Allied Health Education and Accreditation
CAI Computer-Assisted Instruction
CAID Convention of American Instructors of the Deaf
CAIN Computer Anxiety Index
CAIS Canadian Association for Information Science
CAISH Computer Assisted Instruction and Support for the Handicapped
CAITE Computer Aided Instruction for Teacher Education
CAITS Computer-Aided Interactive Testing System
CAJE Coalition for Alternatives in Jewish Education
CAL Center for Applied Linguistics
CAL Composite Assessment of Leverage
CAL Computer-Assisted Learning
CALA Chinese-American Librarians Association
CALIB Computer Assisted Language Instruction Bibliography
CALICO Computer Assisted Language Learning and Instruction Consortium
CALIP Computer Aptitude, Literacy, and Interest Profile
CALL Computer-Assisted Language Learning
CALLS California Academic Libraries List of Serials
CALP Cognitive/Academic Language Proficiency
CAL-SOAP California Student Opportunity and Access Program
CAM Computer-Aided Manufacturing
CAMP College Assistance Migrant Program
CAMPS Cooperative Area Manpower Planning Systems
CAMPUS Comprehensive Analytical Model for Planning in the University Sphere
CANE Classical Association of New England
CAN/OLE Canadian On-Line Enquiry
CANRIS Child Abuse and Neglect Reprint and Inquiry Systems
CAP Client Assistance Program (Rehabilitation Act of 1973)
CAP Concepts About Print Test
CAPE Community Alliance Program for Ex-Offenders
CAPE Council for American Private Education
CAPHE Consortium for the Advancement of Private Higher Education
CAPS ERIC Clearinghouse on Counseling and Personnel Services

CAQ	Computer Aptitude Quotient
CAR	Computer-Assisted Retrieval
CARA	Center for Applied Research in the Apostolate
CARALOC	Children's Attribution of Responsibility and Locus Of Control
C.A.R.E.	Challenging Adults to Read Effectively
CARF	Commission on Accreditation of Rehabilitation Facilities
CARIS	Computer Animated Reading Instruction System
CARISPLAN	Caribbean Information System for Economic and Social Planning
CARS	Classroom Adjustment Rating Scale
CARS	Community Antenna Relay Service
CART	Children's Associative Responding Test
CART	Cultural Attitudes Repertory Technique
CAS	Council for the Advancement of Standards for Student Affairs/Services Programs
CAS	Curriculum Attitude Survey
CASA	Canadian Association of School Administrators
CASETS	Computer Assisted Spanish English Transition Sequence
CASSIP	Computer-Assisted Study Skills Improvement Program
CAST	Council for Agricultural Science and Technology
CASTE	Craig Adapted Sociometric Test Form
CASTLE	Computer Assisted Student Tutorial Learning Environment
CAT	California Achievement Tests
CAT	Committee on Assessment and Testing (Speech Communication Association)
CAT	Computer-Assisted Teaching
CAT	Computer-Assisted Testing
CAT	Computerized Adaptive Testing
CATA	Canadian Advanced Technology Association
CATAM	Computer Aided Teaching of Applied Mathematics (Cambridge University, England)
CATC	Computer-Assisted Test Construction
CATES	Computer Aided Training Evaluation and Scheduling (U.S. Navy)
CATESOL	California Association of Teachers of English to Speakers of Other Languages
CAT-L	California Achievement Test—Language Subtest
CATU	Computer-Assisted Teaching Unit
CATV	Cable Television
CAT-V	Cognitive Abilities Test—Verbal Battery
CATV	Community Antenna Television
CAUSE	Comprehensive Assistance to Undergraduate Science Education
CAUSE	Not an acronym: A professional association for the development, management and use of information systems in higher education
CAUT	Canadian Association of University Teachers
CAV	Continuous Angular Velocity
CAVALIR	Catalog of Virginia Library Resources
CAVD	Completions, Arithmetical Problems, Vocabulary, and Directions Test
CAVE	Catholic Audio-Visual Educators Association
CBA	Catholic Biblical Association of America
CBA	Chemical Bond Approach
CBAE	Competency-Based Administrator Education
CBAE	Competency-Based Adult Education
CBAM	Concerns-Based Adoption Model
CBARC	Conference Board of Associated Research Councils
CBAVE	Competency-Based Adult Vocational Education
CBC	Children's Book Council
CBC	Collective Bargaining Congress (American Association of University Professors)
CBCL	Child Behavior Checklist
CBDNA	College Band Directors National Association
CBE	Community-Based Education
CBE	Competency-Based Education
CBE	Computer-Based Education
CBE	Council for Basic Education
CBE	Counselor Behavior Evaluation Form
CBEA	Connecticut Business Educators Association
CBEDS	California Basic Educational Data System
CBEST	California Basic Educational Skills Test
CBIV	Computer-Based Interactive Video
CBMS	Conference Board on the Mathematical Sciences
CbN	Courses by Newspaper
CBO	Community-Based Organizations
CBP	Child Behavior Profile
CBT	Computer-Based Testing
CBT	Computer-Based Training
CBTE	Competency-Based Teacher Education
CBV	Classroom Business Venture
CCA	Canonical Correlation Analysis
CCA	Cecchetti Council of America
CCAIT	Community College Association for Instruction and Technology
CCALI	Center for Computer-Assisted Legal Instruction
CCAS	Community College Activities Survey
CCAS	Council of Colleges of Arts and Sciences
CCBD	Council for Children with Behavioral Disorders
CCC	Certificate of Clinical Competence
CCC	Christian College Consortium
CCC	Civilian Conservation Corps
CCC	Comprehensive Communication Curriculum
CCC	Copyright Clearance Center

CCC   Core College Curriculum
CCC   Curriculum Coordinating Committees
CCCC   Conference on College Composition and Communication
CCCEI   Conseil Consultatif Canadien de l'Emploi et de l'Immigration
CCDO   Canadian Classification and Dictionary of Occupations
CCEA   Commonwealth Council for Educational Administration (Australia)
CCEFP   Center for Community Education Facility Planning
CCEIS   Community and Continuing Education Information Service
CCEP   Child Care Employee Project
CCEU   Council on the Continuing Education Unit
CCFLT   Colorado Congress of Foreign Language Teachers
CCG   Copyright Copying Guidelines
CCGEA   Community College General Education Association
CCGI   Community College Goals Inventory
CCHA   Community College Humanities Association
CCHE   Carnegie Commission on Higher Education
CCI   College Characteristics Index
CCJA   Community College Journalism Association
CCL   Common Command Language
CCL   Conference on Christianity and Literature
CCLN   Council for Computerized Library Networks
CCMA   Catholic Campus Ministry Association
CCP   Certificate in Computer Programming
CCP   Council of 1890 College Presidents
CCQ   Classroom Climate Questionnaire
CCS   Cartoon Conservation Scales
CCS   Center for Cuban Studies
CC/S   Centralized Correspondence Study (Alaska)
CCS   Council of Communication Societies
CCSA   Children's Cognitive Style Assessment Instrument
CCS/DDC   Cataloging and Classification Section's Descriptive Cataloging Committee (American Library Association)
CCSPU   Committee for Corporate Support of Private Universities
CCSSO   Council of Chief State School Officers
CCT   Children's Checking Test
CCT   Communicative Competence Test
CCTE   Canadian Council of Teachers of English
CDA   Child Development Associate
CDACL   Career Development and Assessment Center for Librarians
CDC   Centers for Disease Control
CDDP   College Discovery and Development Program (New York City)
CDE   Colorado Department of Education

CDER   Center for Death Education and Research
CDF   Children's Defense Fund
CDI   Career Development Inventory
CDI   Children's Depression Inventory
CDI   College Descriptive Index
CDM   Cancer Decision Making Inventory
CDP   Certificate in Data Processing
CDQ   Child Development Questionnaire
CDRSC   Children's Depression Rating Scale for Classrooms
CDRT   Committee on Diagnostic Reading Tests
CDS   Career Decision Scale
CDS   Child Depression Scale
CDSHA   Country Day School Headmasters Association of the United States
CE   Career Education
CE   ERIC Clearinghouse on Adult, Career, and Vocational Education
CEA   Canadian Education Association
CEA   College English Association
CEA   Conservation Education Association
CEA   Cooperative Education Association
CEAFU   Concerned Educators Against Forced Unionism
CEASD   Conference of Educational Administrators Serving the Deaf
CEASE   Concerned Educators Allied for a Safe Environment
CEC   Council for Exceptional Children
CEC   National Council on the Evaluation of Foreign Educational Credentials
CED   Council on Education of the Deaf
CEDA   Cross Examination Debate Association
CEDaR   Council for Educational Development and Research
CEDARC   Confluent Education Development And Research Center
CEDEFOP   European Center for the Development of Vocational Training (West Germany)
CEDS   Council on Educational Diagnostic Services (Council for Exceptional Children)
CEE   Conference on English Education
CEE   Council on Electrolysis Education
CEEB   College Entrance Examination Board
CEEP   Crustal Evolution Education Project (National Association of Geology Teachers)
CEF   Citizens for Educational Freedom
CEF   Creative Education Foundation
CEFA   Council for Educational Freedom in America
CEFPI   Council of Educational Facility Planners, International
CEFT   Children's Embedded Figures Test
CEGEP   Collèges d'Enseignement Général Et Professionel (Quebec)
CEGS   Council on Education in the Geological Sciences

CEI	Center for Education Improvement (U.S. Department of Education)
CEI	Critical Events Interview
CEIA	Career Education Incentive Act of 1977
CEIAC	Canada Employment and Immigration Advisory Council
CEIP	Center for Environmental Intern Programs
CEIQ	Checklist for Ert vs. Inert Qualities
CELF	Clinical Evaluation of Language Functions
CELI	Carrow Elicited Language Inventory
CELT	Comprehensive English Language Test
CEMR	Continuing Education in Mental Retardation Program (American Association on Mental Deficiency)
CEMREL	Central Midwestern Regional Educational Laboratory
CEMYF	Charles Edison Memorial Youth Fund
CENTAUR	Not an acronym: Intelligent computer-aided diagnostic consultation system
CEO	Chief Executive Officer
CEP	Chicano Education Project
CEP	Concentrated Employment Program
CEPM	Center for Educational Policy and Management
CEPR	Center for Educational Policy Research
CEPS	Center for Educational Policy Studies
CEQ	Illinois Course Evaluation Questionnaire
CERC	Consumer Education Research Center
CERI	Centre for Educational Research and Innovation
CERIC	Central ERIC
CERS	Counseling Effectiveness Rating Scale
CES	Classroom Environment Scale
CES	Constructive Error Score
CES	Cooperative Extension Service
CES	Council for European Studies
CESI	Council for Elementary Science International
CESS	Children's English and Services Study
CETA	Comprehensive Employment and Training Act
CETOR	Commission on Education of Teachers of Reading
CEU	Continuing Education Unit
CF	Children's Foundation
CFAE	Council for Financial Aid to Education
CFAT	Carnegie Foundation for the Advancement of Teaching
CFC	Career Factor Checklist
CFEF	Committee for Education Funding
CFNO	Common Fund for Nonprofit Organizations
CFRP	Child and Family Resource Program (Head Start)
CFSoCQ	Change Facilitator Stages of Concern Questionnaire
CFSS	Children's Fear Survey Schedule
CFT	Concealed Figures Test

CG	ERIC Clearinghouse on Counseling and Personnel Services
CGCA	Canadian Guidance and Counseling Association
CGCS	Council of the Great City Schools
CGFPS	Conference Group on French Politics and Society
CGGP	Conference Group on German Politics
CGIP	Conference Group on Italian Politics
CGP	Comparative Guidance and Placement Program
CGPA	Cumulative Grade Point Average
CGS	Council of Graduate Schools in the United States
CGSL	California Guaranteed Student Loans
CGSM	Consortium for Graduate Study in Management
CGT	Computer-Guided Teaching
CHAC	Chicano Humanities and Arts Council
CHART	Children's Attitude toward Reading Test
CHATS	Crabtree-Horsham Affective Trait Scale
Ch.B.	Bachelor of Chemistry
CHEAO	Coalition of Higher Education Assistance Organizations
CHEMLINE	Chemical Information Online Dictionary Key to TOXLINE (National Library of Medicine)
CHFIE	Cordell Hull Foundation for International Education
CHILD	Conductive Hearing Impairment Language Development Program
CHIN	Community Health Information Network (Massachusetts)
CHOICES	Computerized Heuristic Occupational Information and Career Exploration System
CHRIE	Council on Hotel, Restaurant, and Institutional Education
CHTP	Counselling and Home Training Program for Deaf Children (British Colombia)
CIAA	Central Intercollegiate Athletic Association
CIAA	Connecticut Industrial Arts Association
CIBC	Council on Interracial Books for Children
CIC	Committee on Institutional Cooperation
CIC	Council of Independent Colleges
CICHE	Consortium for International Cooperation in Higher Education
CICS	Counselor Interview Competence Scale
CICSB	Coalition of Indian Controlled School Boards
CID	Comfortable Interpersonal Distance Scale
CIDP	International Centre for Parliamentary Documentation
CIDS	Career Information Delivery Systems
CIEE	Council on International Education Exchange
CIES	Comparative and International Education Society
CIES	Council for International Exchange of Scholars

CIHED   Center for International Higher Education Documentation

CII   Computer Integrated Instruction

CIIS   Contemporary Issues In Science Program

CIJE   Current Index to Journals in Education

CIL   Council for Interinstitutional Leadership

CILSDS   Community Independent Living Service Delivery Systems

CILT   Center for Information on Language and Teaching

CIM   Computer Input Microfilm

CIP   Cataloging In Publication

CIP   Classification of Instructional Programs

CIPP   Context, Input, Process, Product

CIPTPP   Cooperative International Pupil-to-Pupil Program

CIRCUIT   Curriculum Improvement Resulting from Creative Utilization of Instructional Two-Way Television Project (Wisconsin)

CIREEH   Carolina Institute for Research on Early Education for the Handicapped

CIS   Career Information System

CIS   Congressional Indexing Service

CIS   Congressional Information Service

CIS   Creative Imagination Scale

CISE   Consortium for International Studies Education

CISP   Council for Intercultural Studies and Programs

CISTI   Canadian Institute for Scientific and Technical Information

CIT   Commission on Instructional Technology

CIT   Critical Incident Technique

CITE   Current Information Transfer in English

CJE   Council for Jewish Education

CL   Computer Literacy

CL   Conceptual Level

CLA   Canadian Library Association

CLA   College Language Association

CLAE   Council of Library Associations Executives

CLAS   California Loans to Assist Students

CLAS   Computerized Lesson-Authoring System

CLASP   College Level Academic Skills Project (Florida)

CLASS   California Library Authority for Systems and Services

CLAST   College-Level Academic Skills Test (Florida)

CLD   Center for Leadership Development

CLD   Council for Learning Disabilities (Council for Exceptional Children)

CLE   Continuing Library Education

CLENE   Continuing Library Education Network and Exchange

CLEO   Council on Legal Education Opportunity

CLEP   College-Level Examination Program

CLIP   Computer Language Instructional Program

CLM   Cognitive Levels Matching

CLP   Career and Life Planning Model

CLR   Council on Library Resources

CLSA   California Library Services Act

CLTA   Chinese Language Teachers Association

CLUE   Computer League for Users in Education

CLUES   Computers, Learners, Users, Educators Association (New Jersey)

CMA   College Media Advisers

CMA   Colleges of Mid-America

C-MAP   Career Motivation and Achievement Planning Inventory

CMAS   Children's Manifest Anxiety Scale

CMC   Council of Mennonite Colleges

CMD   Center for Management Development

CMI   Career Maturity Inventory

CMI   Computer-Managed Instruction

CMIS   Classroom Management Improvement Study

CMITS   Central Maine Interactive Telecommunications System

CML   Computer-Managed Learning

CMLS   Computerized Mastery Learning System

CMMS   Columbia Mental Maturity Scale

CMOS   Classroom Management Observation Scale

CMS   College Music Society

CMT   Concept Memory Test

CMW   Campus Ministry Women

CNA   Canadian Nurses Association

CNCE   Council for Noncollegiate Continuing Education

CNEEUG   Corvus National Educational Enduser's Group, Inc.

CNLIA   Council of National Library and Information Associations

CNPS   Caucus for a New Political Science

COBAS   Council Of Black Architectural Schools

COBOL   Common Business Oriented Language

CODA   Communications among Organizations Dealing with Admissions

CODE   Canadian Organization for Development through Education

COFHE   Consortium On Financing Higher Education

COFOR   Canadian Occupational Forecasting Program

COGME   Council for Opportunity in Graduate Management Education

COGR   Council On Governmental Relations

COIN   Coordinated Occupational Information Network

COKER   Classroom Observations Keyed for Effectiveness Research

COLAND   Council On Library and Network Development

COLT   Council On Library-Media Technical-Assistants

COM   Computer-Output Microcopy

COMcat   Not an acronym: A catalog of library holdings on computer output microfilm

CoMERC	Colorado Migrant Education Resource Center
COMETS	Career Oriented Modules to Explore Topics in Science
COMPENDEX	Computerized Engineering Index
CONAC	El Congreso Nacional de Asuntos Colegiales
CONDUIT	Not an acronym: A consortium of five regional computer centers
CONIT	Connector for Networked Information Transfer
CON PASS	Consortium of Professional Associations for the Study of Special Teacher Improvement Programs
CONSER	Conversion of Serials Project
CONTU	National Commission on New Technological Uses of Copyrighted Text
COO	Committee On Organization (American Library Association)
COPA	Council On Postsecondary Accreditation
COPE	Council Of Program Evaluation
C.O.P.E.	Curriculum Objectives for Physical Education
COPE	Curriculum Organization and Program Evaluation
COPES	Committee On Program Evaluation and Support (American Library Association)
COPES	Community-Oriented Program Environment Scale
COPS	Canadian Occupational Projection System
COPS	Council On Professional Standards in Speech Language Pathology and Audiology (American Speech-Language Hearing Association)
COPS-P	California Occupational Preference System—Form P
COPUS	National Coalition of Independent College and University Students
COR	Chain Of Response
CORD	Center for Occupational Research and Development
CORD	Congress On Research in Dance
CORE	Cohesion, Organization, Resourcefulness and Energy Model
CORMOSEA	Committee On Research Materials On Southeast Asia
CORSAC	Council Of Regional School Accrediting Commissions
CoRT	Cognitive Research Trust
COS	Counseling-Orientation Preference Scale
COSATI	Committee On Scientific And Technical Information
COSLA	Chief Officers of State Library Agencies
COSPA	Council of Student Personnel Associations in Higher Education
COSWL	Committee On the Status of Women in Librarianship (American Library Association)

COU	Council of Ontario Universities
CPA	Critical Path Analysis
CPAA	Colloquia for Presidents and Academic Administrators
CPAE	Certified Public Accountant Examination
CPBI	Cornell Parent Behavior Inventory
CPBI	Counseling Practice Beliefs Inventory
CPBD	Cornell Parent Behavior Description
C/PBTE	Competency/Performance-Based Teacher Education
CPC	College Placement Council
CPC	Council on Professional Certification
CPE	Committee for Positive Education
CPE	Continuing Professional Education
CPEO	Cooperative Program for Educational Opportunity
C.Phil.	Candidate of Philosophy
CPI	California Psychological Inventory
CPI	Consumer Price Index
CPL	Council of Planning Librarians
CPM	Coloured Progressive Matrices
CPM	Critical Path Method
CPQ	Children's Personality Questionnaire
CPS	Career Planning System
CPS	Center for Political Studies (Institute for Social Research)
CPS	Child Protective Services
CPS	College Press Service
CPS	Council for Philosophical Studies
CPSI	Creative Problem-Solving Institute
CPSSC	California Preschool Scale of Social Competence
CRA	Community Rehabilitation Approach
CRC	Career Resource Center
CRC	Conflict Review Curriculum
CREF	College Retirement Equities Fund
CRES	Computer Readability Editing System
CREST	Criterion-Referenced English Syntax Test
CRI	Classroom Reading Inventory
CRIB	Carolina Record of Individual Behavior
CRIPA	Civil Rights of Institutionalized Persons Act of 1980
CRIS	Council for Religion in Independent Schools
CRISP	Child's Report of the Impact of Separation by Parents
CRL	Center for Research Libraries
CRME	Council for Research in Music Education
CRPBI	Child Report of Parent Behavior Inventory
CRSS	College Reading and Study Skills Inventory
CRT	Cathode Ray Tube
CRT	Criterion-Referenced Test
CRUSK	Center for Research on Utilization of Scientific Knowledge (Institute for Social Research)
CS	Cogitive Style
CS	Conditioned Stimulus
CS	ERIC Clearinghouse on Reading and Communication Skills

CSA	Caribbean Studies Association
CSAA	Council of Specialized Accrediting Agencies
CSAB	Cognitive Skills Assessment Battery
CSAB	Counseling Services Assessment Blank
CSAI	Competitive State Anxiety Inventory
CSAO	Chief Student Affairs Officer
CSAR	Characteristic Storage And Retrieval
CSAS	Children's Strategies Assessment System
CSAVR	Council of State Administrators of Vocational Rehabilitation
CSC	Civil Service Commission
CSCC	Center for the Study of Community Colleges
CSD	Coalition on Sexuality and Disability
CSDC	Child Service Demonstration Centers
CSE	Center for the Study of Evaluation (University of California, Los Angeles)
CSFA	Citizen's Scholarship Foundation of America
CSI	Christian Schools International
CSI	Course Structure Inventory
CSLA	Canadian School Library Association
CSLEA	Center for the Study of Liberal Education for Adults
CSMI	Cognitive Style Mapping Inventory
CSMP	Comprehensive School Mathematics Program
CSN	Catholic Scholarships for Negroes
CSO	Community Service Organization
CSOS	Center for Social Organization of Schools (Johns Hopkins University)
CSP	Center for the Study of the Presidency
CSPA	Columbia Scholastic Press Association
CSPAA	Columbia Scholastic Press Advisers Association
C-SPAN	Cable-Satellite Public Affairs Network
CSPC	Conference of Small Private Colleges
CSPD	Comprehensive Systems of Personnel Development
CSPLSP	Canadian Society for Psychomotor Learning and Sport Psychology
CSPT	Conference for the Study of Political Thought
CSR	Center for the Study of Reading
CSR	Council on the Study of Religion
CSRP	Computerized Spelling Remediation Program
CSS	Computer Support Systems
CSSA	Central States Speech Association
CSSC	Classification of Secondary School Courses (National Center for Education Statistics)
CSSE	Canadian Society for the Study of Education
CSSEDC	Conference for Secondary School English Department Chairpersons
CSSO	Chief State School Officer
CSSS	Council of State Science Supervisors
CST	Competency Screening Test

CSWAE	Commission on the Status of Women in Adult Education
CSWE	Council on Social Work Education
CTAC	Center for Teaching About China
CTAI	Cooperating Teacher Attitude Inventory
CTBS	Canadian Test of Basic Skills
CTBS	Comprehensive Test of Basic Skills
CTF	Career Training Foundation
CTFR	Lawson's Classroom Test of Formal Reasoning
CTMM	California Test of Mental Maturity
CTP	California Test of Personality
CTRS	Conner's Teacher Rating Scale
CTS	College Theology Society
CTS	Conflict Tactics Scale
CTSE	Computerized Test of Spelling Errors
CTV	Cable Television
CTW	Children's Television Workshop
CUA	Conference of University Administrators
CUBS	Center for Urban Black Studies
CUE	Computer-Using Educators (California)
CUEBC	Computer-Using Educators of British Columbia
CUE-KY	Computer-Using Educators of Kentucky
CUFA	College and University Faculty Assembly (National Council for the Social Studies)
CUFC	Consortium of University Film Centers
CUMREC	College and University Machine Records Conference
CUPA	College and University Personnel Association
CUPE	Canadian Union of Public Employees
CUPM	Committee on the Undergraduate Program in Mathematics
CUR	Council on Undergraduate Research
CUTHA	Council for the Understanding of Technology in Human Affairs
CVA	Canadian Vocational Association
CVAE	Coordinated Vocational Academic Education (Georgia)
CVIS	Computerized Vocational Information System
CWAS	College Women's Assertion Sample
CWAS	Committee on Women in Asian Studies
CWEEA	Cooperative Work Experience Education Association
CWIS	Council for Women in Independent Schools (National Association of Independent Schools)
CWLA	Child Welfare League of America
CWS	College Work Study
CWSF	Catholic Women's Seminary Fund
CYEP	Consolidated Youth Employment Program
D.A.	Doctor of Arts
DAAD	Deutscher Akademischer Austauschdienst
DABI	Del Greco Assertive Behavior Inventory
DACL	Depression Adjective Checklist

DACUM	Developing A Curriculum
DAF	Denmark-America Foundation
DAI	Dissertation Abstracts International
DARP	Drug Abuse Reporting Program
DART	Division of Actively Retired Teachers (Ohio Education Association)
DAS	Dyadic Adjustment Scale
DASG	Developmental Assessment of Spanish Grammar
DAT	Dental Aptitude Test
DAT	Differential Aptitude Tests
DAT-VR	Differential Aptitude Test—Verbal Reasoning
DATAPAC	Not an acronym: Canada's national telecommunications network
DAVID	Digital And Video Interactive Device
D.B.A.	Doctor of Business Administration
DBC	Disturbing Behavior Checklist
DBMS	Data Base Management System
DBPM	Data-Based Program Modification
DBS	Direct Broadcast Satellite
D.C.	Doctor of Chiropractic
DCAT	Discourse Comprehension Abilities Test
DCBC	Daily Child Behavior Checklist
DCBP	Dissemination Capacity Building Project
DCCA	Day Care Council of America
DCCD	Division for Children with Communication Disorders (Council for Exceptional Children)
DCHM	Development Centers for Handicapped Minors
DCLD	Division for Children with Learning Disabilities (Council for Exceptional Children)
D.C.M.	Doctor of Comparative Medicine
DD	Developmentally Disabled
D.D.	Doctor of Divinity
DDC	Defense Documentation Center
DDC	Dewey Decimal Classification
D.D.S.	Doctor of Dental Surgery
DDST	Denver Developmental Screening Test
DEA	Dance Educators of America
DEA	Dominican Educational Association
DEAS	Delaware Education Accountability System
DECA	Distributive Education Clubs of America
DECS	Dual Employed Coping Scale
DEEP	Diffusion of Exemplary Educational Practices
DEM	Discrepancy Evaluation Model
DEMM	Division of Educational Media Management (Association for Educational Communications and Technology)
D.Eng.	Doctor of Engineering
DESB	Devereaux Elementary School Behavior Rating Scale
DEU	Duplicates Exchange Union
DFA	Dance Films Association
DFC	Designs For Change
DFI	Dynamic Functional Interaction
DGP	Dean's Grant Project
DHAT	Dental Hygiene Aptitude Tests
DHHS	Department of Health and Human Services
DHUD	Department of Housing and Urban Development
DIALOG	Not an acronym: On-line search program of Lockheed Information Systems
DIGA	Dynamics International Gardening Association
DILM	Dartmouth Intensive Language Model
DIOS	Direct Instruction Observation System
DIP	Dissemination and Improvement of Practice
DIQ	Deviation Intelligence Quotient
DIS	Diagnostic Interview Schedule
DISC	Documentation and Integration of Software into the Classroom Project
DISCOVER	Not an acronym: A computer-based career guidance and counselor support system
DISE	Development in Science Education Program
DISTAR	Direct Instructional System for Teaching Arithmetic and Reading
DIT	Defining Issues Test
DLI	Defense Language Institute
D.Lit.	Doctor of Literature
DL-LEA	Directed Listening-Language Experience Approach
DLP	DISTAR Language Program
DLPT	Defense Language Proficiency Tests
DMA	Dance Masters of America
D.M.A.	Doctor of Musical Arts
D.M.D.	Doctor of Dental Medicine
DMF	Detail Matching Figures Test
DMI	DiTomasso Methodology Inventory
DMP	Developing Mathematical Processes
D.Mus.	Doctor of Music
DNAE	Dissemination Network for Adult Educators
D.O.	Doctor of Osteopathy
DOA	Department of Agriculture
DOD	Department Of Defense
DODDS	Department Of Defense Dependents Schools
DOE	Department Of Energy
DOI	Department Of the Interior
DOJ	Department Of Justice
DOL	Department Of Labor
D.O.L.	Doctor Of Library Science
DOPHHH	Division Of Physically Handicapped, Homebound, and Hospitalized (Council for Exceptional Children)
DOS	Disk Operating System
DOSC	Dimensions Of Self-Concept Scales
DOT	Department Of Transportation
DOT	Dictionary Of Occupational Titles
DOT	Division Of Telecommunications (Association for Educational Communications and Technology)

DP	Developmental Play
DPA	Diagnostic Prescriptive Arithmetic
D.P.A.	Doctor of Public Administration
DPC	Dissemination Policy Council
D.Phar.	Doctor of Pharmacy
DPI	Department of Public Instruction
DPICS	Dyadic Parent-Child Interaction Coding System
D.P.M.	Doctor of Podiatric Medicine
DPMA	Data Processing Management Association
DPT	Diagnostic Prescriptive Teacher
DRA	Directed Reading Activity
DREDF	Disability Rights Education and Defense Fund
DRG	Diagnosis Related Groups
DRP	Degrees of Reading Power Test
DRS	Data Retrieval System
DR-TA	Directed Reading-Thinking Activity
D.S.	Doctor of Science
DS	Down's Syndrome
DSAA	Driving School Association of America
DSAB	District School Area Board (Ontario)
DSATHS	Dental Students' Attitudes Toward the Handicapped Scale
DSM	Diagnostic and Statistical Manual of Mental Disorders
DSS	Decision Support System
DSS	Developmental Sentence Scoring
DSU	Dissemination Services Unit
DTA	Documentation and Technical Assistance Project
DTIC	Defense Technical Information System
DTLA	Detroit Tests of Learning Aptitude
DTLA-OC	DTLA-Oral Commissions Subtest
DTLS	Descriptive Tests of Language Skills
DTMS	Descriptive Test of Mathematics Skills
DTS	Domestic Training Site
DTVP	Developmental Test of Visual Perception
DUSO	Developing Understanding of Self and Others
DVH	Division for the Visually Handicapped (Council for Exceptional Children)
D.V.M.	Doctor of Veterinary Medicine
EA	ERIC Clearinghouse on Educational Management
EAA	Education Amendments Act
EAC	Expectations about Counseling Questionnaire
EAHA	Education for All Handicapped Act
EAI	Educational Attitudes Inventory
EAI	Equal-Appearing Intervals
EAIS	Energy Action in Schools
EAJP	East Asia Journalism Program
EASE	Elementary Adult Sex Education
EAT	Eating Attitude Test
EATCQ	Expressed Attitude Toward Confrontation Questionnaire
EBC	Educational Broadcasting Corporation
EBCDIC	Extended Binary-Coded Decimal Interchange Code
EBCE	Experienced-Based Career Education
EBEA	Eastern Business Education Association
EBSI	Educational Beliefs System Inventory
EC	ERIC Clearinghouse on Handicapped and Gifted Children
ECA	Educational Communication Association
ECB	English Composition Board
ECBI	Eyberg Child Behavior Inventory
ECCI	Evening College Characteristics Index
ECCO	Educational Computer Consortium of Ohio
ECCP	Engineering Concepts Curriculum Project
ECCTYC	English Council of California Two-Year Colleges
ECEFT	Early Childhood Embedded Figures Test
ECER	Exceptional Child Education Resources (Council for Exceptional Children)
ECES	Educational and Career Exploration System
ECFMG	Educational Council for Foreign Medical Graduates
ECIA	Education Consolidation and Improvement Act of 1981
ECLP	EDUCOM Computer Literacy Project
ECOO	Educational Computing Organization of Ontario
ECOP	Extension Committee on Organization and Policy
ECRI	Exemplary Center for Reading Instruction (Maine)
ECRS	Earthwork/Center for Rural Studies
ECS	Education Commission of the States
ECS	Experienced Control Scales
ECSU	Educational Cooperative Service Unit
ECT	Electroconvulsive Therapy
ECT	Embedded Conversations Test
ED	Department of Education
ED	Emotionally Disturbed
ED	ERIC Document
EDAC	Evaluation, Dissemination, and Assessment Center for Bilingual Education
EDB	Energy Data Base (U.S. Department of Education)
EDC	Educational Development Center
EdCE	Examen de Colocacion en Español
EDCo	Educational Development Corporation
Ed.D.	Doctor of Education
EDEXS	Education of Exceptional Students
EDGAR	Education Division General Administration Regulations
EdITS	Educational and Industrial Testing Service
EDPRESS	Educational Press Association of America
EdReAn	Educational Research Analysts
EDRS	ERIC Document Reproduction Service

EDUCOM	Educational Communications (Interuniversity Communications Council)
EDUNET	Not an acronym: A computing network for higher education and other nonprofit organizations
EDY	Educationally Disadvantaged Youth
EE	Environmental Education
EEC	Education Exploration Center
EEG	Environmental Education Group
EEO	Equal Employment Opportunity
EEOC	Equal Employment Opportunity Commission
EER	Emergency English for Refugees (Pennsylvania)
EERA	Education Evaluation and Remedial Assistance Program (Connecticut)
EFC	Educational Facilities Center
EFF	Educational Freedom Foundation
EFI	Educational Forces Inventory
EFL	Educational Facilities Laboratories
EFL	English as a Foreign Language
EFLA	Educational Film Library Association
EFPM	EDUCOM Financial Planning Model System
EFRC	Education Funding Research Council
EFT	Embedded Figures Test
EGA	Educational Goals Assessment
EGE	Expected Grade Equivalent
EH	Educationally Handicapped
EHA	Economic History Association
EHA	Education for All Handicapped Children Act
EHCS	Educational and Health Career Services
EI	English Institute
EI	Entayant Institute
EIC	Education Information Center
EIDP	Early Intervention Developmental Profile
EIES	Electronic Information Exchange System
EIL	Experiment in International Living
EIP	Educational Improvement Process (Indiana)
EIT	Environmental Issues Test
EJ	ERIC Journal
EJAA	Emergency Jobs Appropriations Act of 1983
EJPEA	Emergency Jobs Programs Extension Act of 1976
EJS	Ethical Judgement Scale
EL HI	Elementary and High School
ELI	Education Leadership Institute
ELNA	Esperanto League for North America
ELP	Estimated Learning Potential
ELPS	English Language Proficiency Study
EL/SEC/JC	Elementary/Secondary/Junior College Special Interest Group (Association for the Development of Computer-Based Instructional Systems)
ELSEGIS	Elementary and Secondary General Information System

ELSIE	Edmond's Learning Style Identification Exercise
ELT	English Language Teaching
EMC	Electronic Music Consortium
EMG	Electromyogram
EMI	Experiences in Mathematical Ideas
EMIERT	Ethnic Materials Information Exchange Round Table
EMMSE	Educational Modules for Materials Science and Engineering
EMR	Educable Mentally Retarded
EMSI	Educational Micro Systems, Inc.
ENCORE	Not an acronym: A computer-based guidance system
EOC	Evaluation Of Counselors Scale
EOG	Educational Opportunity Grants
EOG	Electrooculograph
EOP	Educational Opportunity Programs
EOPS	Extended Opportunity Programs and Services
EOQ	Educational Orientation Questionnaire
EPA	Educational Paperbacks Association
EPAQ	Extended Personality Attributes Questionnaire
EPAT	Every Pupil Achievement Test
EPDA	Education Professions Development Act
EPF	Established Programme Financing Act (Canada)
EPI	Educational Planning Institute
EPIC	Education Professional for Indian Children
EPIC	Elyria Project for Innovative Curriculum
EPIE	Educational Products Information Exchange
EPPS	Edwards Personal Preference Schedule
EPQ	Eysenck Personality Questionnaire
EPS	Educational Participant Scale
EPSDT	Early and Periodic Screening, Diagnosis and Treatment
EPSIS	Educational Program and Studies Information Services
EPVT	English Picture Vocabulary Test
EQA	Educational Quality Assessment Program (Pennsylvania)
ERAJFS	Emergent Reading Ability Judgements for Favorite Storybooks Scale
ERANDA	Educational Research and Development Associates
ERB	Educational Records Bureau
ERB	Employment Relations Board
ERCA	Educational Research Council of America
ERD	Expressed Reading Difficulty
ERDA	Energy Research and Development Administration
ERDC	Educational Research and Development Committee
ERI	Ekwall Reading Inventory
ERI	Ethical Reasoning Inventory
ERIC	Educational Resources Information Center

ERICA	Effective Reading In Content Areas
ERIC/CAPS	ERIC Clearinghouse on Counseling and Personnel Services
ERIC/CEC	ERIC Clearinghouse on Handicapped and Gifted Children
ERIC/CEM	ERIC Clearinghouse on Educational Management
ERIC/ChESS	ERIC Clearinghouse for Social Studies/Social Science Education
ERIC/CLL	ERIC Clearinghouse on Languages and Linguistics
ERIC/CUE	ERIC Clearinghouse on Urban Education
ERIC/EECE	ERIC Clearinghouse on Elementary and Early Childhood Education
ERIC/RCS	ERIC Clearinghouse on Reading and Communication Skills
ERIC/SMEAC	ERIC Clearinghouse for Science, Mathematics, and Environmental Education
ERIE	Eastern Regional Institute for Education
ERMS	Educational Resource Management System
ERTA	Economic Recovery Tax Act of 1981
ES	Environmental Studies
ESA	Educational Service Agencies
ESAA	Emergency School Aid Act
ESAP	Emergency School Assistance Program
ESC	Education Service Center
ESCS	Early Social Communication Scale
ESD	Educational Service and Demonstration Centers (Washington)
ESD	English as a Second Dialect
ESEA	Elementary and Secondary Education Act
ESI	Early Screening Inventory
ESI	Educational Services, International
ESL	English as a Second Language
ESLAT	English as a Second Language Achievement Test
ESOL	English for Speakers of Other Languages
ESP	English for Specific Purposes
ESRI	Elementary Sex-Role Inventory
ESS	Elementary School Science
ESS	Elementary Science Study
ESSG	Elementary School Study Group
EST	English in Science and Technology
ESU	Educational Service Units
ESWP	Essential Sight Words Program
ESY	Extended School Year
ETA	Electronic Travel Aid
ETI	Effectiveness Training, Inc.
ETS	Educational Testing Service
ETSF	Educational Testing Service Test Collection File
ETS-kit	Educational Testing Service Kit of Reference Abilities
ETV	Educational Television
ETW	Effectiveness Training for Women
EUDISED	European Documentation and Information System for Education
EVAN-G	End Violence Against the Next Generation

EVI	Education Voucher Institute
EVR	Electronic Video Recorder
EWA	Education Writers Association
EWLTP	Earl Warren Legal Training Program
EXTRA	Extended Education in Therapeutic Recreation Administration
F	Frequency
FAAIECE	Fulbright Association of Alumni of International Educational and Cultural Exchange
FACES	Family Adaptability and Cohesion Evaluation Scales
FACSEA	Society for French-American Cultural Services and Educational Aid
FAF	Financial Accounting Foundation
FAF	Financial Aid Form
FAHE	Friends Association for Higher Education
FAME	Fund for the Advancement of Music Education
FAQ	Facts on Aging Quiz
FASAC	Financial Accounting Standards Advisory Council (Financial Accounting Foundation)
FASB	Financial Accounting Standards Boards (Financial Accounting Foundation)
FASCA	Federation of Armenian Students Clubs of America
FAST	Federally Assisted Staff Training
FAST	Florida Association of Science Teachers
FBLA—PBL	Future Business Leaders of America— Phi Beta Lambda
FCC	Federal Communications Commission
FCE	Friends Council on Education
FCIC	Florida Center for Instructional Computing
FD	Field Dependent
FDA	Food and Drug Administration
FDEC	Forum for Death Education and Counseling
FD/I	Field Dependence/Independence
FEC	Faculty Exchange Center
FEC	Foundation for Exceptional Children
FECP	Florida Educational Computing Project
FEDNET	Federal Library Network
FELT	Federal Employee Literacy Training Program
FEP	Fair Employment Practice
FERPA	Family Educational Rights and Privacy Act of 1974
FES	Family Environment Scale
FEU	Further Education Unit (Great Britain)
FFA	Future Farmers of America
FFS	Family Financial Statement
FFTA	Foundation of the Flexographic Technical Association
FFTQ	Four Factor Theory Questionnaire
FGCC	Foundation for Gifted and Creative Children
FGP	Foster Grandparent Program
FHA	Future Homemakers of America

FHSAA	Florida High School Athletics Association		FORT	Formal Operational Reasoning Test
FI	Field Independent		FORTRAN	Formula Translation
FIAC	Flanders Interaction Analysis Categories		FP	Feminist Press
FIAS	Flanders Interaction Analysis System		FPRRE	Foundation for Public Relations Research and Education
FIC	Foundation for International Cooperation		FRMG	Feminist Research Methodology Groups
FICCS	Functional Inventory of Cognitive Communication Strategies		FRSS	Fast Response Survey System (National Center for Education Statistics)
FICE	Federal Interagency Committee on Education		FSC	Foundation for Student Communication
FICS	Freshman Issues and Concerns Survey		FSI	Foreign Service Institute
FID	Fédération Internationale de Documentation		FSIQ	Full Scale Intelligence Quotient
FIDCR	Federal Interagency Day Care Requirements		FSSC	Foreign Student Service Council
			F-T	Full-Time
FIDER	Foundation for Interior Design Education Research		FTCE	Florida Teacher Certification Examination
FILLM	Fédération Internationale des Langues et Litteratures Modernes		FTE	Full-Time Equivalent
			FTEE	Full-Time Equivalent Enrollment
FILM	Film Integrated Learning Modules		FTRF	Freedom To Read Foundation
FIMEM	Fédération Internationale des Mouvements d'École Moderne		FTS	Federal Telecommunications System
			FTT	Failure To Thrive
FIPLV	Fédération Internationale de Professeurs des Langues Vivantes		FWLERD	Far West Laboratory for Educational Research and Development
FIPSE	Fund for the Improvement of Postsecondary Education		FY	Fiscal Year
FIRN	Florida Information Resource Network		GA	Graduate Assistant
FIRO-BC	Fundamental Interpersonal Relations Orientation—Behavior Children Test		GAAFR	Governmental Accounting, Auditing, and Financial Reporting
FISL	Federally Insured Student Loans		GAIN	Gifted Advocacy Information Network
FIT	Figural Intersection Test		GALTS	Generated Author Language Teaching System
FJA	Future Journalists of America			
FL	ERIC Clearinghouse on Languages and Linguistics		GAO	General Accounting Office
			GAS	General Adaptation Scale
			GAS	Global Assessment Scale
FLAG	Foreign Language Arts in the Grades		GATB	General Aptitude Test Battery
FLEDR	Foreign Language Entrance and Degree Requirements		GATE	Gifted And Talented Education Program (California)
FLES	Foreign Languages in Elementary Schools		GCI	General Cognitive Index
FLEX	Federal Licensing Examination		GCI	General Concerns Inventory
FLIC	Film Library Information Council		GCS	Gifted Child Society
FLIP	French Language Intensive Program (Illinois)		GDDQ	Group Dimensions Descriptions Questionnaire
FLIT	Functional Literacy		GDS	Gesell Developmental Schedules
FLRC	Federal Labor Relations Council		GDS	Gordon Diagnostic System
FLRT	Federal Librarians Roundtable (American Library Association)		GED	General Educational Development Test
			GED	General Equivalency Development Test
FLS	Functional Language Survey		GEFT	Group Embedded Figures Test
FLT	Figure Location Test		GEM	General Education Models Project
FLT	Functional Literacy Test		GEPA	General Education Provisions Act
FMA	Financial Management Association		GES	Group Environment Scale
FMCS	Federal Mediation and Conciliation Service		GFBA	Graduate Fellowships for Black Americans
FMS	Flexible Modular Scheduling		GFW	Goldman-Fristoe-Woodcock Auditory Skills Test Battery
FNE	Fear of Negative Evaluation Scale		GIS	Geoscience Information Society
FOI	Freedom Of Information		GIS	Guidance Information System
FOIL	Forward Occupational Imbalance Listing (Canada)		GL	Global Learning
			GLCA	Great Lakes Colleges Association
FORE	Foundation for Oregon Research and Education		GLDP	Ginn Language Development Program
			GMAT	Graduate Management Admissions Test
FORMAS	Feedback to Oral Reading Miscues Analysis System		GMENAC	Graduate Medical Education National Advisory Committee

GMF	Global Matching Figures Test
GODORT	Government Documents Round Table (American Library Association
GODORT FDTF	GODORT Federal Documents Task Force
GODORT IDTF	GODORT International Documents Task Force
GODORT SLDTF	GODORT State and Local Documents Task Force
GOIT	Goyer Organization of Ideas Test
GPA	Grade Point Average
GPE	Global Perspectives in Education, Inc.
GPO	Government Printing Office
GPPS	Guidance Program Preference Scale
GRE	Graduate Record Examination
GREB	Graduate Record Examination Board
GREAT	Gifted Resources Education Action Team Project
GRIP	Group Reading Interaction Pattern (An observation instrument)
GSA	General Services Administration
GSA	Gerontological Association of America
GSFLT	Graduate Student Foreign Language Test
GSL	Guaranteed Student Loans
GSLP	Guaranteed Student Loan Program
GSMT	General Society of Mechanics and Tradesmen
GSRT	Gesell School Readiness Test
G/T	Gifted and Talented
GTA	Graduate Teaching Assistant
GUPH	Group for the Use of Psychology in History
GURC	Gulf Universities Research Consortium
HA	Headmasters Association
HANES	Health and Nutrition Examination Survey
HBEA	Hawaii Business Education Association
HBI	Home-Based Instruction
HC	Hard Copy
HCVRCS	Hill Counselor Verbal Response Category System
HCEEP	Handicapped Children's Early Education Project
HD	Half Day
HDDP	Hospital Discharge Demonstration Project
HDTV	High Definition Television
HE	ERIC Clearinghouse on Higher Education
HEA	Higher Education Act of 1965
HEARS	Higher Education Administration Referral Service
HEATH	Higher Education and the Handicapped Project (American Council on Education)
HECSE	Higher Education Consortium on Special Education
HEDS	Higher Education Data Sharing
HEEA	Home Economics Education Association
HEERA	Higher Education Employer-Employee Relations Act

HEFA	Higher Education Facilities Act
HEGIS	Higher Education General Information Survey
HEITV	Higher Education Instructional Television (West Virginia)
HELDS	Higher Education for Learning Disabled Students
HELP	Human and Environmental Learning Program
HEMI	Higher Education Management Institute
HEN	Holistic Education Network
HEOP	Higher Education Opportunity Program
HEP	High School Equivalence Program
HEP	Higher Education Panel (American Council on Education)
HEPI	Higher Education Price Index
HERC	Home Education Resource Center
HERI	Higher Education Research Institute
HERO	Home Economics Related Occupations
HERS	Higher Education Resource Services
HES	History of Economics Society
HES	History of Education Society
HESB	Hahnemann Elementary School Behavior Rating Scale
HESIG	Health Education Special Interest Group (Association for the Development of Computer-Based Instructional Systems)
HEX	Handicapped Educational Exchange
HFD	Human Figures Drawing Test
HFT	Hidden Frames Test
HHS	Department of Health and Human Services
HIFTO	How I Feel Toward Others
HILT	High Intensity Language Training
HI-MAPS	Program for Hearing-Handicapped Infants Providing Medical, Academic, and Psychological Services
HIS	Health Interview Survey
HISM	How I See Myself Scale
HIT	High Intensity Tutoring
HIT	Holtzman Inkblot Test
HK-WISC	Hong Kong Wechsler Intelligence Scale
HLC	Health Locus of Control
HMCC	Housewife/Mother Career Concept
HML	Horace Mann League of the USA
HNTB	Halstead Neuropsychological Test Battery
H-NTLA	Hiskey-Nebraska Test of Learning Aptitude
HOME	Home Observation for Measurement of the Environment
HOSA	Health Occupations Students of America
HOSTS	Helping One Student To Succeed
HPER	Health, Physical Education, and Recreation
HPI	Health Practices Inventory
HRC	Human Resources Center

HRD	Human Resources Development
HRFT	Health Related Fitness Test
HRI	Health Resources Inventory
HRLSD	Health and Rehabilitative Library Services Division (American Library Association)
HRSA	Health Resources and Services Administration (U.S. Health and Human Services Department)
HSB	High School and Beyond Study
HSCA	Health Sciences Communication Association
HSCI	High School Characteristics Index
HSD	Tukey's Honestly Significant Difference Test
H/SERF	High-Scope Educational Research Foundation
HSI	Home and School Institute
HSP	Hospital School Program
HSPQ	High School Personality Questionnaire
HSTSF	Harry S Truman Scholarship Foundation
HTL	Hearing Threshold Level
HUD	Department of Housing and Urban Development
HumRRO	Human Resources Research Organization
HVAC	Hearing, Ventilating, and Air Conditioning
IAAA	Industrial Arts Association of Alabama
IAALD	International Association of Agricultural Librarians and Documentalists
IABC	International Association of Business Communicators
IABS	International Association of Buddhist Students
IABT	Illinois Association of Biology Teachers
IAC	Instructional Affairs Committee (National Council of Teachers of Mathematics)
IACA	Inter-American College Association
IACCB	Illinois Association of Community College Biologists
IACLEA	International Association of Campus Law Enforcement Administrators
IACP	Industrial Arts Curriculum Project
IACS	International Association of Cooking Schools
IACS	International Association of Counseling Services
IAEA	International Association for Educational Assessment
IAEWP	International Association of Educators for World Peace
IAIA	Institute of American Indian Arts
IALL	International Association for Learning Laboratories
IALL	International Association of Law Libraries
IAMCR	International Association for Mass Communication Research

IAML	International Association of Music Libraries
IAMPTH	International Association of Master Penmen and Teachers of Handwriting
IAOL	International Association Of Orientalist Librarians
IAOT	International Association Of Organ Teachers
IAP	Information Analysis Product (Educational Resources Information Center)
IAP	Inquiry and Assistance Project
IAPC	Institute for the Advancement of Philosophy for Children
IAPD	International Association of Parents of the Deaf
IAPESGW	International Association of Physical Education and Sports for Girls and Women
IAPPW	International Association of Pupil Personnel Workers
IARQ	Intellectual Achievement Responsibility Questionnaire
IAS	Illness Adaptation Scale
IAS	Intelligent Authoring Systems
IASA	International Association of Sound Archives
IASB	Illinois Association of School Boards
IASCE	International Association for the Study of Cooperation in Education
IASL	International Association of School Librarianship
IASSW	International Association of Schools of Social Work
IAST	Instrument for the Analysis of Science Teaching
IASWR	Institute for Advanced Studies of World Religions
IATEFL	International Association of Teachers of English as a Foreign Language
IATUL	International Association of Technological University Libraries
IAU	International Association of Universities
IAUPE	International Association of University Professors of English
IAV	Index of Achievement Values
IAWS	Intercollegiate Association for Women Students
IB	International Baccalaureate
IBBY	International Board on Books for Young People
IBE	Information-Based Education
IBE	International Bureau of Education
IBI	Individualized Bilingual Instruction
IBS	Institute of Black Studies
IBS	Intercollegiate Broadcasting System
IBT	Irrational Beliefs Test
ICA	Industrial Cooperative Association
ICA	International Communication Association
ICA	International Council on Archives

ICAE	International Council for Adult Education
I-CAI	Intelligent Computer-Assisted Instruction
ICB	Interagency Collaborative Boards (Michigan)
ICBS	Impulsive Classroom Behavior Scale
ICCE	International Council for Computers in Education
ICCP	Institute for Certification of Computer Professionals
ICCP	International Camp Counselor Program
ICCP	International Conference on Cataloging Principles
ICE	Indiana Computer Educators
ICEBY	International Council of Educators of Blind Youth
ICEC	Inter-university Consortium for Educational Computing
ICED	International Council for Educational Development
ICEP	Individualized Career Education Planning
ICEQ	Individualized Classroom Environment Questionnaire
ICES	Instructor and Course Evaluation System
ICET	Institute for Certification in Engineering Technologies
ICET	International Council on Education for Teaching
ICFA	Independent College Funds of America
ICFU	International Council on the Future of the University
ICG	Illinois Council for the Gifted
ICG	Indochina Curriculum Group
ICHPER	International Council on Health, Physical Education and Recreation
ICI	Interpersonal Communication Inventory
ICII	International Congress for Individualized Instruction
ICJL	Institute for Computers in Jewish Life
ICLEP	Individualized Computer Literacy Education Plan
ICLM	Induced Course Load Matrix
ICP	International Center of Photography
ICPP	Institutional Child Protection Project (Ohio State University)
ICPS	Interpersonal Cognitive Problem-Solving Program
ICPSR	Inter-University Consortium for Political and Social Research
ICSU	International Council of Scientific Unions
ICSU/AB	International Council of Scientific Unions/Abstracting Board
ICYE	International Christian Youth Exchange
IDDM	Insulin-Dependent Diabetes Mellitus
I/D/E/A	Institute for Development of Education Activities
IDEC	Interior Design Educators Council
IDECC	Interstate Distributive Education Curriculum Consortium

IDRA	Intercultural Development Research Association
IDRC	International Development Research Centre (Canada)
IDRC/MINISIS	Not an acronym: An information retrieval system developed by the IDRC
IDS	Instructional Dimensions Study
IE	Instrumental Enrichment Program
IE	Internal-External Locus of Control
IEA	International Association for the Evaluation of Educational Achievement
IEA	International Study of Educational Achievement
IEC	Imaginative Educational Cooperation Project
IEC	Indian Education Committee
IEC	Industry Education Council
IECA	Independent Educational Counselors Association
IEE	Institute for Environmental Education
IEEE	Institute of Electrical and Electronics Engineers
IEEP	International Environmental Education Programme (UNESCO)
IEL	Institute for Educational Leadership
IEP	Individualized Education Program
IER	Institute of Educational Research
IES	Independent Educational Services
IES	Institute of European Studies
IESMP	Information Exchange System for Minority Personnel
IF	Interfuture
IFCA	International Federation of Catholic Alumnae
IFES	International Fellowship of Evangelical Students
IFLA	International Federation of Library Associations
IFPS	Interactive Financial Planning System (EDUCOM)
IFRT	Intellectual Freedom Roundtable (American Library Association)
IFTDO	International Federation of Training and Development Organizations
IGAEA	International Graphic Arts Education Association
IGCBT	Interagency Group for Computer-Based Training
IGCC	Institute for Global Conflict and Cooperation
IGE	Individually Guided Education
IGI	Institutional Goals Inventory
IGPME	International Group for Psychology and Mathematics Education
IHETS	Indiana Higher Education Telecommunications System
IHS	International Horn Society
IIA	Information Industry Association

IIAS	International Institute for Advanced Studies
IIE	Institute of International Education
IIEP	Illinois Inventory of Educational Progress
IIEP	International Institute for Educational Planning (UNESCO)
IIP	Individualized Instructional Planning
IIS	Interaction Involvement Scale
IIS	International Institutional Services
IISPA	Interactive Instructional Systems— Presentation and Authoring Special Interest Group (Association for the Development of Computer-Based Instructional Systems)
ILAEDS	Illinois Association for Educational Data Systems
ILAR	Institute of Laboratory Animal Resources
ILIAD	Interactive Language Instruction Assistance for the Deaf
ILIC	International Library Information Center
ILIS	Integrated Library Information Systems
ILL	Institute of Lifetime Learning
ILL	Interlibrary Loan
ILLINET	Illinois Library and Information Network
ILP	Inventory of Learning Processes
ILR	Interagency Language Rountables (U.S. Government)
IM	Index Medicus
IMC	Illinois Migrant Council
IMI	Impact Message Inventory
IMPACT	Institute for Manpower Program Analysis, Consultation and Training, Inc.
IMPS	Instructional Management and Presentation System
IMVTS	Industrial Model Vocational Training Systems
INAD	Institute for Native American Development
INICR	Institute for Childhood Resources
INSEA	International Society for Education through Art
IOEHI	International Organization for the Education of the Hearing Impaired
IOSHD	International Organization for the Study of Human Development
IPA	Interaction Process Analysis
IPA	International Phonetic Alphabet
IPA	International Phonetic Association
IPASS	Not an acronym: A computer-managed instruction and testing program for basic mathematics skills in grades 1 through 8
IPAT	Institute for Personality and Ability Testing
IPC	Interparental Conflict Scales
IPCCA	Interassociational Presidents' Committee on Collegiate Athletics

IPDC	International Programme for the Development of Communication (UNESCO)
IPI	Individually Prescribed (or Planned) Instruction
IPLE	Institute for Political/Legal Education
IPM	Interaction Place Map
IQ	Intelligence Quotient
IR	ERIC Clearinghouse on Information Resources
IR	Institutional Research
IRA	Indian Rights Association
IRA	International Reading Association
IRC	Instructional Resources Center
IRC	International Relations Committee (American Library Association)
IRCD	Information Retrieval Center on the Disadvantaged
IR&D	Interactive Research and Development
IRE	Institute for Responsive Education
IREX	International Research and Exchanges Board
IRI	Informal Reading Inventory
IRIS	Individual Reading Instruction System
IRIS	Interagency Research Information System
IRIS	Water Quality Instructional Resources Information System
IRLA	Independent Research Library Association
IRLDP	Pacific Northwest Indian Reading and Language Development Program
IRRT	International Relations Round Table (American Library Association)
IRS	Interpersonal Relationship Scale
IRT	Item Response Theory
ISA	Intermediate Service Agency
ISAD	Information Science and Automation Division (American Library Association)
ISAGA	International Simulation and Gaming Association
ISAM	Institute for Studies in American Music
ISBD	International Standard Bibliographic Description
ISBD(M)	ISBD (Monographs)
ISBD(S)	ISBD (Serials)
ISBE	International Society for Business Education
ISBN	International Standard Book Number
ISCC	Iranian Students Counseling Center
ISEP	Institute for the Study of Educational Policy
ISEP	Instructional Scientific Equipment Program (National Science Foundation)
ISEP	International Society for Educational Planning
ISI	Inter-Sound Interval
ISI	Interstimulus Interval
ISICS	Indian Self-Identified Certified Staff

ISIG	Implementation Special Interest Group (Association for the Development of Computer-Based Instructional Systems)
ISIS	Individualized Science Instructional System
ISLA	International Survey Library Association
ISM	Instructional System in Mathematics Program
ISM	Interpretive Structural Modeling
ISMC	Integrated Sentence-Modeling Curriculum
ISME	International Society for Music Education
ISPCAN	International Society for Prevention of Child Abuse and Neglect
ISPhS	International Society of Phonetic Sciences
ISPN	International Standard Program Number
ISR	Institute for Social Research
ISR	Institute for Study of Regulation
ISRT	Iowa Silent Reading Test
ISS	International Schools Services
ISS	International Student Service
ISSN	International Standard Serial Number
IST	Individualized Study by Telecommunications (Alaska)
IT	Instructional Technologist
ITA	International Teaching Alphabet
ITB	Invitation To Bid
ITBS	Iowa Test of Basic Skills
ITC	Instructional Telecommunications Consortium (American Association of Community and Junior Colleges)
ITED	Iowa Tests of Educational Development
ITFS	Instructional Television Fixed Service
ITP	Individualized Transition Plans
ITPA	Illinois Test of Psycholinguistic Abilities
ITPA-AR	ITPA-Auditory Reception Subtest
ITS	International Thespian Society
ITV	Instructional Television
ITVA	International Television Association
IUC	International University Consortium for Telecommunications in Learning
IULC	Committee on Instruction in the Use of Libraries (American Library Association)
IVCC	Illinois Vocational Curriculum Center
IVD	Interactive Videodisc
IVLA	International Visual Literacy Association
IVP	Individualized Vocational Program
IVSET	Interactive Videodisc for Special Education Technology
IWRI	Informal Word Recognition Inventory
IYC	International Year of the Child
IYDP	International Year for Disabled Persons
JA	Junior Achievement
JACC	Journalism Association of Community Colleges
JACP	Japanese American Curriculum Project

JAG	Jobs for America's Graduates, Inc.
JASC	Japan-America Student Conference
JASIS	Journal of the American Society of Information Science
JASPA	Jesuit Association of Student Personnel Administrators
JC	ERIC Clearinghouse for Junior Colleges
JCAH	Joint Commission on Accreditation of Hospitals
JCCC	Joint Committee on Contemporary China
JCEE	Joint Council on Economic Education
JCET	Joint Council on Educational Telecommunications
J.D.	Juris Doctor
JDI	Job Description Index
JDRP	Joint Dissemination Review Panel (U.S. Department of Education)
JEA	Jewish Educators Assembly
JEA	Journalism Education Association
JESNA	Jewish Education Service of North America
JETS	Junior Engineering Technical Society
JHSN	Junior High School Network Project
JIRI	Johnson Informal Reading Inventory
JMEA	Jewish Music Educators Association
JMRT	Junior Members Round Table (American Library Association)
JNCL	Joint National Committee for Languages
JOBS	Job-Oriented Basic Skills Program (U.S. Navy)
JSA	Junior Statesmen of America
JSEA	Jesuit Secondary Education Association
JSF	Junior Statesmen Foundation
JTPA	Job Training Partnership Act
JV	Junior Varsity
K-ABC	Kaufman Assessment Battery for Children
KACEE	Kansas Advisory Council on Environmental Education
KAHP	Kentucky Allied Health Project
KCPCA	Kansas Committee for Prevention of Child Abuse
KEDDS	Kansas Education Dissemination/Diffusion System
KEEP	Kamehameha Early Education Program (Hawaii)
KEEP	Kentucky Environmental Education Program
KELP	Kindergarten Evaluation of Learning Potential
KFD	Kinetic Family Drawing Method
KHTTA	Kanata High Technology Training Association (Canada)
KICS	Kansas Individualized Curriculum Sequencing
KID	Kent Infant Development Scale
KIDS	Kindling Individual Development Systems Project
KIK	Kentucky's Individualized Kindergartens

KLST	Kindergarten Language Screening Test
KMDAT	Key Math Diagnostic Arithmetic Test
KNOW-NET	Knowledge Network of Washington
KPR	Kuder Preference Record
KPR-V	Kuder Preference Record—Vocational
KSD	Kinetic School Drawing Method
KTSA	Kahn Test of Symbol Arrangement
KWIC	Key Word In Context
KWIT	Key Word In Title
KWOC	Key Word Out of Context
L1	First Language
L2	Second Language
LAB	Language Assessment Battery
LABE	Louisiana Association of Business Educators
LABSTAT	Labor Statistics Database
LAC	Legislative Audit Council (South Carolina)
LAD	Language Acquisition Device
LADB	Laboratory Animal Data Bank
LAIRS	Labor Agreement Information Retrieval System (Civil Service Commission)
LAMA	Library Administration and Management Association
LAMA BES	LAMA Buildings and Equipment Section
LAMA CSS	LAMA Circulation Services Section
LAMA LOMS	LAMA Library Organization and Management Section
LAMA PAS	Library Personnel Administration Section
LAMA PRS	LAMA Public Relations Section
LAMA SS	LAMA Statistics Section
LAP	Goodchild's Location-Allocation Package
LAP	Learning Activity Package
LARC	Learning, Assessment, Retention Consortium (California)
LARR	Linguistic Awareness Reading Test
LAS	Language Assessment Scales
LAS	Leader Authenticity Scale
LASA	Latin American Studies Association
LASPAU	Latin America Scholarship Program of American Universities
LASSO	Linguistic Association of the Southwest
LATC	Language Across the Curriculum
LBD	Learning and/or Behavior Disordered
LBDQ	Leadership Behavior Description Questionnaire
LBR	Library Bill of Rights
LC	Library of Congress
LCA	Library-College Associates
LCCN	Library of Congress Card Number
LCEE	Louisiana Council on Economic Education
LCSH	Library of Congress Subject Headings
LD	Learning Disabled
LDB	Leisure Diagnostic Battery
LDRI	Learning Disabilities Research Institute (University of Virginia)
LDS	Lesson Design System
LEA	Language Experience Approach
LEA	Learning Experience Approach

LEA	Local Education Agency
LEA	Lutheran Education Association
LEAA	Law Enforcement Assistance Act
LEAD	Leadership, Education, and Development Project
LECNA	Lutheran Educational Conference of North America
LEEP	Law Enforcement Education Program
LEF	Lincoln Educational Foundation
LEI	Learning Environment Inventory
LEI	Life Expectancy Inventory
LEP	Limited English Proficiency
LEPUS	Not an acronym: A computing language for teaching programming and for computer-assisted instruction
LEQ	Life Events Questionnaire
LERN	Learning Resources Network
LES	Life Experiences Survey
LES	Limited English Speaking
LGD	Leaderless Group Discussion
LH	Learning Handicapped
L.H.D.	Doctor of Humane Letters
LHRT	Library History Round Table (American Library Association)
LI	Leadership Institute
LIBGIS	Library General Information Survey
LIBS	Library Information Bibliographic System
LICC	League for Innovation in the Community College
LINCS	Language Information Network and Clearinghouse System
LIPC	Levenson's Internal, Powerful Others, and Chance Scales
LIRIC	Language Instruction for Recent Immigrants through Computer Technology
LIRS	Library Information Retrieval System
LIRT	Library Instruction Round Table (American Library Association)
LISA	Library and Information Science Abstracts
LISREL	Linear Structural Relations
LIST	Local Information Sources for Teachers
LIT	Language Inventory Test
LITA	Library and Information Technology Association
LITA AVS	LITA Audiovisual Section
LITA ISAS	LITA Information Science and Automation Section
LITA VCCS	LITA Video and Cable Communications Section
Lit.D.	Doctor of Literature
LL.B.	Bachelor of Laws
LLBA	Language and Language Behavior Abstracts
LL.D.	Doctor of Laws
LLI	Learning and Language Impaired
LL.M.	Master of Laws
LM&AI	Language Measurement and Assessment Inventory

LMET	Leadership and Management Education and Training
LMRA	Labor Management Relations Act
LMRS	Labor Management Relations Service
LMT	Learning Methods Test
LNNB	Luria-Nebraska Neuropsychological Test Battery
LOC	Locus Of Control
LOCI	Local Course Improvement (National Science Foundation)
LORI	Locus Of Responsibility Inventory
LPAD	Learning Potential Assessment Device
LPN	Licensed Practical Nurse
LPRC	Library Public Relations Council
LPT	Language Proficiency Test (National Security Agency)
LPTV	Low-Power Television
LRC	Learning Resources Center
LRDC	Learning Research and Development Center
LRE	Law-Related Education
LREI	Life Role Expectations Inventory
LRPSI	Long-Range Planning for School Improvement (Pennsylvania)
LRRT	Library Research Round Table (American Library Association)
LRTS	Library Resources and Technical Services
LSA	Linguistic Society of America
LSAC	Law School Admission Council
LSAS	Law School Admission Services
LSAT	Law School Admission Test
LSAT	Leveling/Sharpening Aggressions Test
LSCA	Library Services and Construction Act
LSCG	Law School Computer Group
LSCT	Loevinger Sentence Completion Test
LSF	Lloyd Shaw Foundation
LSHT	Leveling/Sharpening House Test
LSI	Learning Styles Inventory
LSI-P	Learning Styles Inventory—Primary Version
LSM	Learning Systems Model
LT	Large Type
M	Mean
M.A.	Master of Arts
MA	Mental Age
MAA	Mathematical Association of America
MAA	Mutual Assistance Associations
MAACL	Multiple Affect Adjective Checklist
MAAI	Modeling Association of America, International
MAB	Man in the Biosphere Programme (Canada)
MAC	MacAndrew Alcoholism Scale
MACL	Mood Adjective Checklist
MACOS	Man: A Course Of Study
MACT	Moral Action Choice Test
MACUL	Michigan Association for Computer Users in Learning
MAEP	Measure of Adult English Proficiency

MAEPS	Model Adoption Exchange Payment System
M-A-F-T	Modified-Adopted-Fernald Technique
MAGERT	Map and Geography Round Table (American Library Association)
M.A. in Ed.	Master of Arts in Education
MAIS	Minnesota Adaptive Instructional System
MALDEF	Mexican-American Legal Defense and Educational Fund
M.A.L.S.	Master of Arts in Library Science
MANA	Mexican-American Women's National Association
MAN-AEDS	Manitoba Association for Educational Data Systems
MANOVA	Multivariate Analysis Of Variance
MANS	Mathematics Applied to Novel Situations Test
MAP	Military Applicant Profile (U.S. Army)
MAP	Musical Aptitude Profile
MAPS	Manpower Assessment and Placement System
MAPS	Middle Atlantic Planetarium Society
MARC	Machine Readable Cataloging
M.Arch.	Master of Architecture
MARS	Machine Assisted Reference Section (American Library Association)
MARS	Mathematics Anxiety Rating Scale
MAS	Math Anxiety Scales
MAS	Mathematics Attitude Scales
MAS	Mathematics Attribution Scale
MASMR	Multidimensional Attitude Scale on Mental Retardation
MASUA	Mid-America State Universities Association
M.A.T.	Masters of Arts in Teaching
MAT	Metropolitan Achievement Tests
MAT	Miller Analogies Test
MATH	Not an acronym: Name for the National Consortium on Uses of Computers in Mathematical Sciences Education (Affiliated with the Association for the Development of Computer-Based Instructional Systems)
MAVE	Model for Articulated Vocational Education
M.B.A.	Master of Business Administration
MBD	Minimal Brain Dysfunction
MBE	Multistate Bar Examination
MBEA	Michigan Business Education Association
MBEA	Missouri Business Education Association
MBEI	Minnesota Business Educators, Inc.
MBI	Maslach Burnout Inventory
MBO	Management By Objectives
MBQ	Management Behavior Questionnaire
MBTI	Myers-Briggs Type Indicator
MCA	Multiple Classification Analysis
MCAAP	Medical College Admissions Assessment Program
MCAI	Microcomputer Assisted Instruction
MCAT	Medical College Admission Test

MCC   Maryland Committee for Children
MCC   Modular Counseling Curriculum
MCCCSA   Michigan Community College Community Services Association
MCCE   Montana Council for Computers in Education
MCCOEES   Michigan Community College Occupational Education Evaluation System
MCDI   Minnesota Child Development Inventory
MCES   Maryland Cooperative Extension Service
MCIP   Manpower Consortium for the Information Professions
MCLAA   Minnesota Computer Literacy and Awareness Assessment
MCPPEP   Medical College of Pennsylvania Pharmaceutical Education Programs
MCREL   Mid-Continent Regional Educational Laboratory
MCT   Minimum Competency Testing
MCTFL   Minnesota Council on the Teaching of Foreign Languages
MCTM   Michigan Council of Teachers of Mathematics
M.D.   Doctor of Medicine
MD   Mathematics Disabled
MDEA   Marketing and Distribution Education Association
MDHES   Manpower Development Higher Education System
MDI   Mental Development Index
M.Div.   Master of Divinity
MDN   Median
MDPI   Mathematics Diagnostic/Prescriptive Inventory
MDS   Microwave Multipoint Distribution Systems
MDS   Multidimensional Scaling
MEAN   Microcomputer Education Application Network
MEAP   Michigan Educational Assessment Program
MEC   Metrolina Educational Consortium (North Carolina)
MECA   Department of Measurement, Evaluation, and Computer Applications (Ontario Institute for Studies in Education)
MECA   Measure of Elementary Communication Apprehension
MECC   Minnesota Educational Computing Consortium
M.Ed.   Master of Education
MEDICI   Melodic Dictation Computerized Instruction
MEDLARS   Medical Literature Analysis Retrieval System (National Library of Medicine)
MEDLINE   Not an acronym: Medical computer bibliographic service of the National Library of Medicine

MEGSSS   Mathematics Education for Gifted Secondary School Students Project
MELA   Middle East Librarians' Association
MELP   Measure of Language Proficiency
MELVYL   Not an acronym: A prototype on-line library catalog at the University of California
MEMO   Minnesota Educational Media Organization
MENC   Music Educators National Conference
MEP   Microelectronics Education Program
MEPE   Michigan English Proficiency Examination
MEPS   Means-Ends Problem Solving Measure
MERA   Michigan Educational Research Association
MERIC   Michigan Educational Resource Information Center
MERP   Minimum Enrollment and Reasonable Progress
MES   Media Evaluation Services (North Carolina)
METCO   Metropolitan Council for Educational Opportunity (Massachusetts)
MF   Microfiche
MF   Microfilm
M.F.A.   Master of Fine Arts
MFD   Memory-For-Designs Test
MFFT   Matching Familiar Figures Test
MFLT   Mathematics Functional Literacy Test
MFMT   Maryland Functional Mathematics Test
MFRT   Maryland Functional Reading Test
MFWP   Maryland Functional Writing Program
MGAP   Middle Grades Assessment Program
MGM   Mentally Gifted Minor
MHHI   Multihandicapped Hearing-Impaired
MHRP   Mental Health Research Project
MHVQ   Mental Health Values Questionnaire
MICCLE   Michigan Interorganizational Committee on Continuing Library Education
MICROCOMP POB Microcomputer Program Oriented Budgeting System
MICRONET   Not an acronym: An Indiana network that promotes microcomputer use in the public schools
MicroSIFT Microcomputer Software and Information For Teachers
MICRO-VERS Microcomputer Vocational Education Reporting System
MID   Measure of Intellectual Development
MIDLNET   Midwestern Regional Library Network
MINI-MICRO Minicomputer User Special Interest Group (Association for the Development of Computer-Based Instructional Systems)
MINITEX   Minnesota Interlibrary Telecommunications Exchange
MINT   Magnetic Information Technology
MIS   Management Information System
MIS   Moody Institute of Science

MISAA	Middle Income Student Assistance Act
MiSIS	Michigan Student Information System
MISSIS	Mississippi Student Information System
MITECS	Multi-International Teacher Education Cooperatives
ML	Mother Language
MLA	Marine Librarians Association
MLA	Medical Library Association
MLA	Modern Language Association of America
MLA	Music Library Association
MLAT	Modern Language Aptitude Test
MLR	Multiple Linear Regression
M.L.S.	Master of Library Science
MLU	Mean Length of Utterance
M.M.	Master of Music
MMCERC	Multiethnic/Multicultural Christian Education Resources Center
MMCS	Multidimensional-Multiattributional Causality Scale
M.M.E.	Master of Music Education
MMEP	Missouri Mathematics Effectiveness Project
MMLA	Midwest Modern Language Association
MMP	Mathematics-Methods Program
MMPI	Minnesota Multi-Phasic Personality Inventory
MMPI-D	MMPI-Depression Scale
M.Mus.	Master of Music
MMY	Mental Measurement Yearbook
MNCP	Math Network Curriculum Project
MNQ	Manifest Needs Questionnaire
M&O	Maintenance and Operations
MOES	Mathematics Olympiads for Elementary Schools
M-PBEA	Mountain-Plains Business Education Association
MPCL	Mooney Problem Checklist
M.P.H.	Master of Public Health
MPLI	Michigan Picture Language Inventory
MPOIS	Multi-Purpose Occupational Information System (North Carolina)
MPSS	Maryland Preschool Self-Concept Scale
MQ	Memory Quotient
MR	Mental Retardation
MRG	Modern Rythmic Gymnastics
MRM	Matter-Relation-Matter Semantic Units
MRT	Metropolitan Reading Test
M.S.	Master of Science
MSA	Measure of Sampling Adequacy Index
MSA	Middle States Association of Colleges and Schools
MSAT	Minnesota Scholastic Aptitude Test
M.Sc.	Master of Science
MSCA	McCarthy Scales of Children's Abilities
M.S.C.E.	Master of Science in Chemical Engineering
M.S.E.E.	Master of Science in Electrical Engineering
MSDAC	Minnesota State Drafting Advisory Committee
MSEM	Mainstreamed Special Educator Model
MSF	Mean Square Fit
MS-GFW	Memory for Sequence Subtest of the Goldman-Fristoe-Woodcock Auditory Skills Test Battery
M.S.in Ed.	Master of Science in Education
MSJ	Master of Science in Journalism
M.S.L.S.	Master of Science in Library Science
M.S.N.	Master of Science in Nursing
MSQ	Minnesota Satisfaction Questionnaire
MSRTS	Migrant Student Record Transfer System
MSS	Movement Shorthand Society
MSSD	Model Secondary School for the Deaf (Gallaudet College)
MSSST	Meeting Street School Screening Test
MST	McCarthy Screening Test
MST	Miniature Situations Test
M.S.W.	Master of Social Work
M.T.	Medical Technologist
MTAI	Minnesota Teacher Attitude Inventory
MTELP	Michigan Test of English Language Proficiency
MTNA	Music Teachers National Association
MURL	Major Urban Resource Libraries
Mus.D.	Doctor of Music
MVPT	Motor-Free Visual Perception Test
MWDAC	Mountain West Desegregation Assistance Centers
MYCIN	Not an acronym: A computer-aided diagnostic consultation system
MZSCS	Martinek-Zaichkowsky Self-Concept Scale
MZT	Man Zeichen Test
N4A	National Association of Academic Athletic Advisors
NA	Not Applicable
NAA	National Academy of Arbitrators
NAAB	National Architectural Accrediting Board
NAABAVE	National Association for the Advancement of Black Americans in Vocational Education
NAACLS	National Accrediting Agency for Clinical Laboratory Sciences
NAACP	National Association for the Advancement of Colored People
NAACSS	National Association for the Accreditation of Colleges and Secondary Schools
NAAEE	North American Association for Environmental Education
NAAPAE	National Association for Asian and Pacific American Education
NAAS	National Association of Academies of Science
NAASFEP	National Association of Administrators of State and Federal Education Programs
NAASS	North American Association of Summer Sessions
NAB	National Alliance of Business

NABE	National Association for Bilingual Education
NABE	National Association of Boards of Education
NABESS	National Association of Business Education State Supervisors
NABP	National Association of Black Professors
NABPR	National Association of Baptist Professors of Religion
NABS	National Association of Barber Schools
NABSE	National Alliance of Black School Educators
NABT	National Association of Biology Teachers
NABT	National Association of Blind Teachers
NABTE	National Association for Business Teacher Education
NAC	National Action Committee on the Status of Women (Canada)
NACA	National Association for Campus Activities
NACAC	National Association of College Admissions Counselors
NACAE	National Advisory Council on Adult Education
NACBE	National Advisory Council for Bilingual Education
NACC	National Association for Core Curriculum
NACCA	National Association for Creative Children and Adults
NACCAS	National Accrediting Commission of Cosmetology Arts and Sciences
NACD	National Association for Community Development
NACDRAO	National Association of College Deans, Registrars, and Admissions Officers
NACEBE	National Association of Classroom Educators in Business Education
NACEEO	National Advisory Council on Equality of Educational Opportunity
NACIE	National Advisory Council on Indian Education
NACME	National Action Council for Minorities in Engineering
NACOME	National Advisory Committee On Mathematics Education
NACS	National Association of College Stores
NACS	National Association of Cosmetology Schools
NACTA	National Association of Colleges and Teachers of Agriculture
NACUA	National Association of College and University Attorneys
NACUBO	National Association of College and University Business Officers
NACUFS	National Association of College and University Food Services
NACURH	National Association of College and University Residence Halls
NACVE	National Advisory Council on Vocational Education
NACWPI	National Assocation of College Wind and Percussion Instructors
NAD	National Association of the Deaf
NAEA	National Art Education Association
NAEB	National Association of Educational Buyers
NAEC	National Association for Education Computing
NAEd	National Academy of Education
NAEEO	National Association for Equal Educational Opportunities
NAEIR	National Association for the Exchange of Industrial Resources
NAEN	National Association of Educational Negotiators
NAEOP	National Association of Educational Office Personnel
NAEP	National Assessment of Educational Progress
NAES	National Association of Episcopal Schools
NAESP	National Association of Elementary School Principals
NAEYC	National Association for the Education of Young Children
NAFEO	National Association For Equal Opportunity in Higher Education
NAFIS	National Association of Federally Impacted Schools
NAFPA	National Association of Federal Program Administration
NAFSA	National Association for Foreign Student Affairs
NAGC	National Association for Gifted Children
NAGT	National Association of Geology Teachers
NAGWS	National Association for Girls and Women in Sport (American Alliance for Health, Physical Education, Recreation, and Dance)
NAHC	National Association of Homes for Children
NAHE	National Association for Humanities Education
NAIA	National Association for Intercollegiate Athletics
NAICU	National Association of Independent Colleges and Universities
NAIEC	National Association for Industry-Education Cooperation
NAIES	National Association of Interdisciplinary Ethnic Studies
NAIS	National Association of Independent Schools
NAIT	National Association of Industrial Technology
NAITTE	National Association of Industrial and Technical Teacher Educators
NAIWA	North American Indian Women's Association
NAJE	National Association of Jazz Educators

NAJSN	North American Jewish Students' Network
NAL	National Agricultural Library
NALSAS	National Association for Legal Support of Alternative Schools
NAM	National Association of Manufacturers
NAME	National Association of Management/Marketing Educators
NAMEPA	National Association of Minority Engineering Program Administrators
NAMESU	National Association of Music Executives in State Universities
NAMSE	National Association of Minority Students and Educators in Higher Education
NANA	Northwest Arctic Inupiat Corporation (Alaska)
NAPAVHEE	National Association of Postsecondary and Adult Vocational Home Economics Educators
NAPCE	National Association of Professors of Christian Education
NAPDEA	North American Professional Driver Education Association
NAPE	National Association of Professional Educators
NAPEHE	National Association for Physical Education in Higher Education
NAPH	National Association of Professors of Hebrew
NAPNSC	National Association of Private, Nontraditional Schools and Colleges
NAPPA	National Association of Pupil Personnel Administrators
NAPSEC	National Association of Private Schools for Exceptional Children
NAPSG	National Association of Principals of Schools for Girls
NARC	National Association of Regional Councils
NARDSPE	National Association for Remedial/Developmental Studies in Postsecondary Education
NARELLO	National Association for Real Estate License Law Officials
NARF	Native American Rights Fund
NARI	Native American Research Institute
NARIC	National Rehabilitation Information Center
NARL	National Assessment of Reading and Literature
NARS	National Archives and Records Service
NARST	National Association for Research in Science Teaching
NARTS	National Association of Reporter Training Schools
NAS	National Academy of Sciences
NAS	Native American Studies
NASA	National Aeronautics and Space Administration
NASAA	National Association of Student Activity Advisers
NASACU	National Association of State Approved Colleges and Universities
NASAD	National Association of Schools of Art and Design
NASAE	National Association of Supervisors of Agricultural Education
NASAGA	North American Simulation And Gaming Association
NASASPS	National Association of State Administrators and Supervisors of Private Schools
NASBE	National Association of State Boards of Education
NASBE	National Association of Supervisors of Business Education
NASC	National Association of Student Councils
NASC	Northwest Association of Schools and Colleges
NASCO	North American Students of Cooperation
NASCUMC	National Association of Schools and Colleges of the United Methodist Church
NASD	National Association of Schools of Dance
NASDSE	National Association of State Directors of Special Education
NASDTEC	National Association of State Directors of Teacher Education Certification
NASDVE	National Association of State Directors of Vocational Education
NASEA	National Association of Student Employment Administrators
NASEDIO	National Association of State Education Department Information Officers
NASFAA	National Association of Student Financial Aid Administrators
NASILP	National Association of Self-Instructional Language Programs
NASM	National Association of Schools of Music
NASN	National Association of School Nurses
NASP	National Association of School Psychologists
NASPA	National Association of Student Personnel Administrators
NASPAA	National Association of Schools of Public Affairs and Administration
NASPE	National Association for Sport and Physical Education
NASPSPA	North American Society for the Psychology of Sport and Physical Activity
NASSD	National Association of School Security Directors
NASSDSE	National Association of State Supervisors and Directors of Secondary Education
NASSM	National Association of State Supervisors of Music
NASSP	National Association of Secondary School Principals

NASSTIE	National Association of State Supervisors of Trade and Industrial Education
NASSVHE	National Association of State Supervisors of Vocational Home Economics
NAST	National Association of Schools of Theatre
NASTA	National Association of State Text Book Administrators
NASULGC	National Association of State Universities and Land-Grant Colleges
NASW	National Association of Social Workers
NATA	National Association of Teachers' Agencies
NATA	National Athletic Trainers Association
NATAL	Not an acronym: Programming Language
NATEBE	National Association of Teacher Educators for Business Education
NATEVHE	National Association of Teacher Educators for Vocational Home Economics
NATIE	National Association for Trade and Industrial Education
NATS	National Association of Teachers of Singing
NATTS	National Association of Trade and Technical Schools
NAUW	National Association of University Women
NAVA	National Audio-Visual Association
NAVAE	National Association for Vietnamese-American Education
NAVEA	National Adult Vocational Education Association
NAVEDTRA	Naval Education and Training Command
NAVESNP	National Association of Vocational Education Special Needs Personnel
NAVH	National Association for the Visually Handicapped
NAVHET	National Association of Vocational Home Economics Teachers
NAVL	National Alliance of Voluntary Learning
NAWDAC	National Association for Women Deans, Administrators, and Counselors
NBAS	Neonatal Behavioral Assessment Scale
NBAS-K	Neonatal Behavioral Assessment Scale—Kansas Revision
NBCDA	National Black Child Development Act
NBCDI	National Black Child Development Institute
NBCGT	National Business Consortium for the Gifted and Talented
NBDHE	National Board Dental Hygiene Examination
NBEA	National Business Education Association
NBLC	National Business Law Council
NBME	National Board of Medical Examiners
NCA	North Central Association of Colleges and Schools
NCAA	National Collegiate Athletic Association
NCAAE	National Council of Administrators of Adult Education

NCACME	National Center for Adult, Continuing and Manpower Education
NCACS	National Coalition of Alternative Community Schools
NCAH	National Committee, Arts for the Handicapped
NCAI	National Congress of American Indians
NCAIE	National Center for American Indian Education
NCAIR	North Carolina Association for Institutional Research
NCAR	National Center for Atmospheric Research (National Science Foundation)
NCARB	National Council of Architectural Registration Boards
NCAS	National Collegiate Association for Secretaries
NCAT	National Center for Audiotape
NCATE	National Council for the Accreditation of Teacher Education
NCAWE	National Council of Administrative Women in Education
NCBE	National Clearinghouse for Bilingual Education
NCBE	National Conference of Bar Examiners
NCBEA	National Catholic Business Education Association
N-CBEA	North-Central Business Education Association
NCBEC	National Center for Business and Economic Communication
NCBFCD	National Council for Black Family and Child Development
NCBFE	National Center for a Barrier Free Environment
NCBIAE	National Council of Bureau of Indian Affairs Educators
NCBPD	National Consortium for Black Professional Development
NCBR	National Center for Bilingual Research
NCBS	National Council for Black Studies
NCC	National Coaches Council
NCCBMI	National Consortium for Computer-Based Music Instruction (Association for the Development of Computer-Based Instructional Systems)
NCCBO	National Council of Community College Business Officials
NCCD	National Council on Communication Disorders
NCCD	National Crisis Center for the Deaf
NCCE	National Center for Community Education
NCCE	National Commission for Cooperative Education
NCCE	National Committee for Citizens in Education
NCCE	Northwest Council for Computer Education

NCCEOA   National Coordinating Council of Educational Opportunities Associations

NCCHE   National Chicano Council on Higher Education

NCCP   National Clearinghouse for Commuter Programs

NCCPA   National Commission on Certification of Physician's Assistants, Inc.

NCCRCU   National Congress of Church-Related Colleges and Universities

NCCSS   North Central Conference on Summer Schools

NCDE   National Coalition for Democracy in Education

NCDTO   National Council of Dance Teacher Organizations

NCE   National Committee on the Emeriti

NCE   Normal Curve Equivalent

NCEA   National Catholic Educational Association

NCEA   National Community Education Association

NCEB   National Center for Education Brokering

NCEC   National Center for Educational Communication

NCEE   National Commission on Excellence in Education

NCEE   National Congress for Educational Excellence

NCEE   National Council of Engineering Examiners

NCEMC   National Committee on the Education of Migrant Children

NCEMMH   National Center on Educational Media and Materials for the Handicapped

NCEOA   National Council of Educational Opportunity Associations

NCER   National Council on Educational Research

NCERD   National Center for Educational Research and Development

NCES   National Center for Education Statistics

NCES   Normal Curve Equivalent Scores

NCFJE   National Committee for the Furtherance of Jewish Education

NCFL   National Catholic Forensic League

NCFLIS   National Council on Foreign Languages and International Studies

NCGA   National Council on Governmental Accounting

NCGE   National Council for Geographic Education

NCHELP   National Council of Higher Education Loan Programs

NCHEMS   National Center for Higher Education Management Systems

NCHS   National Center for Health Statistics

NCI   National Captioning Institute

NCIA   National Council of Instructional Administrators

NCIES   National Center for the Improvement of Educational Systems

NCIL   National Center for the Improvement of Learning (American Association of School Administrators)

NCL   National Character Laboratory

NCLA   National Council of Local Administrators of Vocational Education and Practical Arts

NCLIS   National Commission on Libraries and Information Science

NCMA   National Campus Ministry Association

NCME   National Council on Measurement in Education

NCOA   National Council On the Aging

NCP   Nursing Curriculum Project (Southern Regional Education Board)

NCPERL   National Coalition for Public Education and Religious Liberty

NCPI   National Conference on Parent Involvement

NCQIE   National Coalition for Quality Integrated Education

NCRD   National Council for Resource Development

NCRE   National Conference on Research in English

NCRLS   National Committee for Russian Language Study (American Association for the Advancement of Slavic Studies)

NCRP   National Council for Research and Planning

NCRPE   National Council on Religion and Public Education

NCRVE   National Center for Research in Vocational Education

NCRY   National Commission on Resources for Youth

NCSCBHE   National Center for the Study of Collective Bargaining in Higher Education

NCSCEE   National Council of State Consultants in Elementary Education

NCSCPAS   National Center for the Study of Corporal Punishment and Alternatives in the Schools

NCSDCJC   National Council of State Directors of Community and Junior Colleges

NCSEA   National Council of State Education Associations

NCSI   National Curriculum Study Institute (Association for Supervision and Curriculum Development)

NCSL   National Center for Service-Learning

NCSL   National Conference of State Legislatures

NCSM   National Council of Supervisors of Mathematics

NC SOICC   North Carolina State Occupational Information Coordinating Committee

NCSQ   National Case Study Questionnaire

NCSS	National Council for the Social Studies
NCSSAD	National Council of Secondary School Athletic Directors
NCSSFL	National Council of State Supervisors of Foreign Languages
NCTA	National Cable Television Association
NCTCP	National Coalition of Title 1/Chapter 1 Parents
NCTE	National Council for Textile Education
NCTE	National Council of Teachers of English
NCTM	National Council of Teachers of Mathematics
NCTR	National Council on Teacher Retirement
NCUEA	National Council of Urban Education Associations
NCURA	National Council of University Research Administrators
NCWGE	National Coalition for Women and Girls in Education
NCYP	National Conference of Yeshiva Principals
NCYRE	National Council on Year-Round Education
NDBA	National Data Base on Aging
NDC	New Directions in Creativity Program
NDEA	National Defense Education Act
NDN	National Diffusion Network
NDPCAL	National Development Program in Computer Assisted Learning (Great Britain)
NDRT	Nelson-Denny Reading Test
NDSL	National Direct Student Loans
NEA	National Education Association
NEA	National Endowment for the Arts (National Foundation on the Arts and the Humanities)
NEA-PAC	National Education Association Political Action Committee
NEASC	New England Association of Schools and Colleges
NEBEA	New England Business Educators Association
NEC	Northeast Conference on the Teaching of Foreign Languages
NECA	National Employment Counselors Association (American Personnel and Guidance Association)
NECA	Near East College Association
NECC	National Educational Computing Conference
NECPA	National Energy Conservation Policy Act
NEDCC	Northeast Document Conservation Center
NEDRES	National Environmental Data Referral Service
NEH	National Endowment for the Humanities (National Foundation on the Arts and the Humanities)
NEHC	National Extension Homemakers Council
NEHI	Northwest Educators of the Hearing Impaired
NEIC	New England Information Center
NEL	Network of Education Libraries (Australia)
NELINET	New England Library Information Network
NEMLA	Northeast Modern Language Association
NEOMYCIN	Not an acronym: Intelligent computer-aided diagnostic consultation system
NEPA	National Environmental Policy Act
NEREX	Northeast Regional Exchange
NES	Non-English Speaking
NESDEC	New England School Development Council
NF	Newspaper Fund
NF	Nieman Foundation
NFA	National Forensics Association
NFAH	National Foundation on the Arts and the Humanities
NFAIS	National Federation of Abstracting and Indexing Services
NFC	Northwest Forensics Conference
NFCPO	National Forum of Catholic Parent Organizations
NFDH	National Foundation of Dentistry for the Handicapped
NFE	Non-Formal Education
NFIE	National Foundation for the Improvement of Education
NFL	National Forensic League
NFLCP	National Federation of Local Cable Programmers
NFMLTA	National Federation of Modern Language Teachers Associations
NFSD	National Fraternal Society of the Deaf
NFSM	National Fraternity of Student Musicians
NGAS	Needs-Based Goal Attainment Scale
NGCSA	National Guild of Community Schools of the Arts
NGO	Non-Governmental Organizations
NGPT	National Guild of Piano Teachers
NGTF	National Gay Task Force
NH ACES	New Hampshire Association for Computer Education Statewide
NHD	National History Day
NHF	National Humanities Faculty
NHI	National Health Insurance
NHLBI	National Heart, Lung, and Blood Institute
NHS	National Honor Society
NHSA	National Head Start Association
NHSC	National Home Study Council
NHTAS	National Highway Traffic Safety Administration
NI	National Incidence Study
NIA	National Institute on Aging
NIAAA	National Institute on Alcohol Abuse and Alcoholism
NIAAA	National Interscholastic Athletic Administrators Association

NIAE   National Institute for Architectural Education

NIAID   National Institute of Allergy and Infectious Diseases (National Institutes of Health)

NIC   Neighborhood Info Centers Project

NICA   National Indian Counselors Association

NICEM   National Information Center for Educational Media

NICHHD   National Institute of Child Health and Human Development (National Institutes of Health)

NICSEM/NIMIS   National Information Center for Special Education Material/National Instructional Material Information System

NICOA   National Indian Council On Aging

NIDA   National Institute on Drug Abuse

NIDR   National Institute of Dental Research (National Institutes of Health)

NIE   National Institute of Education (Department of Education)

NIEA   National Indian Education Association

NIEHS   National Institute of Environmental Health Sciences (National Institutes of Health)

NIGP   National Institute of Governmental Purchasing

NIH   National Institutes of Health

NIHR   National Institute of Handicapped Research (U.S. Department of Education)

NIICU   National Institute of Independent Colleges and Universities

NIM   Neurological Impress Method

NIMBL   National Institute for Microcomputer Based Learning

NIME   National Institute for Multicultural Education

NIMH   National Institute of Mental Health

NIN   National Inservice Network

NINCDS   National Institute of Neurological and Communicative Disorders and Stroke (National Institutes of Health)

NIOSH   National Institute for Occupational Safety and Health

NIP   National Identification Program for the Advancement of Women in Higher Education Administration

NIPALS   Nonlinear Iterative Partial Least Squares

NIS   National Institute of Science

NITRAS   Navy Integrated Training Resources and Administration System

NIWL   National Institute for Work and Learning

NIYC   National Indian Youth Council

NJCAA   National Junior College Athletic Association

NJCBSPT   New Jersey College Basic Skills Placement Test

NJCLD   National Joint Committee for Learning Disabilities

NJDDC   New Jersey Developmental Disabilities Council

NJHA   National Junior Horticultural Association

NJHS   National Junior Honor Society

NLA   National Librarians Association

NLAE   National Laboratory for the Advancement of Education

NLC   National Library of Canada

NLM   National Library of Medicine

NLN   National League of Nursing

NLP   Neurolinguistic Programming

NLPP   Natural Language Processing Program

NLPTL   National Lutheran Parent-Teacher League

NLRB   National Labor Relations Board

NLS   National Library Service for the Blind and Physically Handicapped (Library of Congress)

NLS   National Longitudinal Study of the Class of '72

NLSMA   National Longitudinal Study of Mathematical Ability

NLW   National Library Week

NMA   National Micrographics Association

NMEA   National Marine Education Association

NMHSPE   New Mexico High School Proficiency Examination

NMSA   National Middle School Association

NMSC   National Merit Scholarship Corporation

NMSQT   National Merit Scholarship Qualifying Test

NMSRC   National Middle School Resource Center

NNBC   National Network of Bilingual Centers

NNCCVTE   National Network for Curriculum Coordination in Vocational and Technical Education

NNGBSW   National Network of Graduate Business School Women

NNS   Non-native Speakers

NOCERCC   National Organization for the Continuing Education of Roman Catholic Clergy

NOCSAE   National Operating Committee on Standards for Athletic Equipment

NODA   National Orientation Directors Association

NOICC   National Occupational Information Coordinating Committee

NOLPE   National Organization on Legal Problems in Education

NOME   National Origin Minority Education (New Hampshire Department of Education)

NORC   National Opinion Research Center (University of Chicago)

NORDICOM   Nordic Documentation Center for Mass Communication Research (Denmark)

NOW   National Organization for Women

N.P.   Nurse Practitioner

NPC   National Periodicals Center

NPCE   National Project on Career Education

NPF	National Piano Foundation
NPI	Narcissistic Personality Inventory
NPM	National Association of Pastoral Musicians
NPR	National Public Radio
NPS	National Park Service
NR	Norm-Referenced
NRA	National Rifle Association of America
NRC	National Reading Conference
NRC	National Referral Center (Library of Congress)
NRC	National Research Council
NROTC	Naval Reserve Officer Training Corps
NRRS	Nebraska Reading Retrieval System
NRS	New Reading System
NRT	Norm-Referenced Testing
NRTA	National Retired Teachers Association (American Association of Retired Persons)
NS	Native Speaker
NSA	Nepal Studies Association
NSAC	National Student Aid Coalition
NSB	National Science Board of the National Science Foundation
NSBA	National School Boards Association
NSBTN	National Small Business Training Network
NSCEE	National Schools Committee for Economic Education
NSDC	National School Development Council
NSDM	New School for Democratic Management
NSDP	National Serials Data Program
NSE	National Student Exchange
NSEDP	National Sex Equity Demonstration Project
NSEF	National Student Educational Fund
NSF	National Science Foundation
NSF	National Sex Forum
NSGC	National Self-Government Committee
NS-GFW	Noise Subtest of the Goldman-Fristoe-Woodcock Auditory Skills Test Battery
NSIEE	National Society for Internships and Experiential Education
NSKS	Nature of Scientific Knowledge Scale
N/S-LTI-G/T	National/State Leadership Training Institute on Gifted and Talented
NSMR	National Society for Medical Research
NSOA	National School Orchestra Association
NSPA	National Scholastic Press Association
NSPE	National Society of Professional Engineers
NSPI	National Society for Performance and Instruction
NSPRA	National School Public Relations Association
NSRA	National Shorthand Reporters Association
NSSA	National Science Supervisors Association

NSSE	National Society for the Study of Education
NSSE	National Study of School Evaluation
NSSEA	National School Supply and Equipment Association
NSSFNS	National Scholarship Service and Fund for Negro Students
NSSLHA	National Student Speech Language Hearing Association
NSST	Northwestern Syntax Screening Test
NSST-R	NSST-Receptive Portion
NSTA	National School Transportation Association
NSTA	National Science Teachers Association
NSVP	National School Volunteer Programs, Inc.
NSVP	National Student Volunteer Program
NT	Narrower Term
NTAG	Network Technical Architecture Group (Library of Congress)
NTE	National Teachers Examination
NTI	National Theatre Institute
NTID	National Technical Institute for the Deaf
NTIS	National Technical Information Service (U.S. Department of Commerce)
NTL	National Training Laboratories
NUC	National Union Catalog
NUC	National University Consortium
NUCEA	National University Continuing Education Association
NUTN	National University Teleconference Network
NV	Nonverbal
NV	Number of Variables
NVA	Night Vision Aid
NVATA	National Vocational Agricultural Teachers' Association
NVEPDC	National Vocational Educational Professional Development Consortium
NVGA	National Vocational Guidance Association (American Personnel and Guidance Association)
NWEF	National Women's Education Fund
NWF	National Wildlife Federation
NWF	New World Foundation
NWP	National Writing Project
NWREL	Northwest Regional Educational Laboratory
NWRx	Northwest Regional Exchange
NWSA	National Women's Studies Association
NYC	Neighborhood Youth Corps
NYCUC	New York City Urban Corps
NYLS	New York State Longitudinal Study
NYPN	National Youth Practitioners Network
NYSAFLT	New York State Association of Foreign Language Teachers
NYSIAA	New York State Industrial Arts Association
NYSILL	New York State Interlibrary Loan Network

OAA	Older Americans Act of 1965
OAA	Organization of Athletic Administrators
OAH	Organization of American Historians
OAKE	Organization of American Kodaly Educators
OARS	Older Americans Resources and Services
OAS	Organization of American States
OASES	Open Access Satellite Education Services
OB	Outward Bound
OBEA	Oregon Business Education Association
OBEMLA	Office of Bilingual Education and Minority Languages Affairs (Department of Education)
OCCE	Oklahoma Citizen's Commission on Education
OCCI	Organizational Communication Conflict Instrument
OCDQ	Organizational Climate Description Questionnaire
OCI	Organizational Climate Index
OCLC	Not an acronym: A bibliographic data service
OCLDP-K	Open Court Language Development Program: Kindergarten
OCR	Office of Civil Rights (U.S. Department of Education)
OCR	Optical Character Recognition
OCS	Obsessive Compulsive Scale
O.D.	Doctor of Optometry
OD	Organizational Development
ODAP	Office of Drug Abuse Policy
ODAS	Oral Deaf Adults Section (Alexander Graham Bell Association for the Deaf)
ODIN	On-line Database Information Network (Pennsylvania)
ODSE	Open Door Student Exchange
ODT	Oral Directions Test
OE	Operation Enterprise
OE	Outdoor Education
OEA	Office Education Association
OEA	Outdoor Education Association
OEA	Overseas Education Association
OECC	Office on Educational Credit and Credentials (American Council on Education)
OECC	Oregon Educational Computing Consortium
OECD	Organization for Economic Cooperation and Development (France)
OECUP	Oklahoma Educational Computer User's Group
OEES	Organization for Equal Education of the Sexes
OEF	Overseas Education Fund
OEII	O'Neill Educational Ideologies Inventory
OELMA	Ohio Educational Library Media Association
OEO	Office of Economic Opportunity
OEP	Occupational Education Project
OEP	Optional Educational Programs
OERC	Ontario Educational Research Council

OFCCP	Office of Federal Contract Compliance Programs (U.S. Department of Labor)
OGT	Office for the Gifted and Talented (U.S. Department of Education)
OHAPT	Orleans-Hanna Algebra Prognosis Test
OIAS	Occupational Information Access System
OIEP	Office of Indian Education Programs (Bureau of Indian Affairs)
OIF	Office for Intellectual Freedom (American Library Association)
OII	Occupational Interest Inventory
OISE	Ontario Institute for Studies in Education
OJJDP	Office of Juvenile Justice and Delinquency Prevention
OJT	On-the-Job Training
OLA	Ontario Library Association
OLC	Overseas Liaison Committee (American Council on Education)
OLMAT	Otis Lennon Mental Ability Test
OLOS	Office for Library Outreach Services (American Library Association)
OLPR	Office for Library Personnel Resources (American Library Association)
OLS	Ordinary Least Squares
OLSIDI	Oral Langauge Sentence Imitation Diagnostic Inventory
OMB	Office of Management and Budget
OMEA	Ohio Music Education Association
OMEP	Organisation Mondiale pour l'Education Prescolaire (World Organization for Early Childhood Education)
OMLTA	Ohio Modern Language Teachers Association
OMRDD	Office of Mental Retardation and Developmental Disabilities (New York)
OMS	Office of Management Studies (Association of Research Libraries)
ONTERIS	Ontario Educational Research Information System
OOH	Occupational Outlook Handbook
OP	Out of Print
OPAC	Online Public Access Catalog
OPACT	Organization of Professional Acting Coaches and Teachers
OPI	Omnibus Personality Inventory
OPIE	Ohio Program of Intensive English
OPM	U.S. Office of Personnel Management
OPTI	Optimism-Pessimism Test Instrument
ORBIT	Not an acronym: On-line search service of System Development Corporation
ORBS	Off Reservation Boarding School
ORF	Observe Rating Form
ORION	Not an acronym: On-line catalog at the University of California, Los Angeles
ORIS	Omaha Reading Instruction System
ORT	Organization for Rehabilitation through Training
OS	Operating System
OSAS	Ohio Social Acceptance Scale
OSCAR	Observation Schedule And Records

OSE	Office of Special Education (U.S. Department of Education)
OSERS	Office of Special Education and Rehabilitation Services (Department of Education)
OSHA	Occupational Safety and Health Act of 1970
OSI	Open Systems Interconnection
OSIA	Observational System for Instructional Analysis
OSIQA	Offer Self-Image Questionnaire for Adolescents
OSTD	Ontario Society for Training and Development
OSUPE	Ohio State University Psychological Exam
OT	Occupational Therapy
OTA	Office of Technology Assessment (U.S. Congress)
OTID	Office of Talented Identification and Development (Johns Hopkins University)
OVEATP	Ohio Vocational Education Achievement Test Program
OVIS	Ohio Vocational Interest Survey
PA	Psychological Abstracts
PAAT	Parent As A Teacher Inventory
PAC	Parallel Alternate Curriculum
PAC	Parent Advisory Council
PACCE	Providing Professional Developmemt, Assessment, and Coordination of Competency-based Education Project (Illinois)
PACE	Program for Acquiring Competence in Entrepreneurship
PACER	Parent Advocacy Coalition for Educational Rights (Minnesota)
PACES	Parent Attitude toward Child Expressiveness Scale
PACT	Plan of Action for Challenging Times
PACT	Public Action Coalition on Toys
PAEG	Prueba de Admisión para Estudios Graduados (Educational Testing Service)
PAI	Pirchei Agudath Israel
PAIC	Personal Attribute Inventory for Children
PAIS	Public Affairs Information Service
PALA	Polish-American Librarians Association
PALI	Pacific and Asian Linguistics Institute
PALS	Principles of Adult Learning Scale
PAPC	Philological Association of the Pacific Coast
PAQ	Personal Attributes Questionnaire
PARC	Pennsylvania Association for Retarded Children
P.A.R.E.N.T.S.	People of America Responding to Educational Needs of Today's Society
PARS	Program Analysis and Review System
PAS	Personal Attitude Survey

PAS	Pre-conscious Activity Scale
PASE	Programs in the Arts for Special Education Project
PASF	Photographic Art and Science Foundation
PASS	Portable Assisted Study Sequence Program (California)
PAT	Programmer Aptitude Test
PATH	Peer Attitudes Toward the Handicapped Scale
PATHE	Positive Action Through Holistic Evaluation Program
PAVE	Performance-based Adult Vocational Education
PAYES	Program for Assessing Youth Employment Skills
PBEI	Performance-Based Evaluation Instrument
PBS	Public Broadcasting Service
PBTE	Performance-Based Teacher Education
PC	Paired Comparisons
PC	Paper Copy
PCAR	Parent-Child Activity Rating Scale
PCCP	Private Child Care Providers
PCD	Perceptual-Communicative Disorders
PCI	Parent-Child Interaction Scale
PCI	Pupil Control Ideology Form
PCM	Paragraph Completion Method
PCMP	Pennsylvania Comprehensive Mathematics Plan
PCP	Phencyclidine
PCPI	Parent Cooperative Preschools International
PCRP	Pennsylvania Comprehensive Reading Program
PCS	Parent's Confidential Statement
PCS	Public Choice Society
PD	Physically Disabled
PDB	Program Development Branch (Division of Innovation and Development, U.S. Department of Education)
PDC	Project Developmental Continuity (Head Start)
PDI	Program with Developing Institutions
PDI	Psychological Distress Inventory
PDI	Psychomotor Development Index
PDK	Phi Delta Kappa
PDPIC	Professional Development Program Improvement Center
PDR	Parent Daily Telephone Reports
PDS	Personnel Data System
PDU	Protocol Data Unit
PE	Physical Education
PEACESAT	Pan-Pacific Education and Communications Experiments Using Satellites (National Aeronautics and Space Administration)
PECRS	Post-Evaluative Conference Rating Scale
PEEC	Project for an Energy-Enriched Curriculum

PEER	Project on Equal Education Rights (National Organization for Women)
PEF	Packaging Education Foundation
PEF	Plastics Education Foundation
PEFT	Preschool Embedded Figures Test
PEFTP	Parent Education Follow Through Program
PEI	Patriotic Education, Inc.
PEI	Pupil Evaluation Inventory
PEMAP	President's Environmental Merit Awards Program
PEPC	Florida Postsecondary Education Planning Commission
PERB	Public Employment Relations Board
PERC	Public Employment Relations Commission
PERM	Planning, Evaluation, and Resource Management Model (Connecticut)
PERSC	Public Education Religious Studies Center
PERT	Program Evaluation and Review Technique
PES	Philosophy of Education Society
PET	Parent Effectiveness Training
PETREL	Professional Education and Training for Research Librarianship Program
Ph.D.	Doctor of Philosophy
PHEAA	Pennsylvania Higher Education Assistance Agency
PHS	Public Health Service
PHSCS	Pier-Harris Self-Concept Scale
PHT	Paired Hands Test
PI	Proactive Interference
PIA	Plastics Institute of America
P.I.A.G.E.T.	Promoting Intellectual Adaptation Given Experiential Transforming Project
PIAT	Peabody Individual Achievement Test
PIC	Personality Inventory for Children
PIC	Private Industry Council
PICA	Porch Index of Communicative Ability
PILOT	Programmed Instruction Learning On Teaching (A simplified programming language for computer-assisted instruction)
PIN	Peer Intervention Network
PINS	Persons In Need of Supervision
PIPS	Preschool Interpersonal Problem Solving
PIPS	Professional Improvement Points Program (Louisiana)
PIQ	Performance Intelligence Quotient
PIRAMID	Project: Individualized Reading And Mathematics Inter-District
PIRC	Preventive Intervention Research Centers (National Institutes of Mental Health)
PIRG	Public Interest Research Group
PITA	Programming In The Arts (National Endowment for the Arts)
PITA	Provincial Intermediate Teachers Association (Canada)
PL	Public Law
PL/1	Programming Language/Version One
PLA	Private Libraries Association
PLA	Public Library Association
PLA AEPS	Public Library Association Alternative Education Program Section
PLA AFLS	Public Library Association Armed Forces Library Section
PLA CIS	Public Library Association Community Information Section
PLA MLS	Public Library Association Metropolitan Libraries Section
PLA PLSS	Public Library Association Public Library Systems Section
PLA SMLS	Public Library Association Small and Medium-Sized Libraries Section
PLANIT	Programming Language for Interactive Teaching
PLATO	Programmed Logic for Automated Teaching Operations
PLDK-P	Peabody Language Development Kit: Preschool
PLOT	Piagetian Logical Operations Test
PLRA	Pennsylvania Learning Resources Association
PLS	Partial Least Squares
PLS	Preschool Language Scale
PLUS	Parent Loans for Undergraduate Students
PME	Planning, Management, and Evaluation
PMI	Planning, Monitoring, and Implementing Model
PMI	Probe Ministries International
PMR	Profoundly Mentally Retarded
PMSAT	Pre-Medical Student Assessment Test
PNCFL	Pacific Northwest Council on Foreign Languages and Literatures
PNI	Parent Needs Inventory
PNID	Peer Nomination Inventory of Depression
PNP	Pediatric Nurse Practitioner
PNSQ	Porter Need Satisfaction Questionnaire
POD	Professional and Organizational Development Network in Higher Education
Pod.D.	Doctor of Podiatry
PODS	Perceptions Of Developmental Skills Profile
POI	Personal Orientation Inventory
POMS	Profile Of Mood States Inventory
PONS	Profile Of Nonverbal Sensitivity
PONSI	Program On Noncollegiate Sponsored Instruction (American Council on Education)
PONVER	Project On National Vocational Education Resources
POST	Processes Of Science Test
PPBC	Portland Problem Behavior Checklist
PPNA	Pupil-Perceived Needs Assessment
PPNS-IE	Preschool and Primary Nowicki-Strickland Internal-External Control Scale
PPQ	Person Perception Questionnaire

PPSC	Privacy Protection Study Commission
PPSI	Parent Problem-Solving Instrument
PPSQ	Principal Problem Strategy Questionnaire
P-PST	Pre-Professional Skill Test
PPVT	Peabody Picture Vocabulary Test
PQE	Professional Qualification Examination (National Security Agency)
PRAI	Pre-Reading Assessment Inventory
PRECIS	Preserved Context Indexing System
PREPS	Predischarge Remedial Education Program
PREPS	Program of Research and Evaluation for Public Schools
PREST	Not an acronym: A computer-based reading and study skills curriculum developed for Navy recruits
PRFT	Portable Rod-and-Frame Test
PRI	Partnership for Rural Improvement (Washington)
PRISE	Pennsylvania Resources and Information Center for Special Education
PRISM	Pittsburgh's Research-based Instructional Supervising Model
PRISM	Priorities In School Mathematics Project
PROBE	Practical Research into Organizational Behavior and Effectiveness
PROSE	Personal Record Of School Experiences
PROUT	Progressive Utilization Theory
PRPSA	Personal Report of Public Speaking Apprehension
PRS	Primary Representational System
PRSSA	Public Relations Student Society of America
PRT	Passage Reading Test
PRTQ	Peer Role-Taking Questionnaire
PS	ERIC Clearinghouse on Elementary and Early Childhood Education
PSA	Play Schools Association
PSAS	Pre-Speech Assessment Scale
PSAT	Preliminary Scholastic Aptitude Test
PSCI	Perez Self-Concept Inventory
PSCI	Primary Self-Concept Inventory
PSEP	Professional Student Exchange Program (Western Interstate Commission on Higher Education)
PSES	Performance-Self-Esteem Scale
PSEW	Project on the Status and Education of Women
PSI	Palmar Sweat Index
PSI	Parenting Stress Index
PSI	Personalized System of Instruction
PSI	Preschool Inventory
PSI	Problem Solving Inventory
PSIQ	Performance Scales Intelligence Quotient
PSP	Professional and Scholarly Publishing Division (Association of American Publishers)
PSPT	Parisi Spanish Proficiency Test
PSSC	Physical Science Study Committee
PSSC	Public Service Satellite Consortium

PSSS	Philosophic Society for the Study of Sport
P-T	Part-Time
PTA	Parent Teacher Association
PTAVE	Parents and Teachers Against Violence in Education
PTI	Pictorial Test of Intelligence
PTI	Principal-Teacher Interaction Study
PTS	Primary Trait System
PTSD	Post-Traumatic Stress Disorder
PTST	Prime Time School Television
PT-WEX	Texas Part-Time Work Experience Program
PUG	PLATO Users Group (Association for the Development of Computer-Based Instructional Systems)
PUOS	Public Understanding Of Science Program
PURCHASE	Not an acronym: Name of a software program for the management of school purchasing systems
P.U.S.H.	Play Units for Severely Handicapped
PWI	Projects With Industry Program
PWP	Parents Without Partners
QACUE	Quebec Association of Computer Users in Education
QAR	Question-Answer Relations Technique
QAT	Quick Assessment Test
QC	Quality Circles
QL/SEARCH	Not an acronym: The on-line system developed by QL Systems Ltd., Ontario
QRRS	Quality Response Rating Scale
QSL	Quality of School Life Scale
QT	Quick Test
QUESTA	Questionnaire for Students, Teachers, and Administrators
QUILL	Not an acronym: Computer-based writing program
QWL	Quality of Working Life
QWT	Quick Word Test
R&D	Research & Development
RA	Resident Advisor
RA	Resident Assistant
RAC	Research Advisory Committee (National Council of Teachers of Mathematics)
RAIT	Reading Attitude Imagination Technique
RAM	Random Access Memory
RAMP	Records and Archives Management Programme (UNESCO)
RAMP	Research Association of Minority Professors
RAMP	Resource Allocation and Management Program
RAMOS	Reading And Mathematics Observation System
RAP	Resource Access Projects (Administration for Children, Youth, and Families)

RAPYHT	Retrieval and Acceleration of Promising Young Handicapped and Talented Program
RAS	Rathus Assertiveness Scale
RASD	Reference and Adult Services Division (American Library Association)
RASD HS	RASD History Section
RASD MARS	RASD Machine-Assisted Reference Service Section
RAT	Remote Associations Test
RBSDS	Revised Bogardus Social Distance Scale
RBTA	Road Builders Training Association
RC	ERIC Clearinghouse on Rural Education
RCGD	Research Center for Group Dynamics (Institute for Social Research)
RCI	Reading Comprehension Interview
RCM	Resource Cost Model
RCQ	Role Category Questionnaire
RCSE	Resource Centers for Science Education (National Science Foundation)
RD	Reading-Disabled
R.D.	Registered Dietitian
RDCEHCY	Research and Demonstration Center for the Education of Handicapped Children and Youth
RDCTE	Research and Development Center for Teacher Education (University of Texas, Austin)
RDIM	Revolving Door Identification Model
REA	Religious Education Association
REA	Research in Accrediting Efforts Project (Illinois)
REA	Rural Education Association
REACH	Research on the Early Abilities of Children with Handicaps Project
RECDC	Regional Early Childhood Direction Centers
RECON	Retrospective Conversion of Cataloging Records (Library of Congress)
REDE	Regents External Degree Examinations (New York)
REED	Resources on Educational Equity for the Disabled Project
REES	Regular Educator Expectancy Scale
RELC	Regional Educational Laboratory for the Carolinas
REP	Role Construct Repertory Test
REPI	Ross Educational Philosophical Inventory
RESA	Regional Educational Service Agencies
RESA	Regional Educational Service Areas
RESC	Regional Educational Service Centers
RESNA	Rehabilitation Engineering Society of North America
RET	Rational Emotive Therapy
RETAP	Regular Education Teachers and Principals Project
REWARD	Reading, Writing and Arithmetic Development System
RFB	Recording For the Blind, Inc.
RFP	Request For Proposals

RFVII	Reading-Free Vocational Interest Inventory
RGEPS	Rucker-Gable Educational Programming Scale
RIBEA	Rhode Island Business Educators Association
RICE	Resources In Computer Education
RID	Registry of Interpreters for the Deaf
RIE	Resources In Education
RIF	Reading Is Fundamental
RIF	Reduction In Force
RIM	Readiness-Instruction-Maintenance Model
RISE	Register for International Service in Education (Institute of International Education)
RISE	Research and Information Services for Education
RISE	Research In Science Education (National Science Foundation)
RLG	Research Libraries Group
RLIN	Research Libraries Information Network
RMBS	Responsive Multicultural Basic Skills Approach
RMMLA	Rocky Mountain Modern Language Association
RN	Registered Nurse
ROCTAPUS	Really Outstanding Color Television About Practically Unlimited Subjects (Australia)
ROL	Record of Oral Language
ROM	Read Only Memory
ROPES	Regional Occupation Planning and Evaluation System
ROSES	Retired Operating Staff Employment Services (University of New Hampshire)
ROTC	Reserve Officers Training Corps
RP	Retinitis Pigmentosa
RPM	Raven's Progressive Matrices Test
RPRS	Rorschach Prognostic Rating Scale
R.P.T.	Registered Physical Therapist
RRC	Regional Resource Centers
RRF	Reading Reform Foundation
RRPM	Resource Requirement Prediction Model
RRT	Reading Resource Teacher
RSA	Rehabilitation Services Administration
RSA	Responsibility for Student Achievement Scale
RSCA	Religious Speech Communication Association
RSLSI	Renzulli/Smith Learning Style Inventory
RSP	Resource Specialist Program (California)
RSS	Response-sensitive Sequencing Strategy
RSVP	Response System with Variable Prescriptions
RSVP	Retired Senior Volunteer Program
RSVP	Rural Student Vocational Program (Washington)
RT	Related Term
RT	Round Table

RTDVHPEP	Rural Texas Domestic Violence Health Professionals Education Program
RTNOBE	Round Table of National Organizations for Better Education
RTSD	Resources and Technical Services Division (American Library Association)
RTSD CCS	RTSD Cataloging and Classification Section
RTSD RLMS	RTSD Reproduction of Library Materials Section
RTSD RS	RTSD Resources Section
RTSD SS	RTSD Serials Section
RTT	Revised Token Test
RUI	Research in Undergraduate Institutions (National Science Foundation)
RWRT	Real World Reading Test
SAA	Society for Academic Achievement
SAA	Society of American Achivists
SAA	Suzuki Association of the Americas
SAAS	Southern Association of Agricultural Scientists
SAB	Specific Adaptive Strategy
SACCR	Southeastern Association of Community College Researchers
SACE	Saskatchewan Association for Computers in Education
SACNAS	Society for the Advancement of Chicanos and Native Americans in Science
SACS	Southern Association of Colleges and Schools
SACUS	Southern Association for Children Under Six
SACVE	State Advisory Councils for Vocational Education
SADS	Schedule for Affective Disorders and Schizophrenia
SAE	Society for the Advancement of Education
SAGE	Society for the Advancement of Good English
SAGE	Statistical Analysis Group in Education
SAIR	Southern Association for Institutional Research
SALALM	Seminar on the Acquisition of Latin American Library Materials
Sallie Mae	Student Loan Marketing Association
SALT	Society for Applied Learning Technology
SALT	Society of American Law Teachers
SALT	Suggestive-Accelerative Learning and Teaching
SAM	School-Aged Maternity
SAM	Something About Myself Inventory
SAM	Student Accountability Model (California)
SAMLA	South Atlantic Modern Language Association
S-APA	Science—A Process Approach

SAPIENS	Spreading Activation Processor for Information Encoded in Network Structures
SARB	School Attendance Review Board
SARS	Scholarly Activities Rating Scale
SAS	Statistical Analysis System
SAS	Sverige-Amerika Stiftelsen (Sweden-America Foundation)
SASS	Society for the Advancement of Scandinavian Study
SASW	Situational Attitude Scale—Women
SAT	Scholastic Aptitude Test
SAT	Stanford Achievement Test
SATB	Specific Aptitude Test Battery
SAT-HI	Stanford Achievement Test, Special Edition for Hearing Impaired Students
SAT-M	Scholastic Aptitude Test-Mathematical
SAT-V	Scholastic Aptitude Test-Verbal
SBA	Small Business Administration
SBA	Social Behavior Assessment
SBAA	Southern Business Administration Association
SBCT	Schilling Body Coordination Test
SBDQ	Supervisory Behavior Description Questionnaire
SBE	Society for Business Ethics
SBEA	Southern Business Education Association
SBI	Study Behavior Inventory
SBIS	Stanford-Binet Intelligence Scale
SBIT	Stanford-Binet Intelligence Test
SBMT	Small Business Management Training
SBN	Standard Book Number
SBS	Sharing Business Success Program (Association of School Business Officials of the United States and Canada)
SCA	Speech Communication Association
SCA	Subsidiary Communications Authorization
SCABT	South Carolina Association of Biology Teachers
SCAN	Schedule for Classroom Activity Norms
SCAT	School and College Ability Tests
SCAT	Science College Ability Test
SCATT	Scientific Communications And Technology Transfer System (National Science Foundation)
SCB	State Capacity Building
SCBQ	Science Classroom Behavior Q-Sort
SCC	State Computer Committee (North Dakota)
Sc.D.	Doctor of Science
SCDEs	Schools, Colleges, and Departments of Education
SCE	Sentence Combining Exercise
SCE	Society of Christian Ethics
SCE	State Compensatory Education
SCEE	Société Canadienne pour l'Étude de l'Éducation
SCH	Student Contact Hours
SCH	Student Credit Hours

SCHSIS	South Carolina Handicapped Services Information System
SCI	Science Citation Index
SCII	Strong-Campbell Interest Inventory
SCIPPY	Social Competence Intervention Package for Preschool Youngsters
SCIS	Science Curriculum Improvement Study
SCLS	Study of Children's Learning Styles
SCMLA	South Central Modern Language Association
SCNS	Statewide Course Numbering System (Florida)
SCOC	Société Canadienne d'Orientation et de Consultation
SCOLT	Southern Conference On Language Teaching, Inc.
SCOPE	Standardized Curriculum Oriented Pupil Evaluation
SCORE	Service Corps Of Retired Executives
SCRIPT	Screenwriting Coalition for Industry Professionals and Teachers
SCSA	Soil Conservation Society of America
SCSPP	Southern Center for Studies in Public Policy
SCST	Society for College Science Teachers
SCT	Sentence Completion Test
SCUP	Society for College and University Planning
SD	Semantic Differential
SDC	System Development Corporation
SDE	Society of Data Educators
SDE	State Department of Education
SDE-IS	State Department of Education—Information System (Minnesota)
SDI	Selective Dissemination of Information
SDIP	Strengthening Developing Institutions Program
SDMIX	South Dakota Medical Information Exchange
SDQ	Student Descriptive Questionnaire
SDRS	Spache's Diagnostic Reading Scales
SDRT	Stanford Diagnostic Reading Test
SDS	Self-Directed Search
SDS	Self-Rating Depression Scale
SDS	Social Desirability Scale
SDS	Syntactic Density Score
SDSI	Staff Development for School Improvement Program
SDTI	Student Developmental Task Inventory
SE	ERIC Clearinghouse for Science, Mathematics, and Environmental Education
SE	Standard English
SEA	Sea Education Association
SEA	State Education Agency
SEA	Survival Education Association
SEALLING	Southeast Louisiana Library Network Cooperative
SEAMEO	Southeast Asian Ministers of Education Organization
SEARCH	Not an acronym: Kentucky's capacity building project
SEAS	Spiral-Ecological Approach to Supervision
SECA	Southern Educational Communications Association
SED	State Education Department
SEDL	Southwest Educational Development Laboratory
SEDR	Science Education Development and Research Division (National Science Foundation)
SEE	Seeing Essential English
SEECA	State Environmental Education Coordinators Association
SEED	Schoolhouse Energy Efficiency Demonstration Project
SEED	Structured Environment for the Emotionally Disturbed Project
SEEK	Sooner Exchange for Educational Knowledge (Oklahoma)
SEEL	Sex Equity in Educational Leadership Project (Oregon)
SEEN	Seeing-Eye Elephant Network (a computer-assisted instruction program)
SEEQ	Students' Evaluations of Educational Quality
SEF	Southern Education Foundation
SEGCE	Scale for the Evaluation of Group Counseling Experiences
SEI	Coopersmith Self-Esteem Inventory
SEI	Social-Emotional Inventory
SEL	Southeastern Education Laboratory
SELA	Southeastern Library Association
SELO	Some Essential Learner Outcomes (Minnesota)
SELPA	Special Education Local Planning Agency
S/ELPS	Spanish/English Language Performance Screening
SEM	Self-Evaluation Maintenance Model
SEM	Standard Error of the Mean
SEOG	Supplemental Educational Opportunity Grants
SEPA	School Employment Procedures Act of 1977
SEQ	Self-Estimate Questionnaire
SER	Society for Educational Reconstruction
SER	Student Eligibility Report
SERC	Special Education in the Regular Classroom Project (U.S. Office of Special Education and Rehabilitation Services)
SERCH	State Education Research Clearinghouse (California)
SERP	Secondary Education Review Project
SES	Socioeconomic Status
SES	Symptom Evaluation Survey
SESAT	Stanford Early School Achievement Test

SESE	Search for Excellence in Science Education (National Science Teacher Association)
SESS	Society of Ethnic and Special Studies
SFA	Semantic Feature Analysis
SFAS	Self-Feeling Awareness Scale
SFAT	Scott, Foresman Achievement Test
SFEC	Southeast Florida Educational Consortium
SFEMS	School Finance Equalization Management System
SFLRP	Society of Federal Labor Relations Professionals
SFRA	Science Fiction Research Association
SFSP	Summer Food Service Program
SFTAA	Short Form Test of Academic Aptitude
SGIS	Student Guidance Information Service (Ontario)
SH	Speech Handicapped
SHAC	School Heads Advisory Commitee (National Association of Independent Schools)
SHE	Society for History Education
SHEEO	State Higher Education Executive Officers Association
SHH	Sociedad Honoraria Hispanica
SIAM	Society for Industrial and Applied Mathematics
SIB	Self-Injurious Behavior
SICD	Sequenced Inventory of Communication Development
SICN	New York Statewide Instructional Computing Network
SIDS	Sudden Infant Death Syndrome
SIEC	Société Internationale pour l'Enseignement Commercial
SIECUS	Sex Information and Education Council of the United States
SIETAR/INTL	International Society for Intercultural Education, Training And Research
SIG	Special Interest Group
SIG CSE	Special Interest Group for Computer Science Education (Association for Computing Machinery)
SIG CUE	Special Interest Group for Computer Uses in Education
SIGHAN	Educators of the Handicapped Special Interest Group (Association for the Development of Computer-Based Instructional Systems)
SIG/HomEc	Home Economics Special Interest Group (Association for the Development of Computer-Based Instructional Systems)
SIGI	System of Interactive Guidance and Information
SIG IVA	Interactive Video/Audio Special Interest Group (Association for the Development of Computer-Based Instructional Systems)

SIG/TAR	Theory and Research Special Interest Group (Association for the Development of Computer-Based Instructional Systems)
SIGUCCS	Special Interest Group for University and College Computing Sciences
SIM	School Improvement Model
SIMPAR	Not an acronym: Simulation game focusing on parent-child relations
SIMULA	Simulation Language
SIP	School Improvement Program
SIPA	Systems Information Processing Analysis
SIPS	Simulated Interpersonal Problem Situation
SIRS	School Information and Research Service
SIRS	Structure of Instruction Rating Scale
SISS	Second International Science Study
SIT	Slosson Intelligence Test
SITE	Satellite Instructional Television Experiment
SITES	Smithsonian Institute Traveling Exhibition Service
SITIP	School Improvement Through Instructional Process (Maryland)
SIV	Survey of Interpersonal Value
SJTCC	State Job Training Coordinating Councils
SKEEC	Southern Central Kansas Environmental Education Center
SLA	Second Language Acquisition
SLA	Sleep-Learning Association
SLA	Special Libraries Association
SLATE	State Leadership Assistance for Technology in Education (U.S. Department of Education)
SLEP	Secondary Level English Proficiency Test
SLIF	Student Loan Insurance Fund
SLMA	Student Loan Marketing Association
SLMP	School Library Manpower Project
SLT	Sociolinguistic Test
SMAST	Short Michigan Alcoholism Screening Test
SMERC	San Mateo Educational Resources Center (California)
SMILE	Society for Microcomputers In Life and Education
SMIS	Society for Management Information Systems
SMMA	Social Mapping Matrix Assessment
SMNC	Self-Monitoring Negative Checklist
SMPY	Study of Mathematically Precocious Youth
SMS	Self-Monitoring Scale
SMS	Sociometric Status
SMSA	Standard Metropolitan Statistical Areas
SMSG	School Management Study Group
SMSG	School Mathematics Study Group
SMTP	Simple Mail Transfer Protocol
SN	Scope Note
SNAS	Student Needs Assessment Survey
SNE	Society for Nutrition Education
SNMA	Student National Medical Association

SNP	School Nurse Practitioner
SO	ERIC Clearinghouse for Social Studies/Social Science Education
SOA	Stimulus Onset Asynchrony
SOC	Servicemembers Opportunity Colleges
SOC	Standard Occupational Classification
SOCAD	Servicemembers Opportunity Colleges Associate Degree
SOCMATICAS	Not an acronym: Bilingual, multicultural, English/Spanish curriculum
SOCP	Servicemembers Opportunity College Program
SoCQ	Stages of Concern Questionnaire
SOD	Student Organization Development
SOE	Supervised Occupational Experience
SOICC	State Occupational Information Coordinating Committee
SOI-LA	Structure Of Intellect-Learning Abilities Test
SOLAT	Your Style Of Learning And Thinking Inventory
SOLINET	Southeast Library Network
SOMPA	System Of Multicultural, Pluarlistic Assessment
SOPHE	Society for Public Health Education
SORT	Slosson Oral Reading Test
SORT	Spanish Oral Reading Text
SORT	Staff Organizations Round Table (American Library Association)
SOS	Grillingham-Stillman Simultaneous-Oral-Spelling
SOS	Self-Observational Scales
SOSF	Schedule Of Social Functioning
SOV	Study Of Values Test
SP	ERIC Clearinghouse on Teacher Education
SPA	Spacial Appreciation Test
SPACES	Solving Problems of Access to Careers in Engineering and Science
SPAF	Student Product Assessment Form
SPAN	Social Studies Priorities, Practices, And Needs
SPAS	Student's Perception of Ability Scale
SPCA	School Projectionist Club of America
SPCT	Science Process Competency Test
SPE	Society for Photographic Education
SPE	Society of Professors of Education
SPEC	Systems and Procedures Exchange Center (Association of Research Libraries)
SPEL-2	Standardized Proficiency Entry Level 2 Test (National Security Agency)
SPFA	Société des Professeurs Français et Francophones en Amerique
SPH	Severely and Profoundly Handicapped
SPI	Edwards Situational Preference Inventory
SPICE	Self Paced Instruction for Competency Education
SPICE	Stanford Program on International and Cross Cultural Education

SPIDR	Society of Professionals In Dispute Resolution
SPIES	Stanford Preschool Internality-Externality Scale
SPIF	School Practices Information File
SPIRES	Stanford Public Information Retrieval System
SPIRIT	Sensible Policy for Information Resources and Information Technology Group
SPL	Sound Pressure Level
SPLC	Student Press Law Center
SPLT	Structured Photographic Language Test
SPM	Standard Progressive Matrices
SPMSQ	Short Portable Mental Status Questionnaire
SPPC	Systeme de projections des professions au Canada
SPPED	System for Pupil and Program Evaluation and Development
SPPI	Structured Pediatric Psychosocial Interview
SPR	Society for Philosophy of Religion
SPRE	Society of Park and Recreation Educators
SPS	Science Participation Scales
SPSS	Statistical Package for the Social Sciences
SPST	Social Problem-Solving Test
SQ3R	Survey, Question, Read, Recite, and Review Method of Reading Instruction
SQ4R	Surveying, Questioning, Reading, Recording, Reciting, and Reflecting Method
SQT	Skill Qualifications Test
SRBR	Storage and Retrieval of Bibliographic References Program
SRC	Survey Research Center (Institute for Social Research)
SRCD	Society for Research in Child Development
SRD	Self-Reported Delinquency
SRDAS	School Retrofit Design Analysis System
SREB	Southern Regional Education Board
SRHE	Society for Research into Higher Education (Great Britain)
SRM	Sociomoral Reflection Measures
SRMS	Sociomoral Reflection Maturity Score
SROM	Sociomoral Relfection Objective Measure
SRQ	Self-Righteousness Questionnaire
SRRS	Social Readjustment Rating Scale
SRRT	Social Responsibilities Round Table (American Library Association)
SS	Sample Size
SS	Scandinavian Summer
SSA	Semiotic Society of America
SSAT	Secondary School Admission Test
SSAT	State Student Assessment Test (Florida)
SSATB	Secondary School Admission Test Board
SSAVE	Special Student Access to Vocational Education Project

SSCA	Southern Speech Communication Association
SSCI	Social Science Citation Index
SSCQT	Selective Service College Qualification Test
SSD	Science and Self-Determination Project (Upward Bound)
SSDHPER	Society of State Directors of Health, Physical Education and Recreation
SSDI	Social Security Disability Insurance
SSEC	Social Science Education Consortium
SSEC	Society for the Study of Early China
SSH	Student Semester Hours
SSHA	Survey of Study Habits and Attitudes
SSI	Supplemental Security Income
SSIG	State Student Incentive Grants
SSIS	Society for South India Studies
SSPO	Survey of Student Personnel Objectives
SSPT	Speech Sounds Perception Test
SSR	Sustained Silent Reading
SSRC	Social Science Research Council
SSS	Society for Slovene Studies
SSTA	Secondary School Theatre Association
SSTP	Student Science Training Program
STABS	Suinn Test Anxiety Behavior Scale
STAD	Student Teams-Achievement Divisions
STAI	Speilberger's Trait-Anxiety Inventory
STAI	State-Trait Anxiety Inventory
STAIC	State-Trait Anxiety Inventory for Children
STAIRS	Storage and Information Retrieval System
STAL	Screening Test of Adolescent Language
STAP	Supplemental Tuition Assistance Program (New York)
STAR	Scientific and Technical Aerospace Reports (National Aeronautics and Space Administration)
STAR	Students Taking Action with Recognition (Kentucky)
STARS	Secondary Training for Alaskan Rural Students
STARS	Spaulding Teacher Activity Rating Schedule
STBDQ	Supervising Teacher Behavior Description Questionnaire
STC	Society for Technical Communication
STC	Student Teacher Concerns Instrument
STEMBOR	Supervision Through Educational Management By Objectives and Results
STEP	Sequential Tests of Educational Progress
STEP	Systematic Training for Effective Parenting
STEPS	Surviving Today's Experiences and Problems Successfully Curriculum (West Virginia)
STEP-W	Sequential Test of Educational Progress—Writing Test
STEWS	Standardized Test of Essential Writing Skills
STIN	Science Teacher Inventory of Need
STM	Short-Term Memory
STN	Symmetric Tonic Neck
STOI	Science Teaching Observational Instrument
STORE	Standardized Test Of Reading Effectiveness
STRS	State Teachers Retirement System (Ohio)
STS	Science Talent Search
STS	Self-Testimony Scale
STSG	Screening Test of Spanish Grammar
STUCENFL	Student Census-date Report File
STV	Subscription Television
SUCCESS	Sources to Upgrade the Career Counseling and Employment of Special Students (Florida)
SUMIT	Single-concept User-adaptable Microcomputer-based Instructional Technique
SUREA	Syracuse University Resources for Educators of Adults
SURPO	Survey of Pupil Opinion
SVIB	Strong Vocational Interest Blank
SWAT	Study With A Teacher Program (Ohio)
SWCEL	Southwestern Cooperative Educational Laboratory
SWE	Society of Wine Educators
TA	Teaching Assistant
TA	Transactional Analysis
TABE	Tests of Adult Basic Education
TABE	Texas Association for Bilingual Education
TABS	Teaching Analysis By Students
TABS	Texas Assessment of Basic Skills
TAC	Technical Assistance Centers
TACL	Test of Auditory Comprehension of Language
TACSCE	Texas Association for Community Service and Continuing Education
TADS	Technical Assistance Development System (Handicapped Children's Early Education Program)
TAEDS	Texas Association for Educational Data Systems
TAEG	Training Analysis and Evaluation Group (Department of the Navy)
TAFE	Technical And Further Education (Australia)
TAG	Talented And Gifted
TAG	The Association for the Gifted
TAI	Team-Assisted Individualization
TAI	Test Anxiety Inventory
TA III	Teaching Appraisal for Instructional Improvement Instrument
TAL	Teacher Assessment of Leverage
TALC	Tutoring Adults through Literacy Councils
TAMS	Texas Assessment Modeling Systems
TAP	Tapping Achievement Potential Project
TAP	Technical Assistance Project
TAP	Tests of Achievement and Proficiency

TAP	Tuition Assistance Program (New York)	TGT	DeVries' Teams-Games-Tournaments
TAQ	Task Attribution Questionnaire	Th.B.	Bachelor of Theology
TAS	Teacher Authoring System	Th.M.	Master of Theology
TASC	Test Anxiety Scale for Children	TIAA	Teachers Insurance and Annuity Association
TASH	The Association for the Severely Handicapped	TIAA-CREF	TIAA-College Retirement Equities Fund
TASK	Stanford Test of Academic Skills	TIC	Technical Information Center (U.S. Department of Energy)
TAT	Thematic Appreciation Test	TICCIT	Time-Shared, Interactive, Computer-Controlled Information Television
TBEA	Tennessee Business Education Association	TIERS	Title I Evaluation and Reporting System
TBI	Teacher-Based Instruction	TIPS	Test of Integrated Process Skills
TBI	Traditionally Black Institutions	TJDP	Targeted Jobs Demonstration Program
TCAM	Thinking Creatively in Action and Movement Test	TJTC	Targeted Jobs Tax Credit
TCEA	Texas Computer Education Association	TLA	Theatre Library Association
TCIAS	Texas Council of Industrial Arts Supervisors	TLC	Teaching, Learning and Curriculum Model
TCIATE	Texas Council on Industrial Arts Teacher Education	TLE	The Learning Exchange
TCQ	Teacher Concerns Questionnaire	TM	ERIC Clearinghouse on Tests, Measurement and Evaluation
TCT	Teacher Certification Test	TMH	Trainable Mentally Handicapped
TDBS	Texas Data Base System	TMP	The Madison Project
TDD	Telecommunications Device for the Deaf	TMR	Trainable Mentally Retarded
TDF	Transborder Data Flow	TOBC	Transportation Officer Basic Course (U.S. Army)
TDTA	Templin-Darley Test of Articulation	TOBE	Test Of Basic Experiences
TE	Tuition Exchange	TOEFL	Test Of English as a Foreign Language
TEAL	Teachers of English as an Additional Language (British Columbia)	TOEIC	Test Of English for International Communication
TEAM	Teacher Education And Mathematics Project	TOLD	Test Of Language Development
TEC	Teacher Education Centers	TOLT	Test Of Logical Thinking
TEC	Technician Education Council (Great Britain)	TORC	Test Of Reading Comprehension
TEC	Test of Ecology Comprehension	TOSFQ	Teacher Occupational Stress Factor Questionnaire
TECC	Teacher Education and Computer Centers (California)	TOTAL	Teacher Organized Training for the Acquisition of Language
TECV	Test of Engery Concepts and Values	TOWL	Test Of Written Language
TEFL	Teaching English as a Foreign Language	TOXLINE	Toxicology Information Online (National Library of Medicine)
TEFL	Test of English as a Foreign Language	TPAI	Teacher Performance Assessment Instruments
TEFRA	Tax Equity and Fiscal Responsibility Act	TPE	Teacher Performance Evaluation
TELD	Test of Early Language Development	TPE	Training Program Evaluation
TELE	Trilanguage Education Learning Environment Program (New York City)	TPP	Teacher Participation Project
		TPR	Asher's Total Physical Response Method
TEMAS	"Tell-Me-A-Story" Thematic Appreciation Test	TPSI	Texas Preschool Screening Inventory
		TQI	Teacher's Questionnaire Inventory
TERC	Technical Education Research Center, Inc.	TQLR	Tune-in, Question, Listen, Review Technique
TESI	Teaching Events Stress Inventory	TRAC	Training Access (British Columbia)
TESL	Teaching English as a Second Language	TRACES	Training, Research and Assistance Cooperative Extension Service
TESOL	Teachers of English to Speakers of Other Languages	TRADEC	Trades Education (Great Britain)
TESS	The Educational Software Selector (A handbook of software and hardware)	TRADOC	Army Training and Doctrine Command
		TREE	Teacher Recruitment for Educational Excellence
TET	Teacher Effectiveness Training	TRF	Teacher Rating Form
TEXSIS	Texas Student Information System	TRF	Teacher's Report Form of the Child Behavior Checklist
TFCCE	Task Force on Computers in Chemical Education (American Chemical Society)		
TFLA	Texas Foreign Language Association	TRIP	The Research Instruments Project
TGI	Test of General Information		

TRIS	Transportation Research Information Service
TSA	Tax Sheltered Annuity
TSA	Test of Syntactic Abilities
TSA	Tripoli Science Association
TSBI	Texas Social Behavior Inventory
TSCS	Tennessee Self-Concept Scale
TSE	Test of Spoken English
TSH	Tendency to Seek Help Questionnaire
TSLNC	Texas State Library Communications Network
TSP	Traveling Scholar Program
TSPC	Tri-State Parenting Collaborative Project (Minnesota, North Dakota, South Dakota)
TSS	Teacher Stress Scale
TSTP	Talking Screen Textwriting Program
TSWE	Test of Standard Written English
TT	Token Test
TTC	Tuition Tax Credit
TTCT	Torrance Test of Creative Thinking
TTR	Type-Token Ratio
TTVIT	Tetreau-Trahan Visual Interest Test
TVCAI	Television Computer Assisted Instruction
UAA	University Aviation Association
UAA	Urban Affairs Association
UAF	University Affiliated Facility
UB	Upward Bound
UBC	Universal Bibliographic Control
UCCE	Utah Council for Computers in Education
UCCJA	Uniform Child Custody Jurisdiction Act
UCDA	University and College Designers Association
UCEA	University Council for Educational Administration
UCIDT	University Consortium for Instructional Development and Technology
UCPNW	United Campuses to Prevent Nuclear War
UCPP	Urban Crime Prevention Program
UCTA	University and College Theatre Association
UD	ERIC Clearinghouse on Urban Education
UDAG	Urban Development Action Grant
UDC	Universal Decimal Classification
UECU	Union for Experimenting Colleges and Universities
UF	Used For
UFCT	United Federation of College Teachers
UFSI	University Field Staff International
UFSI-IWA	University Field Staff International— Institute of World Affairs
UFT	United Federation of Teachers
UFVA	University Film and Video Association
UFVF	University Film and Video Foundation
UIATF	United Indians of All Tribes Foundation
ULAA	Ukranian Library Association of America
ULC	Urban Libraries Council
ULISYS	Universal Library System Ltd.
ULOSSOM	Union List of Selected Serials of Michigan
UMI	University Microfilms International
UMREL	Upper Midwest Regional Educational Laboratory
UMTA	Urban Mass Transportation Administration (U.S. Department of Transportation)
UNCF	United Negro College Fund
UNEP	United Nations Education Project
UNESCO	United Nations Educational, Scientific, and Cultural Organization
UNIACT	Unisex Edition of the American College Testing Program Interest Inventory
UNICEF	United Nations Children's Fund
UNISIST	World Science Information System (UNESCO)
UPAA	University Photographers Association of America
UPAO	University Professors for Academic Order
UPAS	Uniform Performance Assessment System
UPE	Universal Primary Education
UPSA	Ukranian Political Science Association in the United States
UPSF	Universal Proutist Student Federation
UPSTEP	Undergraduate Pre-Service Science Teacher Education Program (Iowa)
UPTA	United Parent-Teachers Association of Jewish Schools
URMIA	University Risk Management and Insurance Association
USA Funds	United Student Aid Funds
USBE	Universal Serials and Book Exchange
USCJE	United Synagogue Commission on Jewish Education
USD	Unified School District
USIA	United States Information Agency
USITT	United States Institute for Theatre Technology
USMES	Unified Sciences and Mathematics for Elementary Schools
USSA	United States Student Association
USSR	Uninterrupted Sustained Silent Reading
USSTS	United States Student Travel Service
USTED	United Students and Techers for Educational Development
USYSA	United States Youth Soccer Association
UWP	Up With People
VA	Veterans Administration
VABS	Vineland Adaptive Behavior Scale
VAIR	Virginia Association for Institutional Research
VAPS	Videodisc Authoring and Production Systems
VAST	Vocational Adult Secondary Training (British Columbia)
VAT	Value-Added Tax
VAT	Veterinary Aptitude Test

VBE	Vernacular Black English
VBLS	Voice-Based Learning System
VBTA	Vermont Business Teachers Association
VCR	Videocassette Recorder
VD	Venereal Disease
VDC	Video-Documentary Clearinghouse
VDC	Vocational Development Checklist
VDI	Vocational Development Inventory
VDMD	Vocational Decision-Making Difficulty Scale
VDP	Videodisc Player
VEA	Vocational Education Act
VEAP	Veterans' Educational Assistance Program
VECM	Vocational Education Curriculum Materials
VEDS	Vocational Education Data System
VEEAP	Vocational Education Evaluation and Assessment Process (Pennsylvania)
VEH	Vocational Education for the Handicapped
VESL	Vocational English as a Second Langauge
VICA	Vocational Industrial Clubs of America
VICI	Ventures in Community Improvement Demonstration Project
VIEW	Vital Information on Education and Work
VIM	Videodiscs Interactive with Microcomputers Project (U.S. Department of Education)
VISTA	Volunteers in Service to America
VITA	Volunteers in Technical Assistance
VLP	Video Long Play
VMT	Vowel Matching Test
VNS	Validity Network Schema
VOICE	Vocational and Occupational Information Center for Educators (California)
VPI	Vocational Preference Inventory
VR	Vocational Rehabilitation
VRG	Vocabulary Review Group (Educational Resources Information Center)
VRPSES	Vocational Rehabilitation Program Standards Evaluation System
VSC	Navy Verbal Skills Curriculum
VSIQ	Verbal Scale Intelligence Quotient
VSMS	Vineland Social Maturity Scale
V-T	Vocational-Technical
VTAE	Vocational Technical and Adult Education
VTDS	Videodisc Training Delivery System
V-TECS	Vocational-Technical Education Consortium of States
VTR	Videotape Recorder
VVQ	Visualizer-Verbalizer Questionnaire
VVT	Validation, Verification, and Testing (of Software)
WAIS	Wechsler Adult Intelligence Scale
WAML	Wide Angle Mobility Light
WAMS	Women As Manager Scales
WANDAH	Writing-Aid And Author's Helper
WARC	World Administration Radio Conference
WASC	Western Association of Schools and Colleges
WASTE	Working at Student Time-Saving in Education Project (Illinois)
WATS	Wide-Area Telecommunications Service
WBNA	Women Band Directors National Association
WCA	Western College Association
WCC	Women's College Coalition
WCCC	Western Curriculum Coordination Center
WCCE	World Conference on Computers in Education
WCCI	World Council for Curriculum and Instruction
WCDC	Washington Child Development Council (District of Columbia)
WCET	Weighted Common Examination Total
WCF	Winston Churchill Foundation
WCGTC	World Council for Gifted and Talented Children
WCIS	Wisconsin Career Information System
WCLA	Washington Center for Learning Alternatives
WCLP	Women's Computer Literacy Project
WCML	Women's Caucus for the Modern Languages
WCOTP	World Confederation of Organizations of the Teaching Profession
WCPS	Women's Caucus for Political Science
WCRA	Western College Reading Association
WCRLA	Western College Reading and Learning Association
WC:RS	Women's Caucus: Religious Studies
WCST	Wisconsin Card Sorting Test
WDRSD	Wisconsin Design for Reading Skill Development
WE	Women Educators
WE	World Education
WEA	Wilderness Education Association
WEAL	Women's Equity Action League
WECC	Wyoming Educational Computing Council
WECEP	Work Experience Career Exploration Program
WEEA	Women's Education Equity Act
WEEAP	Women's Education Equity Act Program
WEF	World Education Fellowship
WEIS	World Event/Interaction Survey
WELAP	Work Experience Liberal Arts Program
WEP	Work Experience Program
WESSAS	Wisconsin Elementary and Secondary School Accounting System
WEST	Western Educational Society for Telecommunications
WFD	World Federation of the Deaf
WFOS	Work and Family Orientation Scale
WGCTA	Watson-Glaser Critical Thinking Appraisal
WHO	World Health Organization

WIA	Western Interpreters Association
WICC	Wisconsin Instructional Computing Consortium
WICHE	Western Interstate Commission for Higher Education
WIEDS	Ways to Improve Education in Desegregated Schools Project (Southwest Educational Development Laboratory)
WILCO	Western Interstate Library Coordinating Organization
WIRE	Wisconsin Information Resources for Education
WISC	Wechsler Intelligence Scale for Children
WisCom	Wisconsin Competency Based Occupational Curriculum Data System
WISC-R	Wechsler Intelligence Scale for Children—Revised
WISP	Women In Scholarly Publishing
WISP	Wyoming Infant Stimulation Program
WiSS	Women in Science Scale
WIS-SIM	Wisconsin System for Instructional Management
WITF	What I Think and Feel
WJPEB	Woodcock-Johnson Psycho-Educational Battery
WJTCA	Woodcock-Johnson Tests of Cognitive Ability
WLI	Wilderness Leadership International
WLN	Washington Library Network
WLW	Woman Library Workers
WM	Working Memory
WMA	World Modeling Association
WME	Women in Mathematics Education
WMI	Wildlife Management Institute
WMS	Wechsler Memory Scale
WOCMDC	Warrent Officer Candidate Military Development Course (U.S. Army)
WORK	Widening Occupational Roles Kit
WORLDS	Western Ohio Regional Library Development System
WOWI	Women On Words and Images
WP	Word Processing
WPA	Western Psychological Association
W-PACC	Wisconsin Procedure for Appraisal of Clinical Competence
WPBIC	Walker Problem Behavior Identification Checklist
WPC	Washington Pre-College Test
WPERS	Washington Public Employees Retirement System
WPPSI	Wechsler Preschool and Primary Scale of Intelligence
WPSS	Work Performance Survey System
WRAT	Wide-Range Achievement Test
WRISE	Wisconsin Program for the Renewal and Improvement of Secondary Education
WRMT	Woodcock Reading Mastery Test
WRQ	Willingness to Risk Questionnaire
WRQ	Women's Role Questionnaire Scale

WSAT	Writing Skills Assessment Test
WSCS	Wallace Self-Concept Scale
WST	Wiig-Semel Test of Linguistic Concepts
WSTRS	Washington State Teachers Retirement System
WVAATS	West Virginia Assessment And Tracking System
WVBEA	West Virginia Business Education Association
WWF	Washington Workshop Foundation
WWNFF	Woodrow Wilson National Fellowship Foundation
YA	Young Adults
YASD	Young Adult Services Division (American Library Association)
YCCIP	Youth Community Conservation and Community Improvement Programs
YCIP	Youth Career Information Project (Northwest Regional Educational Laboratory)
YCSDS	Young Children's Social Desirability Scale
YEDPA	Youth Employment and Demonstration Project Act
YET	Youth Effectiveness Training
YETP	Youth Employment and Training Program
YFU	Youth For Understanding
YIEPP	Youth Entitlement Incentive Pilot Projects
YPLA	Young People's LOGO Association
YR	Youth Resources
YRE	Year Round Education

PART II

Reverse List of Acronyms, Abbreviations, and Initialisms

AASL Non-Public Schools Section, AASL NPSS
AASL Supervisors Section, AASL SS
Abbreviated Conners Parent/Teacher Rating Scale, ACRS
Ability Grouped Active Teaching, AGAT
Abstracts of Instructional and Research Materials in Vocational and Technical Education, AIM/ARM
Academic Collective Bargaining Information Service, ACBIS
Academic Learning Time, ALT
Academic Library Program, ALP
Academic Program Evaluation Project, APEP
Academic Ranking, AR
Academic Self-Concept Scale, ASCS
Academic Senate for California Community Colleges, ASCCC
Academic Travel Abroad, ATA
Academy for Educational Development, AED
Academy of Independent Scholars, AIS
Academy of International Business, AIB
Academy of Management, AM
Academy of Marketing Science, AMS
Academy of Political Science, APS
Academy of Security Educators and Trainees, ASET
Acceptance of Others Scale, AOS
Accepting Individual Differences Curriculum, AID
Acclimizatization Experiences Institute, AEI
Accreditation Board for Engineering and Technology, ABET
Accreditation Council for Graduate Medical Education, ACGME
Accreditation Council for Services for Mentally Retarded and other Developmentally Disabled Persons, AC/MRDD
Accrediting Commission for Specialized Colleges, ACSC
Accrediting Commission on Education for Health Services Administration, ACEHSA
Accrediting Council on Education in Journalism and Mass Communication, ACEJMC
Achenbach Child Behavior Checklist, ACBC
Achievement Anxiety Test, AAT
ACRL Anthroplogy and Sociology Section, ACRL ANSS
ACRL Arts Section, ACRL ARTS
ACRL Asian and African Section, ACRL AAS
ACRL Bibliographic Instruction Section, ACRL BIS
ACRL Community and Junior College Libraries Section, ACRL CJCLS
ACRL Education and Behavioral Sciences Section, ACRL EBSS
ACRL Law and Political Science Section, ACRL LPSS
ACRL Rare Books and Manuscripts Section, ACRL RBMS
ACRL Science and Technology Section, ACRL STS
ACRL Slavic and East European Section, ACRL SEES
ACRL University Libraries Section, ACRL ULS
ACRL Western European Specialists Section, ACRL WESS
Action Committee for Higher Education, ACHE
Actualization of Mainstream Experience Skills Project (Iowa), AMES

Adapted Uzgiris-Hunt Scales, AUHS
Adaptive Behavior Inventory for Children, ABIC
Adaptive Behavior Scale—Public School Version, ABS-PS
Adaptive Behavior Scales, ABS
Adaptive Learning Environments Model, ALEM
Adjective Check List, ACL
Adjusted Agreement Index, AAI
Adkins Life Skills Program, ALSP
Administration for Children, Youth, and Families, ACYF
Administration for Native Americans Research Analysis Project, ANARAP
Administration on Aging, AoA
Administrative Management by Objectives Appraisal System, AMOAS
Administrative Management Society, AMS
Administrator Performance Evaluation, APE
Admission Test for Graduate Study in Business, ATGSB
Admissions Testing Program, ATP
Adolescent Abuse Inventory, AAI
Adolescent-Family Inventory of Life Events and Changes, A-FILE
Adult Basic and Continuing Education, ABCE
Adult Basic Education, ABE
Adult Basic Learning Examination, ABLE
Adult Inventory of Reading Interests and Attitudes, AIRIA
Adult Learning Association, ALA
Adult Performance Level, APL
Adult Secondary Education, ASE
Advanced Institutional Development Program, AIDP
Advanced Placement, AP
Advanced Progressive Matrices, APM
Advanced Research Projects Agency, ARPA
Advanced Research Projects Agency Network, ARPANET
Advisory Role Play, ARP
Aerospace Education Foundation, AEF
Affective Perception Inventory, API
Affective Work Competencies Inventory, AWCI
Affirmative Action Plan, AAP
African Studies Association, ASA
Afro-Asian Center, AAC
Agency for Instructional Television, AIT
Agricultural Online Access (U.S. Department of Agriculture), AGRICOLA
Aid to Families with Dependent Children, AFDC
Air Force Reading Abilities Test, AFRAT
Airman Classification Battery, ACB
Alabama Basic Competency Tests, ABCT
Alabama High School Graduation Examination, AHSGE
Alabama Initial Teacher Certification Test, AITCT
Alaska Association for Computers in Education, AACE
Alaska Early Childhood Certification Process, AECCP
Alaska Resources for the Moderately/Severely Impaired, ARMSI
Alaska Rural Teacher Training Corps, ARTTC
All But Dissertation, ABD
Alliance for Arts Education, AAE

Alliance for Environmental Education, AEE

Alliance of Associations for the Advancement of Education, AAAE

Alliance of Independent Colleges of Art, AICA

Alumi Presidents' Council of Independent Secondary Schools, APCISS

American Academy of Advertising, AAA

American Academy of Physical Education, AAPE

American Academy of Political and Social Science, AAPSS

American Academy of Teachers of Singing, AATS

American Alliance for Health, Physical Education, Recreation and Dance, AAHPERD

American and French Research on the Treasury of the French Language Project, ARTFL

American Arbitration Association, AAA

American Assembly of Collegiate Schools of Business, AACSB

American Association for Adult and Continuing Education, AAACE

American Association for Applied Linguistics, AAAL

American Association for Career Education, AACE

American Association for Chinese Studies, AACS

American Association for Counseling and Development, AACD

American Association for Gifted Children, AAGC

American Association for Higher Education, AAHE

American Association for Leisure and Recreation, AALR

American Association for State and Local History, AASLH

American Association for the Advancement of Science, AAAS

American Association for the Advancement of Slavic Studies, AAASS

American Association for the Education of Severely/Profoundly Handicapped, AAESPH

American Association for Vocational Instructional Materials, AAVIM

American Association of Academic Editors, AAAE

American Association of Bible Colleges, AABC

American Association of Christian Schools, AACS

American Association of Colleges for Teacher Education, AACTE

American Association of Colleges of Nursing, AACN

American Association of Collegiate Registrars and Admissions Officers, AACRAO

American Association of Community and Junior Colleges, AACJC

American Association of Diabetes Educators, AADE

American Association of Educational Service Agencies, AAESA

American Association of Evangelical Students, AAES

American Association of Housing Educators, AAHE

American Association of Law Libraries, AALL

American Association of Phonetic Sciences, AAPS

American Association of Physics Teachers, AAPT

American Association of Presidents of Independent Colleges and Universities, AAPICU

American Association of Professors of Yiddish, AAPY

American Association of School Administrators, AASA

American Association of School Librarians, AASL

American Association of School Personnel Administrators, AASPA

American Association of Sex Educators, Counselors, and Therapists, AASECT

American Association of Special Educators, AASE

American Association of Specialized Colleges, AASC

American Association of State Colleges and Universities, AASCU

American Association of Students of German, AASG

American Association of Teacher Educators in Agriculture, AATEA

American Association of Teachers of Arabic, AATA

American Association of Teachers of Esperanto, AATE

American Association of Teachers of French, AATF

American Association of Teachers of German, AATG

American Association of Teachers of Italian, AATI

American Association of Teachers of Slavic and East European Languages, AATSEEL

American Association of Teachers of Spanish and Portuguese, AATSP

American Association of University Administrators, AAUA

American Association of University Professors, AAUP

American Association of University Professors of Italian, AAUPI

American Association of University Students, AAUS

American Association of University Women, AAUW

American Association of University Women Educational Foundation, AAUWEF

American Association of Women in Community and Junior Colleges, AAWCJC

American Association of Workers for the Blind, AAWB

American Association on Mental Deficiency, AAMD

American Astronomical Society, AAS

American Bar Association, ABA

American Board of Funeral Service Education, ABFSE

American Business Communication Association, ABCA

American Business Law Association, ABLA

American Catholic Personnel Association, ACPA

American Chemical Society, ACS

American Classical League, ACL

American College Admissions Advisory Center, ACAAC

American College of Musicians, ACM

American College of Obstetricians and Gynecologists, ACOG

American College Personnel Association, ACPA

American College Test, ACT

American College Testing Program, ACT

American College Testing Program, ACTP

American Collegiate Retailing Association, ACRA

American Comparative Literature Association, ACLA

American Computer Science League, ACSL

American Conference of Academic Deans, ACAD

American Council for Construction Education, ACCE

American Council for Elementary School Industrial Arts, ACESIA

American Council for University Planning and Academic Excellence, ACUPAE

American Council of Industrial Arts State Association Officers, ACIASAO

American Council of Industrial Arts Supervisors, ACIAS

American Council of Learned Societies, ACLS

American Council of Teachers of Russian, ACTR

American Council on Cosmetology Education, ACCE

American Council on Education, ACE

American Council on Education for Journalism, ACEJ

American Council on Industrial Arts Teacher Education, ACIATE

American Council on International Sports, ACIS

American Council on Rural Special Education, ACRES

American Council on Schools and Colleges, ACSC

American Council on the Teaching of Foreign Languages, ACTFL

American Dialect Society, ADS

American Disability Evaluation Research Institute, ADERI

American Driver and Traffic Safety Education Association, ADTSEA

American Economic Association, AEA

American Economic Development Council, AEDC

American Education Association, AEA

American Education Finance Association, AEFA

American Educational Research Association, AERA

American Educational Studies Association, AESA

American Federation of Information Processing Societies, AFIPS

American Federation of Labor—Congress of Industrial Occupations, AFL-CIO

American Federation of School Administrators, AFSA

American Federation of State, County and Municipal Employees, AFSCME

American Federation of Teachers, AFT

American Federation of Teachers—Teacher Center Resource Exchange, AFT-TCRE

American Field Service, AFS

American Foundation for Negro Affairs, AFNA

American Foundation for the Blind, AFB

American Friends of the Alliance Israelite Universelle, AFAIU

American Friends of the Hebrew University, AFHU

American Geological Institute, AGI

American Historical Association, AHA

American Hominological Association, AHA

American Humanics, AH

American Hungarian Educators' Association, AHEA

American Indian Development Association, AIDA

American Indian Law Students Association, AILSA

American Indian Scholarships, AIS

American Indian Studies, AIS

American Industrial Arts Association, AIAA

American Industrial Arts Student Association, AIASA

American Institute for Character Education, AICE

American Institute for Decision Sciences, AIDS

American Institute for Professional Education, AIPE

American Institute of Biological Sciences, AIBS

American Institute of Chemical Engineers, AIChE

American Institute of Indian Studies, AIIS

American Institute of Musical Studies, AIMS

American Institutes for Research in the Behavioral Sciences, AIR

American Legal Studies Association, ALSA

American Library Association, ALA

American Library Trustee Association, ALTA

American Lutheran Education Association, ALEA

American Management Association, AMA

American Mathematical Association of Two-Year Colleges, AMATYC

American Mathematical Society, AMS

American Mental Health Counselor Association (American Personnel and Guidance Association), AMHCA

American Mideast Educational and Training Services, Inc., AMIDEAST

American Montessori Society, AMS

American National Standards Institute, ANSI

American Nature Study Society, ANSS

American Nurses' Association, ANA

American Personnel and Guidance Association, APGA

American Philological Association, APA

American Philosophical Association, APA

American Press Institute, API

American Psychiatric Association, APA

American Psychological Association, APA

American Public Health Association, APHA

American Reading Council, ARC

American Reading Forum, ARF

American Registry of Research and Research-Related Organizations, ARROE

American Rehabilitation Counseling Association (American Personnel and Guidance Association), ARCA

American Risk and Insurance Association, ARIA

American School Band Directors' Association, ASBDA

American School Counselor Association, ASCA

American School Food Service Association, ASFSA

American School Health Association, ASHA

American Schools Association, ASA

American Schools of Oriental Research, ASOR

American Society for Engineering Education, ASEE

American Society for Environmental Education, ASEE

American Society for Environmental History, ASEH

American Society for Information Science, ASIS

American Society for Technion—Israel Institute of Technology, ASTIIT

American Society for the Study of Religion, ASSR

American Society for Training and Development, ASTD

American Society of Allied Health Professions, ASAHP

American Society of Educators, ASE

American Society of Interior Designers, ASID

American Society of Journalism School Administrators, ASJSA

American Society of Medical Technology, ASMT

American Society of University Composers, ASUC

American Sociological Association, ASA

American Speech-Language-Hearing Association, ASHA

American Speech-Language-Hearing Association, ASLHA

American Sports Education Institute, ASEI

American Standard Code for Information Interchange, ASCII

American String Teachers Association, ASTA

American Student Association, ASA

American Studies Association, ASA

American Technical Education Association, ATEA

American Technical Society, ATS

American Theological Library Association, ATLA

American Vocational Education Personnel Development Association, AVEPDA

American Vocational Education Research Association, AVERA

American Yoga Association, AYA

American-Nepal Education Foundation, ANEF

Analysis of Covariance, ANCOVA

Analysis Of Variance, ANOVA

Anglo-American Cataloging Rules, AACR

Annual Program Plan, APP

Appalachia Preschool Test, APT

Appalachian Community Service Network, ACSN

Appalachian Educational Laboratory, AEL

Appalachian Educational Satellite Project, AESP

Apple University Consortium, AUC

Applied Performance Tests, APT

Approaches to Behavior Change Inventory, ABC

Aptitude Treatment Interaction, ATI

Architectural and Transportation Barriers Compliance Board, A&TBCB

Area Health Education Centers (California), AHEC

Area Library Service Authority, ALSA

Area Vocational and Technical Institute, AVTI

Area Vocational Schools, AVS

Area Wide Library Network (California), AWLNET

Areawide Agency on Aging, AAA

Arizona Basic Assessment and Curriculum Utilization System, ABACUS

Armed Forces Health Professional Scholarship Program, AFHPSP

Armed Services Vocational Aptitude Battery, ASVAB

Armenian Educational Foundation, AEF

Army Continuing Education System, ACES

Army Research Office, ARO

Army Training and Doctrine Command, TRADOC

Art Library Society of North America, ARLIS/NA

Art Self-Concept Inventory, ASCI

Art Students' League of New York, ASLNY

Articulation Test of Intelligibility, ATI

Artists In the Schools Program, AIS

Artium Baccalaureus, A.B.

Artium Magister, A.M.

Arts, Education and Americans, Inc., AEA

Arts Recognition and Talent Search, ARTS

Asher's Total Physical Response Method, TPR

Asian and Pacific Professional Language and Education Services, APPLES

Asian Program of Educational Innovation for Development, APEID

Asociation of Collegiate Schools of Architecture, ACSA

Assembly of National Postsecondary Educational Organizations, ANPEO

Assembly of State Conferences (American Association of University Professors), ASC

Assessing the Cognitive Consequences of Computer Environments for Learning Project, ACCCEL

Assessment of Instructional Terms, AIT

Assessment of Language And Reading Maturity Test, ALARM

Assessment of Language Proficiency of Bilingual Persons Project, ALPBP

Assessment Policy Committee (National Assessment of Educational Progress), APC

Assessments of Performance in Teaching (South Carolina), APT

Assisting Women to Advance through Resources and Encouragement Project, AWARE

Associate Degree Nursing, ADN

Associate in Applied Arts, AAA

Associate in Applied Nursing, AAN

Associate in Applied Science, AAS

Associate in Arts, AA

Associate in Arts in Business, AAB

Associate in Arts in Law Enforcement, AALE

Associated Colleges of the Midwest, ACM

Associated Collegiate Press, ACP

Associated Information Managers, AIM

Associated Organizations for Professionals in Education, AOPE

Associated Schools of Construction, ASC

Association Canadienne de la Formation Professionelle, ACFP

Association Canadienne de Technologie Advancée, ACTA

Association Canadienne d'Éducation, ACE

Association Council for Policy Analysis and Research, ACPAR

Association for Advancement of Behavior Therapy, AABT

Association for Asian Studies, AAS

Association for Business Simulation and Experiential Learning, ABSEL

Association for Canadian Studies in the United States, ACSUS

Association for Childhood Education International, ACEI

Association for Children and Adults with Learning Disabilities, ACLD

Association for Communication Administration, ACA

Association for Community-Based Education, ACBE

Association for Computational Linguistics, ACL

Association for Computing Machinery, ACM

Association for Continuing Higher Education, ACHE

Association for Continuing Professional Education, ACPE

Association for Counselor Education and Supervision, ACES

Association for Education in Journalism and Mass Communication, AEJMC

Association for Education of the Visually Handicapped, AEVH

Association for Educational Communications and Technology, AECT

Association for Educational Data Systems, AEDS

Association for Environmental Engineering Professors, AEEP

Association for Experiential Education, AEE

Association for General and Liberal Studies, AGLS

Association for Gerontology in Higher Education, AGHE

Association for Humanistic Education, AHE

Association for Individually Guided Education, AIGE

Association for Innovation in Higher Education, AIHE

Association for Institutional Research, AIR

Association for Intercollegiate Athletics for Women, AIAW

Association for International Practical Training, AIPT

Association for Library and Information Science Education, ALISE

Association for Library Service to Children (American Library Association), ALSC

Association for Measurement and Evaluation in Guidance, AMEG

Association for Media-based Continuing Education for Engineers, Inc., AMCEE

Association for Multi-Image, AMI

Association for Politics and the Life Sciences, APLS

Association for Population/Family Planning Libraries and Information Centers, International, APLIC

Association for Professional Education for Ministry, APEM

Association for Religious and Value Issues In Counseling, ARVIC

Association for Research, Administration, Professional Councils and Societies, ARAPCS

Association for School, College, and University Staffing, ASCUS

Association for Specialists in Group Work, ASGW

Association for Supervision and Curriculum Development, ASCD

Association for the Advancement of Health Education, AAHE

Association for the Advancement of International Education, AAIE

Association for the Care of Children's Health, ACCH

Association for the Coordination of University Religious Affairs, ACURA

Association for the Development of Computer-based Instructional Systems, ADCIS

Association for the Education of Teachers in Science, AETS

The Association for the Gifted, TAG

Association for the Improvement of Community College Teaching, AICCT

The Association for the Severely Handicapped, TASH

Association for the Sociological Study of Jewry, ASSJ

Association for the Study of Higher Education, ASHE

Association for University Business and Economic Research, AUBER

Association for World Education, AWE

Association for World University, AWU

Association Internationale de Linguistique Appliquée, AILA

Association Internationale des Écoles des Sciences de l'Information, AIESI

Association Internationale des Étudiants en Sciences Économiques et Commerciales, AIESEC

Association Internationale pour la Recherche et la Diffusion des Méthodes Audio-Visuelles et Structo-Globales, AIMAV

Association of Academic Health Centers, AAHC

Association of Academic Health Sciences Library Directors, AAHSLD

Association of Advanced Rabbinical and Talmudic Schools, AARTS

Association of American Colleges, AAC

Association of American Law Schools, AALS

Association of American Medical Colleges, AAMC

Association of American Publishers, AAP

Association of American Universities, AAU

Association of American University Presses, AAUP

Association of American Veterinary Medical Colleges, AAVMC

Association of Arts Administration Educators, AAAE

Association of Atlantic Universities (Canada), AAU

Association of Atlantic University Business Officers (Canada), AAUBO

Association of Black Women Historians, ABWH

Association of Black Women in Higher Education, ABWHE

Association of Business Officers of Preparatory Schools, ABOPS

Association of Canadian Community Colleges, ACCC

Association of Caribbean Studies, ACS

Association of Catholic Colleges and Universities, ACCU

Association of Chairmen of Departments of Mechanics, ACDM

Association of Christian Schools International, ACSI

Association of College and Research Libraries, ACRL

Association of College and University Auditors, ACUA

Association of College and University Housing Officers—International, ACUHO-I

Association of College and University Telecommunications Administrators, ACUTA

Association of College Unions—International, ACU-I

Association of College, University, and Community Arts Administrators, ACUCAA

Association of Collegiate Entrepreneurs, ACE

Association of Collegiate Schools of Planning, ACSP

Association of Community College Trustees, ACCT

Association of Cooperative Educators, ACE

Association of Counseling Center Training Agents, ACCTA

Association of Data Processing Service Organizations, ADPSO

Association of Departments of English, ADE

Association of Departments of Foreign Languages, ADFL

Association of Governing Boards of Universities and Colleges, AGB

Association of Graduate Liberal Studies Programs, AGLSP

Association of Graduate Schools, AGS

Association of Hillel/Jewish Campus Professionals, AHJCP

Association of Independent Colleges and Schools, AICS

Association of Independent Colleges of Music, AICM

Association of Independent Liberal Arts Colleges for Teacher Education, AILACTE

Association of Independent Maryland Schools, AIMS

Association of Information and Dissemination Centers, ASIDIC

Association of Information Systems Professionals, AISP

Association of International Colleges and Universities, AICU

Association of Jesuit Colleges and Universities, AJCU

Association of Jewish Libraries, AJL

Association of Labor Mediation Agencies, ALMA

Association of Lutheran College Faculties, ALCF

Association of Lutheran Secondary Schools, ALSS

Association of Mercy Colleges, AMC

Association of Mexican American Educators, AMAE

Association of Military Colleges and Schools of the U.S., AMCS

Association of Orthodox Jewish Teachers, AOJT

Association of Overseas Educators, AOE

Association of Physical Plant Administrators of Universities and Colleges, APPA

Association of Presbyterian Colleges and Universities, APCU

Association of Professors and Researchers in Religious Education, APRRE

Association of Records Managers and Administrators, ARMA

Association of Rehabiliation Programs in Data Processing, ARPDP

Association of Research Libraries, ARL

Association of Retarded Citizens, ARC

Association of School Business Officials of the United States and Canada, ASBO

Association of Schools of Journalism and Mass Communication, ASJMC

Association of Southern Baptist Colleges and Schools, ASBCS

Association of Specialized and Cooperative Library Agencies, ASCLA

Association of Student Chapters, American Institute of Architects, ASC/AIA

Association of Teacher Educators, ATE

Association of Teachers of English as a Second Language, ATESL

Association of Teachers of Japanese, ATJ

Association of Teachers of Preventive Medicine, ATPM

Association of Teachers of Technical Writing, ATTW

Association of Theological Schools, ATS

Association of Universities and Colleges of Canada, AUCC

Association of University Programs in Health Administration, AUPHA

Association of Urban Universities, AUU

Association of U.S. University Directors of International Agricultural Programs, AUSUDIAP

Association of Visual Science Librarians, AVSL

Association on American Indian Affairs, AAIA

Association on Handicapped Student Services Programs in Postsecondary Education, AHSSPPE

Athletic Training Council, ATC

Attention Deficit Disorders, ADD

Attitudes Toward Blindness Questionnaire, ATBQ

Attitudes Toward College Inventory, ATCI

Attitudes Toward Disabled Persons Questionnaire, ATDP

Attitudes Toward Educational Research Scale, ATERS

Attitudes Toward Feminist Issues Scales, ATFI

Attitudes Toward Handicapped Individuals Scale, ATHI

Attitudes Toward Mainstreaming Scale, ATMS

Attitudes Toward Sex Roles Instrument, ATSR

Attitudes Toward Women Scale, AWS

Audio, Visual, Kinesthetic, and Oral, AVKO

Audio-Visual, AV

Auditory Attending Task, AAT

Auditory Comprehension Test for Sentences, ACTS

Auditory Reception, AR

Augustinian Educational Association, AEA

Australian Earth Sciences Information System, AESIS

Auto Regressive Integrated Moving Average Model, ARIMA

Automated Instructional Materials Service, AIMS

Automated Library Information System, ALIS

Automatic Vocal Transaction Analyzer, AVTA

Automobile Mechanic Training Evaluation Project (Southern Association of Colleges and Schools), AMTEP

Automotive Service Education Program (General Motors), ASEP

Autonomic Perception Questionnaire, APQ

Auxiliary Loans to Assist Students, ALAS

Average Daily Attendance, ADA

Average Daily Membership, ADM

Aviation Technician Education Council, ATEC

AVKO Educational Research Foundation, AVKOERF

Bachelor of Arts, B.A.

Bachelor of Arts in Education, B.A.in Ed.

Bachelor of Arts in Science, B.A.S.

Bachelor of Business Administration, B.B.A.

Bachelor of Chemistry, Ch.B.

Bachelor of Divinity, B.D.

Bachelor of Domestic Arts, B.D.A.

Bachelor of Education, B.Ed.

Bachelor of Electrical Engineering, B.E.E.

Bachelor of Engineering, B.E.

Bachelor of Fine Arts, B.F.A.

Bachelor of Laws, LL.B.

Bachelor of Music, B.M.

Bachelor of Music Education, B.M.E.

Bachelor of Music Education, B.Mus.Ed.

Bachelor of Science, B.S.

Bachelor of Science in Chemical Engineering, B.S.Ch.E.

Bachelor of Science in Civil Engineering, B.S.C.E.

Bachelor of Science in Education, B.S.Ed.

Bachelor of Science in Electrical Engineering, B.S.E.E.

Bachelor of Science in Engineering, B.S.E.

Bachelor of Science in Mechanical Engineering, B.S.M.E.

Bachelor of Science in Medical Technology,
B.S.Med.Tech.
Bachelor of Science in Nursing, B.S.N.
Bachelor of Science in Pharmacy, B.S.Phar.
Bachelor of Theology, Th.B.
Bahia Oral Language Test, BOLT
Bakersfield Individualized Process, BIP
Bankson Language Screening Test, BLST
Barclay Early Childhood Skill Assessment Center,
BECSAS
Barrett-Lennard Relationship Inventory, BLRI
Baruch Retrieval of Automated Information for
Negotiations, BRAIN
Basic Achievement Skills Individual Screener, BASIS
Basic Education Opportunity Grants, BEOG
Basic Education Program, BEP
Basic Educational Skills through Technology Project
(U.S. Department of Education), BEST
Basic Interpersonal Communicative Skills, BICS
Basic Organizing/Optimizing Training Schedules (U.S.
Navy), BOOTS
Basic Reading Inventory, BRI
Basic Skills Assessment Program (South Carolina),
BSAP
Basic Skills Learning System, BSLS
Battelle Automated Search Information System, BASIS
Bay Area Bilingual Education League (California),
BABEL
Bayley Scales of Infant Development, BSID
Beck Depression Inventory, BDI
Beginner's All-Purpose Symbolic Instruction Code,
BASIC
Beginning Assessment Test of Reading, BATR
Beginning Teacher Evaluation Study, BTES
Behavior Disorder or Behaviorally Disordered, BD
Behavior Engineering Model, BEM
Behavior Problem Checklist, BPC
Behavior Rating Profile, BRP
Behavioral Assertiveness Test, BAT
Behavioral Assessment of Speech Anxiety, BASA
Behavioral Role-Playing Test, BRPT
Behaviorally Anchored Rating Scales, BARS
Beliefs about Science and Science Education Scale, BSSE
Bell Adjustment Inventory, BAI
Bellevue Index of Depression, BID
Bem Sex Role Inventory, BSRI
Best Asymptotically Normal, BAN
A Better Chance, ABC
Better Educational Services through Testing Project
(Kansas), BEST
Bibliographic Access System, BAS
Bibliographic Automation of Large Library Operations
using a Timesharing System, BALLOTS
Bibliographic Center for Research, BCR
Bibliographic Records Conversion, BIBCON
Bibliographic Retrieval Service, BRS
Bibliographic Society of America, BSA
Big Eight Council on Black Student Government,
BECBSG
Bilingual Education, BE
Bilingual Education Act of 1968, BEA

Bilingual Education Bibliographic Abstracts, BEBA
Bilingual Evaluation Technical Assistance Project,
BETA
Bilingual Inventory of Natural Languages, BINL
Bilingual Syntax Measure, BSM
Biological Sciences Curriculum Study, BSCS
Biology Classroom Activity Checklist, BCAC
Biosciences Information Service, BIOSIS
Black English, BE
Black Law Student Association, BLSA
Black Librarians Caucus (American Library
Association), BCALA
Black United Front, BUF
Board of Cooperative Educational Services, BOCES
Boehm Test of Basic Concepts, BTBC
Book Inventory Building and Library Oriented System,
BIBLIOS
Border College Consortium, BCC
Boston Diagnostic Aphasia Examination, BDAE
Boston Theological Institute, BTI
Braille Institute of America, BIA
Brain Injured, BI
Brighton Reading and Individualized Skills Continuum,
BRISC
British Ability Scales, BAS
British American Educational Foundation, BAEF
British Columbia Teachers' Federation, BCTF
British Library, BL
British Schools and Universities Foundation, BSUF
Broadcast Education Association, BEA
Broader Term, BT
Building Better Boards for Community Organizations
Project (American Association of Community and
Junior Colleges), BBB
Bureau of Apprenticeship and Training (U.S.
Department of Labor), BAT
Bureau of Indian Affairs (U.S. Department of the
Interior), BIA
Bureau of Labor Statistics (U.S. Department of Labor),
BLS
Business Education Association of Maine, BEAM
Business Education Research of America, BERA
Business Industry Community College Coalition,
BICCC
Business Teachers Association of New York State,
BTANYS
Business-Higher Education Forum, BHEF
Buss Durkee Hostility Inventory, BDHI
Cable Television, CATV
Cable Television, CTV
Cable-Satellite Public Affairs Network, C-SPAN
California Academic Libraries List of Serials, CALLS
California Achievement Test—Language Subtest, CAT-
L
California Achievement Tests, CAT
California Association of Teachers of English to
Speakers of Other Languages, CATESOL
California Basic Educational Data System, CBEDS
California Basic Educational Skills Test, CBEST
California Guaranteed Student Loans, CGSL

California Library Authority for Systems and Services, CLASS

California Library Services Act, CLSA

California Loans to Assist Students, CLAS

California Occupational Preference System—Form P, COPS-P

California Preschool Scale of Social Competence, CPSSC

California Psychological Inventory, CPI

California Student Opportunity and Access Program, CAL-SOAP

California Test of Mental Maturity, CTMM

California Test of Personality, CTP

Campus Ministry Women, CMW

Canada Employment and Immigration Advisory Council, CEIAC

Canadian Advanced Technology Association, CATA

Canadian Association for Adult Education, CAAE

Canadian Association for Information Science, CAIS

Canadian Association of School Administrators, CASA

Canadian Association of University Teachers, CAUT

Canadian Classification and Dictionary of Occupations, CCDO

Canadian Council of Teachers of English, CCTE

Canadian Education Association, CEA

Canadian Guidance and Counseling Association, CGCA

Canadian Institute for Scientific and Technical Information, CISTI

Canadian Library Association, CLA

Canadian Nurses Association, CNA

Canadian Occupational Forecasting Program, COFOR

Canadian Occupational Projection System, COPS

Canadian On-Line Enquiry, CAN/OLE

Canadian Organization for Development through Education, CODE

Canadian School Library Association, CSLA

Canadian Society for Psychomotor Learning and Sport Psychology, CSPLSP

Canadian Society for the Study of Education, CSSE

Canadian Test of Basic Skills, CTBS

Canadian Union of Public Employees, CUPE

Canadian Vocational Association, CVA

Cancer Decision Making Inventory, CDM

Candidate of Philosophy, C.Phil.

Canonical Correlation Analysis, CCA

Career and Life Planning Model, CLP

Career Decision Scale, CDS

Career Development and Assessment Center for Librarians, CDACL

Career Development Inventory, CDI

Career Education, CE

Career Education Incentive Act of 1977, CEIA

Career Factor Checklist, CFC

Career Information Delivery Systems, CIDS

Career Information System, CIS

Career Maturity Inventory, CMI

Career Motivation and Achievement Planning Inventory, C-MAP

Career Oriented Modules to Explore Topics in Science, COMETS

Career Planning System, CPS

Career Resource Center, CRC

Career Training Foundation, CTF

Caribbean Information System for Economic and Social Planning, CARISPLAN

Caribbean Studies Association, CSA

Carnegie Commission on Higher Education, CCHE

Carnegie Foundation for the Advancement of Teaching, CFAT

Carolina Institute for Research on Early Education for the Handicapped, CIREEH

Carolina Record of Individual Behavior, CRIB

Carrow Elicited Language Inventory, CELI

Cartoon Conservation Scales, CCS

Catalog of Virginia Library Resources, CAVALIR

Cataloging and Classification Section's Descriptive Cataloging Committee (American Library Association), CCS/DDC

Cataloging In Publication, CIP

Cathode Ray Tube, CRT

Catholic Alumni Clubs, International, CACI

Catholic Audio-Visual Educators Association, CAVE

Catholic Biblical Association of America, CBA

Catholic Campus Ministry Association, CCMA

Catholic Scholarships for Negroes, CSN

Catholic Women's Seminary Fund, CWSF

Caucus for a New Political Science, CNPS

Cecchetti Council of America, CCA

Center for Applied Linguistics, CAL

Center for Applied Research in the Apostolate, CARA

Center for Community Education Facility Planning, CCEFP

Center for Computer-Assisted Legal Instruction, CCALI

Center for Cuban Studies, CCS

Center for Death Education and Research, CDER

Center for Education Improvement (U.S. Department of Education), CEI

Center for Educational Policy and Management, CEPM

Center for Educational Policy Research, CEPR

Center for Educational Policy Studies, CEPS

Center for Environmental Intern Programs, CEIP

Center for Information on Language and Teaching, CILT

Center for International Higher Education Documentation, CIHED

Center for Leadership Development, CLD

Center for Management Development, CMD

Center for Occupational Research and Development, CORD

Center for Political Studies (Institute for Social Research), CPS

Center for Research Libraries, CRL

Center for Research on Utilization of Scientific Knowledge (Institute for Social Research), CRUSK

Center for Social Organization of Schools (Johns Hopkins University), CSOS

Center for Teaching About China, CTAC

Center for the Study of Community Colleges, CSCC

Center for the Study of Evaluation (University of California, Los Angeles), CSE

Center for the Study of Liberal Education for Adults, CSLEA
Center for the Study of Reading, CSR
Center for the Study of the Presidency, CSP
Center for Urban Black Studies, CUBS
Centers for Disease Control, CDC
Central ERIC, CERIC
Central Intercollegiate Athletic Association, CIAA
Central Maine Interactive Telecommunications System, CMITS
Central Midwestern Regional Educational Laboratory, CEMREL
Central States Speech Association, CSSA
Centralized Correspondence Study (Alaska), CC/S
Centre for Educational Research and Innovation, CERI
Certificate in Adult Education, CAE
Certificate in Computer Programming, CCP
Certificate in Data Processing, CDP
Certificate of Clinical Competence, CCC
Certified Public Accountant Examination, CPAE
Chain Of Response, COR
Challenging Adults to Read Effectively, C.A.R.E.
Change Facilitator Stages of Concern Questionnaire, CFSoCQ
Characteristic Storage And Retrieval, CSAR
Charles Edison Memorial Youth Fund, CEMYF
Checklist for Ert vs. Inert Qualities, CEIQ
Cheffers' Adaptation of Flanders' Interaction Analysis System, CAFIAS
Chemical Abstracts, CA
Chemical Bond Approach, CBA
Chemical Information Online Dictionary Key to TOXLINE (National Library of Medicine), CHEMLINE
Chicano Education Project, CEP
Chicano Humanities and Arts Council, CHAC
Chief Executive Officer, CEO
Chief Officers of State Library Agencies, COSLA
Chief State School Officer, CSSO
Chief Student Affairs Officer, CSAO
Child Abuse and Neglect Reprint and Inquiry Systems, CANRIS
Child and Family Resource Program (Head Start), CFRP
Child Behavior Checklist, CBCL
Child Behavior Profile, CBP
Child Care Employee Project, CCEP
Child Depression Scale, CDS
Child Development Associate, CDA
Child Development Questionnaire, CDQ
Child Protective Services, CPS
Child Report of Parent Behavior Inventory, CRPBI
Child Service Demonstration Centers, CSDC
Child Welfare League of America, CWLA
Children's Associative Responding Test, CART
Children's Attitude toward Reading Test, CHART
Children's Attribution of Responsibility and Locus Of Control, CARALOC
Children's Book Council, CBC
Children's Checking Test, CCT

Children's Cognitive Style Assessment Instrument, CCSA
Children's Defense Fund, CDF
Children's Depression Inventory, CDI
Children's Depression Rating Scale for Classrooms, CDRSC
Children's Embedded Figures Test, CEFT
Children's English and Services Study, CESS
Children's Fear Survey Schedule, CFSS
Children's Foundation, CF
Children's Manifest Anxiety Scale, CMAS
Children's Personality Questionnaire, CPQ
Children's Strategies Assessment System, CSAS
Children's Television Workshop, CTW
Child's Report of the Impact of Separation by Parents, CRISP
Chinese Language Teachers Association, CLTA
Chinese-American Educational Foundation, CAEF
Chinese-American Librarians Association, CALA
Christian College Consortium, CCC
Christian Schools International, CSI
Chronological Age, CA
Citizens for Educational Freedom, CEF
Citizen's Scholarship Foundation of America, CSFA
Civil Rights of Institutionalized Persons Act of 1980, CRIPA
Civil Service Commission, CSC
Civilian Conservation Corps, CCC
Classical Association of New England, CANE
Classification of Instructional Programs, CIP
Classification of Secondary School Courses (National Center for Education Statistics), CSSC
Classroom Adjustment Rating Scale, CARS
Classroom Business Venture, CBV
Classroom Climate Questionnaire, CCQ
Classroom Environment Scale, CES
Classroom Management Improvement Study, CMIS
Classroom Management Observation Scale, CMOS
Classroom Observations Keyed for Effectiveness Research, COKER
Classroom Reading Inventory, CRI
Client Assistance Program (Rehabilitation Act of 1973), CAP
Clinical Evaluation of Language Functions, CELF
Coalition for Alternatives in Jewish Education, CAJE
Coalition of Adult Education Organizations, CAEO
Coalition of Higher Education Assistance Organizations, CHEAO
Coalition of Indian Controlled School Boards, CICSB
Coalition on Sexuality and Disability, CSD
Cogitive Style, CS
Cognitive Abilities Test—Verbal Battery, CAT-V
Cognitive/Academic Language Proficiency, CALP
Cognitive Levels Matching, CLM
Cognitive Research Trust, CoRT
Cognitive Skills Assessment Battery, CSAB
Cognitive Style Mapping Inventory, CSMI
Cohesion, Organization, Resourcefulness and Energy Model, CORE
Collèges d'Enseignement Général Et Professionel (Quebec), CEGEP

Collective Bargaining Congress (American Association of University Professors), CBC

College and University Faculty Assembly (National Council for the Social Studies), CUFA

College and University Machine Records Conference, CUMREC

College and University Personnel Association, CUPA

College Art Association of America, CAA

College Assistance Migrant Program, CAMP

College Band Directors National Association, CBDNA

College Characteristics Index, CCI

College Descriptive Index, CDI

College Discovery and Development Program (New York City), CDDP

College English Association, CEA

College Entrance Examination Board, CEEB

College Language Association, CLA

College Level Academic Skills Project (Florida), CLASP

College Media Advisers, CMA

College Music Society, CMS

College Placement Council, CPC

College Press Service, CPS

College Reading and Study Skills Inventory, CRSS

College Retirement Equities Fund, CREF

College Theology Society, CTS

College Women's Assertion Sample, CWAS

College Work Study, CWS

College-Level Academic Skills Test (Florida), CLAST

College-Level Examination Program, CLEP

Colleges of Applied Arts and Technology (Ontario), CAAT

Colleges of Mid-America, CMA

Collegial Association for the Development and Renewal of Educators, CADRE

Colloquia for Presidents and Academic Administrators, CPAA

Colorado Congress of Foreign Language Teachers, CCFLT

Colorado Department of Education, CDE

Colorado Migrant Education Resource Center, CoMERC

Coloured Progressive Matrices, CPM

Columbia Mental Maturity Scale, CMMS

Columbia Scholastic Press Advisers Association, CSPAA

Columbia Scholastic Press Association, CSPA

Comfortable Interpersonal Distance Scale, CID

Commission on Accreditation of Rehabilitation Facilities, CARF

Commission on Education of Teachers of Reading, CETOR

Commission on Instructional Technology, CIT

Commission on the Status of Women in Adult Education, CSWAE

Committee for Corporate Support of Private Universities, CCSPU

Committee for Education Funding, CFEF

Committee for Positive Education, CPE

Committee on Allied Health Education and Accreditation, CAHEA

Committee on Assessment and Testing (Speech Communication Association), CAT

Committee on Diagnostic Reading Tests, CDRT

Committee on Institutional Cooperation, CIC

Committee on Instruction in the Use of Libraries (American Library Association), IULC

Committee On Organization (American Library Association), COO

Committee On Program Evaluation and Support (American Library Association), COPES

Committee On Research Materials On Southeast Asia, CORMOSEA

Committee On Scientific And Technical Information, COSATI

Committee On the Status of Women in Librarianship (American Library Association), COSWL

Committee on the Undergraduate Program in Mathematics, CUPM

Committee on Women in Asian Studies, CWAS

Common Business Oriented Language, COBOL

Common Command Language, CCL

Common Fund for Nonprofit Organizations, CFNO

Commonwealth Council for Educational Administration (Australia), CCEA

Communications among Organizations Dealing with Admissions, CODA

Communicative Competence Test, CCT

Community Alliance Program for Ex-Offenders, CAPE

Community and Continuing Education Information Service, CCEIS

Community Antenna Relay Service, CARS

Community Antenna Television, CATV

Community College Activities Survey, CCAS

Community College Association for Instruction and Technology, CCAIT

Community College General Education Association, CCGEA

Community College Goals Inventory, CCGI

Community College Humanities Association, CCHA

Community College Journalism Association, CCJA

Community Health Information Network (Massachusetts), CHIN

Community Independent Living Service Delivery Systems, CILSDS

Community Rehabilitation Approach, CRA

Community Service Organization, CSO

Community-Based Education, CBE

Community-Based Organizations, CBO

Community-Oriented Program Environment Scale, COPES

Comparative and International Education Society, CIES

Comparative Guidance and Placement Program, CGP

Competency/Performance-Based Teacher Education, C/PBTE

Competency Screening Test, CST

Competency-Based Administrator Education, CBAE

Competency-Based Adult Education, CBAE

Competency-Based Adult Vocational Education, CBAVE

Competency-Based Education, CBE

Competency-Based Teacher Education, CBTE

Competitive State Anxiety Inventory, CSAI
Completions, Arithmetical Problems, Vocabulary, and
    Directions Test, CAVD
Composite Assessment of Leverage, CAL
Comprehensive Ability Battery, CAB
Comprehensive Analytical Model for Planning in the
    University Sphere, CAMPUS
Comprehensive Assistance to Undergraduate Science
    Education, CAUSE
Comprehensive Communication Curriculum, CCC
Comprehensive Employment and Training Act, CETA
Comprehensive English Language Test, CELT
Comprehensive School Mathematics Program, CSMP
Comprehensive Systems of Personnel Development,
    CSPD
Comprehensive Test of Basic Skills, CTBS
Computer Aided Instruction for Teacher Education,
    CAITE
Computer Aided Teaching of Applied Mathematics
    (Cambridge University, England), CATAM
Computer Aided Training Evaluation and Scheduling
    (U.S. Navy), CATES
Computer Animated Reading Instruction System,
    CARIS
Computer Anxiety Index, CAIN
Computer Aptitude, Literacy, and Interest Profile,
    CALIP
Computer Aptitude Quotient, CAQ
Computer Assisted Diagnostic and Prescription
    Instruction, CAD PI
Computer Assisted Instruction and Support for the
    Handicapped, CAISH
Computer Assisted Language Instruction Bibliography,
    CALIB
Computer Assisted Language Learning and Instruction
    Consortium, CALICO
Computer Assisted Spanish English Transition
    Sequence, CASETS
Computer Assisted Student Tutorial Learning
    Environment, CASTLE
Computer Input Microfilm, CIM
Computer Integrated Instruction, CII
Computer Language Instructional Program, CLIP
Computer League for Users in Education, CLUE
Computer Literacy, CL
Computer Readability Editing System, CRES
Computer Support Systems, CSS
Computer-Aided Design, CAD
Computer-Aided Engineering, CAE
Computer-Aided Interactive Testing System, CAITS
Computer-Aided Manufacturing, CAM
Computer-Assisted Guidance, CAG
Computer-Assisted Instruction, CAI
Computer-Assisted Language Learning, CALL
Computer-Assisted Learning, CAL
Computer-Assisted Retrieval, CAR
Computer-Assisted Study Skills Improvement Program,
    CASSIP
Computer-Assisted Teaching, CAT
Computer-Assisted Teaching Unit, CATU
Computer-Assisted Test Construction, CATC

Computer-Assisted Testing, CAT
Computer-Based Education, CBE
Computer-Based Interactive Video, CBIV
Computer-Based Testing, CBT
Computer-Based Training, CBT
Computer-Graphics Augmented Design and
    Manufacturing System, CADAM
Computer-Guided Teaching, CGT
Computerized Adaptive Testing, CAT
Computerized Engineering Index, COMPENDEX
Computerized Heuristic Occupational Information and
    Career Exploration System, CHOICES
Computerized Lesson-Authoring System, CLAS
Computerized Mastery Learning System, CMLS
Computerized Spelling Remediation Program, CSRP
Computerized Test of Spelling Errors, CTSE
Computerized Vocational Information System, CVIS
Computer-Managed Instruction, CMI
Computer-Managed Learning, CML
Computer-Output Microcopy, COM
Computers, Learners, Users, Educators Association
    (New Jersey), CLUES
Computer-Using Educators (California), CUE
Computer-Using Educators of British Columbia,
    CUEBC
Computer-Using Educators of Kentucky, CUE-KY
Concealed Figures Test, CFT
Concentrated Employment Program, CEP
Concept Memory Test, CMT
Concepts About Print Test, CAP
Conceptual Level, CL
Concerned Educators Against Forced Unionism,
    CEAFU
Concerned Educators Allied for a Safe Environment,
    CEASE
Concerns-Based Adoption Model, CBAM
Conditioned Stimulus, CS
Conductive Hearing Impairment Language
    Development Program, CHILD
Conference Board of Associated Research Councils,
    CBARC
Conference Board on the Mathematical Sciences, CBMS
Conference for Secondary School English Department
    Chairpersons, CSSEDC
Conference for the Study of Political Thought, CSPT
Conference Group on French Politics and Society,
    CGFPS
Conference Group on German Politics, CGGP
Conference Group on Italian Politics, CGIP
Conference of Educational Administrators Serving the
    Deaf, CEASD
Conference of Small Private Colleges, CSPC
Conference of University Administrators, CUA
Conference on Christianity and Literature, CCL
Conference on College Composition and
    Communication, CCCC
Conference on English Education, CEE
Conflict Review Curriculum, CRC
Conflict Tactics Scale, CTS
Confluent Education Development And Research
    Center, CEDARC

Congress On Research in Dance, CORD
Congressional Indexing Service, CIS
Congressional Information Service, CIS
Connecticut Assessment of Educational Progress, CAEP
Connecticut Business Educators Association, CBEA
Connecticut Industrial Arts Association, CIAA
Connector for Networked Information Transfer, CONIT
Conner's Teacher Rating Scale, CTRS
Conseil Consultatif Canadien de l'Emploi et de
    l'Immigration, CCCEI
Conservation Education Association, CEA
Consolidated Youth Employment Program, CYEP
Consortium for Graduate Study in Management,
    CGSM
Consortium for International Cooperation in Higher
    Education, CICHE
Consortium for International Studies Education, CISE
Consortium for the Advancement of Private Higher
    Education, CAPHE
Consortium of Professional Associations for the Study of
    Special Teacher Improvement Programs, CON PASS
Consortium of University Film Centers, CUFC
Consortium On Financing Higher Education, COFHE
Constructive Error Score, CES
Consumer Education Research Center, CERC
Consumer Price Index, CPI
Contemporary Issues In Science Program, CIIS
Context, Input, Process, Product, CIPP
Continuing Education in Mental Retardation Program
    (American Association on Mental Deficiency),
    CEMR
Continuing Education Unit, CEU
Continuing Library Education, CLE
Continuing Library Education Network and Exchange,
    CLENE
Continuing Professional Education, CPE
Continuous Angular Velocity, CAV
Convention of American Instructors of the Deaf, CAID
Conversion of Serials Project, CONSER
Cooperating Teacher Attitude Inventory, CTAI
Cooperative Area Manpower Planning Systems,
    CAMPS
Cooperative Assessment of Experiential Learning
    Project, CAEL
Cooperative Education Association, CEA
Cooperative Extension Service, CES
Cooperative International Pupil-to-Pupil Program,
    CIPTPP
Cooperative Program for Educational Opportunity,
    CPEO
Cooperative Work Experience Education Association,
    CWEEA
Coopersmith Self-Esteem Inventory, SEI
Coordinated Occupational Information Network, COIN
Coordinated Vocational Academic Education (Georgia),
    CVAE
Copyright Clearance Center, CCC
Copyright Copying Guidelines, CCG
Cordell Hull Foundation for International Education,
    CHFIE
Core College Curriculum, CCC

Cornell Parent Behavior Description, CPBD
Cornell Parent Behavior Inventory, CPBI
Corvus National Educational Enduser's Group, Inc.,
    CNEEUG
Costing and Data Management System (National
    Center for Higher Education Management Systems),
    CADMS
Council for Accreditation of Counseling and Related
    Educational Programs, CACREP
Council for Agricultural Science and Technology, CAST
Council for American Private Education, CAPE
Council for Basic Education, CBE
Council for Children with Behavioral Disorders, CCBD
Council for Computerized Library Networks, CCLN
Council for Educational Development and Research,
    CEDaR
Council for Educational Freedom in America, CEFA
Council for Elementary Science International, CESI
Council for European Studies, CES
Council for Exceptional Children, CEC
Council for Financial Aid to Education, CFAE
Council for Intercultural Studies and Programs, CISP
Council for Interinstitutional Leadership, CIL
Council for International Exchange of Scholars, CIES
Council for Jewish Education, CJE
Council for Learning Disabilities (Council for
    Exceptional Children), CLD
Council for Noncollegiate Continuing Education, CNCE
Council for Opportunity in Graduate Management
    Education, COGME
Council for Philosophical Studies, CPS
Council for Religion in Independent Schools, CRIS
Council for Research in Music Education, CRME
Council for the Advancement of Experiential Learning,
    CAEL
Council for the Advancement of Standards for Student
    Affairs/Services Programs, CAS
Council for the Understanding of Technology in Human
    Affairs, CUTHA
Council for Women in Independent Schools (National
    Association of Independent Schools), CWIS
Council of 1890 College Presidents, CCP
Council Of Black Architectural Schools, COBAS
Council of Chief State School Officers, CCSSO
Council of Colleges of Arts and Sciences, CCAS
Council of Communication Societies, CCS
Council of Educational Facility Planners, International,
    CEFPI
Council of Graduate Schools in the United States, CGS
Council of Independent Colleges, CIC
Council of Library Associations Executives, CLAE
Council of Mennonite Colleges, CMC
Council of National Library and Information
    Associations, CNLIA
Council of Ontario Universities, COU
Council of Planning Librarians, CPL
Council Of Program Evaluation, COPE
Council Of Regional School Accrediting Commissions,
    CORSAC
Council of Specialized Accrediting Agencies, CSAA

Council of State Administrators of Vocational Rehabilitation, CSAVR

Council of State Science Supervisors, CSSS

Council of Student Personnel Associations in Higher Education, COSPA

Council of the Great City Schools, CGCS

Council on Anthropology and Education, CAE

Council on Education in the Geological Sciences, CEGS

Council on Education of the Deaf, CED

Council on Educational Diagnostic Services (Council for Exceptional Children), CEDS

Council on Electrolysis Education, CEE

Council On Governmental Relations, COGR

Council on Hotel, Restaurant, and Institutional Education, CHRIE

Council on International Education Exchange, CIEE

Council on Interracial Books for Children, CIBC

Council on Legal Education Opportunity, CLEO

Council On Library and Network Development, COLAND

Council on Library Resources, CLR

Council On Library-Media Technical-Assistants, COLT

Council On Postsecondary Accreditation, COPA

Council on Professional Certification, CPC

Council On Professional Standards in Speech Language Pathology and Audiology (American Speech-Language Hearing Association), COPS

Council on Social Work Education, CSWE

Council on the Continuing Education Unit, CCEU

Council on the Study of Religion, CSR

Council on Undergraduate Research, CUR

Counseling Effectiveness Rating Scale, CERS

Counseling Practice Beliefs Inventory, CPBI

Counseling Services Assessment Blank, CSAB

Counseling-Orientation Preference Scale, COS

Counselling and Home Training Program for Deaf Children (British Colombia), CHTP

Counselor Behavior Evaluation Form, CBE

Counselor Interview Competence Scale, CICS

Country Day School Headmasters Association of the United States, CDSHA

Course Structure Inventory, CSI

Courses by Newspaper, CbN

Crabtree-Horsham Affective Trait Scale, CHATS

Craig Adapted Sociometric Test Form, CASTE

Creative Education Foundation, CEF

Creative Imagination Scale, CIS

Creative Problem-Solving Institute, CPSI

Criterion-Referenced English Syntax Test, CREST

Criterion-Referenced Test, CRT

Critical Events Interview, CEI

Critical Incident Technique, CIT

Critical Path Analysis, CPA

Critical Path Method, CPM

Cross Examination Debate Association, CEDA

Crustal Evolution Education Project (National Association of Geology Teachers), CEEP

Cultural and Social Center for the Asian and Pacific Region (South Korea), ASPAC

Cultural Attitudes Repertory Technique, CART

Cumulative Grade Point Average, CGPA

Current Index to Journals in Education, CIJE

Current Information Transfer in English, CITE

Curriculum Attitude Survey, CAS

Curriculum Coordinating Committees, CCC

Curriculum Improvement Resulting from Creative Utilization of Instructional Two-Way Television Project (Wisconsin), CIRCUIT

Curriculum Objectives for Physical Education, C.O.P.E.

Curriculum Organization and Program Evaluation, COPE

Daily Child Behavior Checklist, DCBC

Dance Educators of America, DEA

Dance Films Association, DFA

Dance Masters of America, DMA

Dartmouth Intensive Language Model, DILM

Data Base Management System, DBMS

Data Processing Management Association, DPMA

Data Retrieval System, DRS

Data-Based Program Modification, DBPM

Day Care Council of America, DCCA

Dean's Grant Project, DGP

Decision Support System, DSS

Defense Documentation Center, DDC

Defense Language Institute, DLI

Defense Language Proficiency Tests, DLPT

Defense Technical Information System, DTIC

Defining Issues Test, DIT

Degrees of Reading Power Test, DRP

Del Greco Assertive Behavior Inventory, DABI

Delaware Education Accountability System, DEAS

Denmark-America Foundation, DAF

Dental Aptitude Test, DAT

Dental Hygiene Aptitude Tests, DHAT

Dental Students' Attitudes Toward the Handicapped Scale, DSATHS

Denver Developmental Screening Test, DDST

Department of Agriculture, DOA

Department Of Defense, DOD

Department Of Defense Dependents Schools, DODDS

Department of Education, ED

Department Of Energy, DOE

Department of Health and Human Services, DHHS

Department of Health and Human Services, HHS

Department of Housing and Urban Development, DHUD

Department of Housing and Urban Development, HUD

Department Of Justice, DOJ

Department Of Labor, DOL

Department of Measurement, Evaluation, and Computer Applications (Ontario Institute for Studies in Education), MECA

Department of Public Instruction, DPI

Department Of the Interior, DOI

Department Of Transportation, DOT

Depression Adjective Checklist, DACL

Descriptive Test of Mathematics Skills, DTMS

Descriptive Tests of Language Skills, DTLS

Designs For Change, DFC

Detail Matching Figures Test, DMF

Detroit Tests of Learning Aptitude, DTLA

Deutscher Akademischer Austauschdienst, DAAD
Developing A Curriculum, DACUM
Developing Mathematical Processes, DMP
Developing Understanding of Self and Others, DUSO
Development Centers for Handicapped Minors, DCHM
Development in Science Education Program, DISE
Developmental Assessment of Spanish Grammar, DASG
Developmental Play, DP
Developmental Sentence Scoring, DSS
Developmental Test of Visual Perception, DTVP
Developmentally Disabled, DD
Devereaux Elementary School Behavior Rating Scale, DESB
Deviation Intelligence Quotient, DIQ
DeVries' Teams-Games-Tournaments, TGT
Dewey Decimal Classification, DDC
Diagnosis Related Groups, DRG
Diagnostic and Statistical Manual of Mental Disorders, DSM
Diagnostic Interview Schedule, DIS
Diagnostic Prescriptive Arithmetic, DPA
Diagnostic Prescriptive Teacher, DPT
Dictionary Of Occupational Titles, DOT
Differential Aptitude Test—Verbal Reasoning, DAT-VR
Differential Aptitude Tests, DAT
Diffusion of Exemplary Educational Practices, DEEP
Digital And Video Interactive Device, DAVID
Dimensions Of Self-Concept Scales, DOSC
Direct Broadcast Satellite, DBS
Direct Instruction Observation System, DIOS
Direct Instructional System for Teaching Arithmetic and Reading, DISTAR
Directed Listening-Language Experience Approach, DL-LEA
Directed Reading Activity, DRA
Directed Reading-Thinking Activity, DR-TA
Disability Rights Education and Defense Fund, DREDF
Discourse Comprehension Abilities Test, DCAT
Discrepancy Evaluation Model, DEM
Disk Operating System, DOS
Dissemination and Improvement of Practice, DIP
Dissemination Capacity Building Project, DCBP
Dissemination Network for Adult Educators, DNAE
Dissemination Policy Council, DPC
Dissemination Services Unit, DSU
Dissertation Abstracts International, DAI
DISTAR Language Program, DLP
Distributive Education Clubs of America, DECA
District School Area Board (Ontario), DSAB
Disturbing Behavior Checklist, DBC
DiTomasso Methodology Inventory, DMI
Division for Children with Communication Disorders (Council for Exceptional Children), DCCD
Division for Children with Learning Disabilities (Council for Exceptional Children), DCLD
Division for the Visually Handicapped (Council for Exceptional Children), DVH
Division of Actively Retired Teachers (Ohio Education Association), DART

Division of Educational Media Management (Association for Educational Communications and Technology), DEMM
Division Of Physically Handicapped, Homebound, and Hospitalized (Council for Exceptional Children), DOPHHH
Division Of Telecommunications (Association for Educational Communications and Technology), DOT
Doctor of Business Administration, D.B.A.
Doctor of Chiropractic, D.C.
Doctor of Comparative Medicine, D.C.M.
Doctor of Dental Medicine, D.M.D.
Doctor of Dental Surgery, D.D.S.
Doctor of Divinity, D.D.
Doctor of Education, Ed.D.
Doctor of Engineering, D.Eng.
Doctor of Humane Letters, L.H.D.
Doctor of Laws, LL.D.
Doctor Of Library Science, D.O.L.
Doctor of Literature, D.Lit.
Doctor of Literature, Lit.D.
Doctor of Medicine, M.D.
Doctor of Music, D.Mus.
Doctor of Music, Mus.D.
Doctor of Musical Arts, D.M.A.
Doctor of Optometry, O.D.
Doctor of Osteopathy, D.O.
Doctor of Pharmacy, D.Phar.
Doctor of Philosophy, Ph.D.
Doctor of Podiatric Medicine, D.P.M.
Doctor of Podiatry, Pod.D.
Doctor of Public Administration, D.P.A.
Doctor of Science, D.S.
Doctor of Science, Sc.D.
Doctor of Veterinary Medicine, D.V.M.
Documentation and Integration of Software into the Classroom Project, DISC
Documentation and Technical Assistance Project, DTA
Domestic Training Site, DTS
Dominican Educational Association, DEA
Down's Syndrome, DS
Driving School Association of America, DSAA
Drug Abuse Reporting Program, DARP
DTLA-Oral Commissions Subtest, DTLA-OC
Dual Employed Coping Scale, DECS
Duplicates Exchange Union, DEU
Dyadic Adjustment Scale, DAS
Dyadic Parent-Child Interaction Coding System, DPICS
Dynamic Functional Interaction, DFI
Dynamics International Gardening Association, DIGA
Earl Warren Legal Training Program, EWLTP
Early and Periodic Screening, Diagnosis and Treatment, EPSDT
Early Childhood Embedded Figures Test, ECEFT
Early Intervention Developmental Profile, EIDP
Early Screening Inventory, ESI
Early Social Communication Scale, ESCS
Earthwork/Center for Rural Studies, ECRS
East Asia Journalism Program, EAJP
Eastern Business Education Association, EBEA
Eastern Regional Institute for Education, ERIE

Eating Attitude Test, EAT
Economic History Association, EHA
Economic Recovery Tax Act of 1981, ERTA
Edmond's Learning Style Identification Exercise, ELSIE
Educable Mentally Retarded, EMR
Education Amendments Act, EAA
Education Commission of the States, ECS
Education Consolidation and Improvement Act of 1981, ECIA
Education Division General Administration Regulations, EDGAR
Education Evaluation and Remedial Assistance Program (Connecticut), EERA
Education Exploration Center, EEC
Education for All Handicapped Act, EAHA
Education for All Handicapped Children Act, EHA
Education Funding Research Council, EFRC
Education Information Center, EIC
Education Leadership Institute, ELI
Education of Exceptional Students, EDEXS
Education Professional for Indian Children, EPIC
Education Professions Development Act, EPDA
Education Service Center, ESC
Education Voucher Institute, EVI
Education Writers Association, EWA
Educational and Career Exploration System, ECES
Educational and Health Career Services, EHCS
Educational and Industrial Testing Service, EdITS
Educational Attitudes Inventory, EAI
Educational Beliefs System Inventory, EBSI
Educational Broadcasting Corporation, EBC
Educational Communication Association, ECA
Educational Communications (Interuniversity Communications Council), EDUCOM
Educational Computer Consortium of Ohio, ECCO
Educational Computing Organization of Ontario, ECOO
Educational Cooperative Service Unit, ECSU
Educational Council for Foreign Medical Graduates, ECFMG
Educational Development Center, EDC
Educational Development Corporation, EDCo
Educational Facilities Center, EFC
Educational Facilities Laboratories, EFL
Educational Film Library Association, EFLA
Educational Forces Inventory, EFI
Educational Freedom Foundation, EFF
Educational Goals Assessment, EGA
Educational Improvement Process (Indiana), EIP
Educational Micro Systems, Inc., EMSI
Educational Modules for Materials Science and Engineering, EMMSE
Educational Opportunity Grants, EOG
Educational Opportunity Programs, EOP
Educational Orientation Questionnaire, EOQ
Educational Paperbacks Association, EPA
Educational Participant Scale, EPS
Educational Planning Institute, EPI
Educational Press Association of America, EDPRESS
Educational Products Information Exchange, EPIE
Educational Program and Studies Information Services, EPSIS

Educational Quality Assessment Program (Pennsylvania), EQA
Educational Records Bureau, ERB
Educational Research Analysts, EdReAn
Educational Research and Development Associates, ERANDA
Educational Research and Development Committee, ERDC
Educational Research Council of America, ERCA
Educational Resource Management System, ERMS
Educational Resources Information Center, ERIC
Educational Service Agencies, ESA
Educational Service and Demonstration Centers (Washington), ESD
Educational Service Units, ESU
Educational Services, International, ESI
The Educational Software Selector (A handbook of software and hardware), TESS
Educational Television, ETV
Educational Testing Service, ETS
Educational Testing Service Kit of Reference Abilities, ETS-kit
Educational Testing Service Test Collection File, ETSF
Educationally Disadvantaged Youth, EDY
Educationally Handicapped, EH
Educators of the Handicapped Special Interest Group (Association for the Development of Computer-Based Instructional Systems), SIGHAN
EDUCOM Computer Literacy Project, ECLP
EDUCOM Financial Planning Model System, EFPM
Edwards Personal Preference Schedule, EPPS
Edwards Situational Preference Inventory, SPI
Effective Reading In Content Areas, ERICA
Effectiveness Training for Women, ETW
Effectiveness Training, Inc., ETI
Ekwall Reading Inventory, ERI
El Congreso Nacional de Asuntos Colegiales, CONAC
Electroconvulsive Therapy, ECT
Electromyogram, EMG
Electronic Information Exchange System, EIES
Electronic Music Consortium, EMC
Electronic Travel Aid, ETA
Electronic Video Recorder, EVR
Electrooculograph, EOG
Elementary Adult Sex Education, EASE
Elementary and High School, EL HI
Elementary and Secondary Education Act, ESEA
Elementary and Secondary General Information System, ELSEGIS
Elementary School Science, ESS
Elementary School Study Group, ESSG
Elementary Science Study, ESS
Elementary/Secondary/Junior College Special Interest Group (Association for the Development of Computer-Based Instructional Systems), EL/SEC/JC
Elementary Sex-Role Inventory, ESRI
Elyria Project for Innovative Curriculum, EPIC
Embedded Conversations Test, ECT
Embedded Figures Test, EFT
Emergency English for Refugees (Pennsylvania), EER
Emergency Jobs Appropriations Act of 1983, EJAA

Emergency Jobs Programs Extension Act of 1976, EJPEA

Emergency School Aid Act, ESAA

Emergency School Assistance Program, ESAP

Emergent Reading Ability Judgements for Favorite Storybooks Scale, ERAJFS

Emotionally Disturbed, ED

Employment Relations Board, ERB

End Violence Against the Next Generation, EVAN-G

Energy Action in Schools, EAIS

Energy Data Base (U.S. Department of Education), EDB

Energy Research and Development Administration, ERDA

Engineering Concepts Curriculum Project, ECCP

English as a Foreign Language, EFL

English as a Second Dialect, ESD

English as a Second Language, ESL

English as a Second Language Achievement Test, ESLAT

English Composition Board, ECB

English Council of California Two-Year Colleges, ECCTYC

English for Speakers of Other Languages, ESOL

English for Specific Purposes, ESP

English in Science and Technology, EST

English Institute, EI

English Language Proficiency Study, ELPS

English Language Teaching, ELT

English Picture Vocabulary Test, EPVT

Entayant Institute, EI

Environmental Education, EE

Environmental Education Group, EEG

Environmental Issues Test, EIT

Environmental Studies, ES

Equal Employment Opportunity, EEO

Equal Employment Opportunity Commission, EEOC

Equal-Appearing Intervals, EAI

ERIC Clearinghouse for Junior Colleges, JC

ERIC Clearinghouse for Science, Mathematics, and Environmental Education, ERIC/SMEAC

ERIC Clearinghouse for Science, Mathematics, and Environmental Education, SE

ERIC Clearinghouse for Social Studies/Social Science Education, ERIC/ChESS

ERIC Clearinghouse for Social Studies/Social Science Education, SO

ERIC Clearinghouse on Adult, Career, and Vocational Education, CE

ERIC Clearinghouse on Counseling and Personnel Services, CAPS

ERIC Clearinghouse on Counseling and Personnel Services, CG

ERIC Clearinghouse on Counseling and Personnel Services, ERIC/CAPS

ERIC Clearinghouse on Educational Management, EA

ERIC Clearinghouse on Educational Management, ERIC/CEM

ERIC Clearinghouse on Elementary and Early Childhood Education, ERIC/EECE

ERIC Clearinghouse on Elementary and Early Childhood Education, PS

ERIC Clearinghouse on Handicapped and Gifted Children, EC

ERIC Clearinghouse on Handicapped and Gifted Children, ERIC/CEC

ERIC Clearinghouse on Higher Education, HE

ERIC Clearinghouse on Information Resources, IR

ERIC Clearinghouse on Languages and Linguistics, ERIC/CLL

ERIC Clearinghouse on Languages and Linguistics, FL

ERIC Clearinghouse on Reading and Communication Skills, CS

ERIC Clearinghouse on Reading and Communication Skills, ERIC/RCS

ERIC Clearinghouse on Rural Education, RC

ERIC Clearinghouse on Teacher Education, SP

ERIC Clearinghouse on Tests, Measurement and Evaluation, TM

ERIC Clearinghouse on Urban Education, ERIC/CUE

ERIC Clearinghouse on Urban Education, UD

ERIC Document, ED

ERIC Document Reproduction Service, EDRS

ERIC Journal, EJ

Esperanto League for North America, ELNA

Essential Sight Words Program, ESWP

Established Programme Financing Act (Canada), EPF

Estimated Learning Potential, ELP

Ethical Judgement Scale, EJS

Ethical Reasoning Inventory, ERI

Ethnic Materials Information Exchange Round Table, EMIERT

European Center for the Development of Vocational Training (West Germany), CEDEFOP

European Documentation and Information System for Education, EUDISED

Evaluation, Dissemination, and Assessment Center for Bilingual Education, EDAC

Evaluation Of Counselors Scale, EOC

Evening College Characteristics Index, ECCI

Every Pupil Achievement Test, EPAT

Examen de Colocación en Español, EdCE

Exceptional Child Education Resources (Council for Exceptional Children), ECER

Exemplary Center for Reading Instruction (Maine), ECRI

Expectations about Counseling Questionnaire, EAC

Expected Grade Equivalent, EGE

Experienced Control Scales, ECS

Experienced-Based Career Education, EBCE

Experiences in Mathematical Ideas, EMI

Experiment in International Living, EIL

Expressed Attitude Toward Confrontation Questionnaire, EATCQ

Expressed Reading Difficulty, ERD

Extended Binary-Coded Decimal Interchange Code, EBCDIC

Extended Education in Therapeutic Recreation Administration, EXTRA

Extended Opportunity Programs and Services, EOPS

Extended Personality Attributes Questionnaire, EPAQ

Extended School Year, ESY

Extension Committee on Organization and Policy, ECOP

Eyberg Child Behavior Inventory, ECBI

Eysenck Personality Questionnaire, EPQ

Facts on Aging Quiz, FAQ

Faculty Exchange Center, FEC

Failure To Thrive, FTT

Fair Employment Practice, FEP

Family Adaptability and Cohesion Evaluation Scales, FACES

Family Educational Rights and Privacy Act of 1974, FERPA

Family Environment Scale, FES

Family Financial Statement, FFS

Far West Laboratory for Educational Research and Development, FWLERD

Fast Response Survey System (National Center for Education Statistics), FRSS

Fédération Internationale de Documentation, FID

Fédération Internationale de Professeurs des Langues Vivantes, FIPLV

Fédération Internationale des Langues et Litteratures Modernes, FILLM

Fédération Internationale des Mouvements d'École Moderne, FIMEM

Fear of Negative Evaluation Scale, FNE

Federal Communications Commission, FCC

Federal Employee Literacy Training Program, FELT

Federal Interagency Committee on Education, FICE

Federal Interagency Day Care Requirements, FIDCR

Federal Labor Relations Council, FLRC

Federal Librarians Roundtable (American Library Association), FLRT

Federal Library Network, FEDNET

Federal Licensing Examination, FLEX

Federal Mediation and Conciliation Service, FMCS

Federal Telecommunications System, FTS

Federally Assisted Staff Training, FAST

Federally Insured Student Loans, FISL

Federation of Armenian Students Clubs of America, FASCA

Feedback to Oral Reading Miscues Analysis System, FORMAS

Feminist Press, FP

Feminist Research Methodology Groups, FRMG

Field Dependence/Independence, FD/I

Field Dependent, FD

Field Independent, FI

Figural Intersection Test, FIT

Figure Location Test, FLT

Film Integrated Learning Modules, FILM

Film Library Information Council, FLIC

Financial Accounting Foundation, FAF

Financial Accounting Standards Advisory Council (Financial Accounting Foundation), FASAC

Financial Accounting Standards Boards (Financial Accounting Foundation), FASB

Financial Aid Form, FAF

Financial Management Association, FMA

First Language, L1

Fiscal Year, FY

Flanders Interaction Analysis Categories, FIAC

Flanders Interaction Analysis System, FIAS

Flexible Modular Scheduling, FMS

Florida Association of Science Teachers, FAST

Florida Center for Instructional Computing, FCIC

Florida Educational Computing Project, FECP

Florida High School Athletics Association, FHSAA

Florida Information Resource Network, FIRN

Florida Postsecondary Education Planning Commission, PEPC

Florida Teacher Certification Examination, FTCE

Food and Drug Administration, FDA

Foreign Language Arts in the Grades, FLAG

Foreign Language Entrance and Degree Requirements, FLEDR

Foreign Languages in Elementary Schools, FLES

Foreign Service Institute, FSI

Foreign Student Service Council, FSSC

Formal Operational Reasoning Test, FORT

Formula Translation, FORTRAN

Forum for Death Education and Counseling, FDEC

Forward Occupational Imbalance Listing (Canada), FOIL

Foster Grandparent Program, FGP

Foundation for Exceptional Children, FEC

Foundation for Gifted and Creative Children, FGCC

Foundation for Interior Design Education Research, FIDER

Foundation for International Cooperation, FIC

Foundation for Oregon Research and Education, FORE

Foundation for Public Relations Research and Education, FPRRE

Foundation for Student Communication, FSC

Foundation of the Flexographic Technical Association, FFTA

Four Factor Theory Questionnaire, FFTQ

Freedom Of Information, FOI

Freedom To Read Foundation, FTRF

French Language Intensive Program (Illinois), FLIP

Frequency, F

Freshman Issues and Concerns Survey, FICS

Friends Association for Higher Education, FAHE

Friends Council on Education, FCE

Fulbright Association of Alumni of International Educational and Cultural Exchange, FAAIECE

Full Scale Intelligence Quotient, FSIQ

Full-Time, F-T

Full-Time Equivalent, FTE

Full-Time Equivalent Enrollment, FTEE

Functional Inventory of Cognitive Communication Strategies, FICCS

Functional Language Survey, FLS

Functional Literacy, FLIT

Functional Literacy Test, FLT

Fund for the Advancement of Music Education, FAME

Fund for the Improvement of Postsecondary Education, FIPSE

Fundamental Interpersonal Relations Orientation— Behavior Children Test, FIRO-BC

Further Education Unit (Great Britain), FEU

Future Business Leaders of America—Phi Beta Lambda, FBLA—PBL
Future Farmers of America, FFA
Future Homemakers of America, FHA
Future Journalists of America, FJA
General Accounting Office, GAO
General Adaptation Scale, GAS
General Aptitude Test Battery, GATB
General Cognitive Index, GCI
General Concerns Inventory, GCI
General Education Models Project, GEM
General Education Provisions Act, GEPA
General Educational Development Test, GED
General Equivalency Development Test, GED
General Services Administration, GSA
General Society of Mechanics and Tradesmen, GSMT
Generated Author Language Teaching System, GALTS
Geoscience Information Society, GIS
Gerontological Association of America, GSA
Gesell Developmental Schedules, GDS
Gesell School Readiness Test, GSRT
Gifted Advocacy Information Network, GAIN
Gifted and Talented, G/T
Gifted And Talented Education Program (California), GATE
Gifted Child Society, GCS
Gifted Resources Education Action Team Project, GREAT
Ginn Language Development Program, GLDP
Global Assessment Scale, GAS
Global Learning, GL
Global Matching Figures Test, GMF
Global Perspectives in Education, Inc., GPE
GODORT Federal Documents Task Force, GODORT FDTF
GODORT International Documents Task Force, GODORT IDTF
GODORT State and Local Documents Task Force, GODORT SLDTF
Goldman-Fristoe-Woodcock Auditory Skills Test Battery, GFW
Goodchild's Location-Allocation Package, LAP
Gordon Diagnostic System, GDS
Government Documents Round Table (American Library Association, GODORT
Government Printing Office, GPO
Governmental Accounting, Auditing, and Financial Reporting, GAAFR
Goyer Organization of Ideas Test, GOIT
Grade Point Average, GPA
Graduate Assistant, GA
Graduate Fellowships for Black Americans, GFBA
Graduate Management Admissions Test, GMAT
Graduate Medical Education National Advisory Committee, GMENAC
Graduate Record Examination, GRE
Graduate Record Examination Board, GREB
Graduate Student Foreign Language Test, GSFLT
Graduate Teaching Assistant, GTA
Great Lakes Colleges Association, GLCA
Grillingham-Stillman Simultaneous-Oral-Spelling, SOS

Group Dimensions Descriptions Questionnaire, GDDQ
Group Embedded Figures Test, GEFT
Group Environment Scale, GES
Group for the Use of Psychology in History, GUPH
Group Reading Interaction Pattern (An observation instrument), GRIP
Guaranteed Student Loan Program, GSLP
Guaranteed Student Loans, GSL
Guidance Information System, GIS
Guidance Program Preference Scale, GPPS
Gulf Universities Research Consortium, GURC
Hahnemann Elementary School Behavior Rating Scale, HESB
Half Day, HD
Halstead Neuropsychological Test Battery, HNTB
Handicapped Children's Early Education Project, HCEEP
Handicapped Educational Exchange, HEX
Hard Copy, HC
Harry S Truman Scholarship Foundation, HSTSF
Hawaii Business Education Association, HBEA
Headmasters Association, HA
Health and Rehabilitative Library Services Division (American Library Association), HRLSD
Health Education Special Interest Group (Association for the Development of Computer-Based Instructional Systems), HESIG
Health Interview Survey, HIS
Health Locus of Control, HLC
Health Occupations Students of America, HOSA
Health, Physical Education, and Recreation, HPER
Health Practices Inventory, HPI
Health Related Fitness Test, HRFT
Health Resources and Services Administration (U.S. Health and Human Services Department), HRSA
Health Resources Inventory, HRI
Health Sciences Communication Association, HSCA
Hearing Threshold Level, HTL
Hearing, Ventilating, and Air Conditioning, HVAC
Helping One Student To Succeed, HOSTS
Hidden Frames Test, HFT
High Definition Television, HDTV
High Intensity Language Training, HILT
High Intensity Tutoring, HIT
High School and Beyond Study, HSB
High School Characteristics Index, HSCI
High School Equivalence Program, HEP
High School Personality Questionnaire, HSPQ
Higher Education Act of 1965, HEA
Higher Education Administration Referral Service, HEARS
Higher Education and the Handicapped Project (American Council on Education), HEATH
Higher Education Consortium on Special Education, HECSE
Higher Education Data Sharing, HEDS
Higher Education Employer-Employee Relations Act, HEERA
Higher Education Facilities Act, HEFA
Higher Education for Learning Disabled Students, HELDS

Higher Education General Information Survey, HEGIS
Higher Education Instructional Television (West Virginia), HEITV
Higher Education Management Institute, HEMI
Higher Education Opportunity Program, HEOP
Higher Education Panel (American Council on Education), HEP
Higher Education Price Index, HEPI
Higher Education Research Institute, HERI
Higher Education Resource Services, HERS
High-Scope Educational Research Foundation, H/SERF
Hill Counselor Verbal Response Category System, HCVRCS
Hiskey-Nebraska Test of Learning Aptitude, H-NTLA
History of Economics Society, HES
History of Education Society, HES
Holistic Education Network, HEN
Holtzman Inkblot Test, HIT
Home and School Institute, HSI
Home Economics Education Association, HEEA
Home Economics Related Occupations, HERO
Home Economics Special Interest Group (Association for the Development of Computer-Based Instructional Systems), SIG/HomEc
Home Education Resource Center, HERC
Home Observation for Measurement of the Environment, HOME
Home-Based Instruction, HBI
Hong Kong Wechsler Intelligence Scale, HK-WISC
Horace Mann League of the USA, HML
Hospital Discharge Demonstration Project, HDDP
Hospital School Program, HSP
Housewife/Mother Career Concept, HMCC
How I Feel Toward Others, HIFTO
How I See Myself Scale, HISM
Human and Environmental Learning Program, HELP
Human Figures Drawing Test, HFD
Human Resources Center, HRC
Human Resources Development, HRD
Human Resources Research Organization, HumRRO
Illinois Association for Educational Data Systems, ILAEDS
Illinois Association of Biology Teachers, IABT
Illinois Association of Community College Biologists, IACCB
Illinois Association of School Boards, IASB
Illinois Council for the Gifted, ICG
Illinois Course Evaluation Questionnaire, CEQ
Illinois Inventory of Educational Progress, IIEP
Illinois Library and Information Network, ILLINET
Illinois Migrant Council, IMC
Illinois Test of Psycholinguistic Abilities, ITPA
Illinois Vocational Curriculum Center, IVCC
Illness Adaptation Scale, IAS
Imaginative Educational Cooperation Project, IEC
Impact Message Inventory, IMI
Implementation Special Interest Group (Association for the Development of Computer-Based Instructional Systems), ISIG
Impulsive Classroom Behavior Scale, ICBS
Independent College Funds of America, ICFA

Independent Educational Counselors Association, IECA
Independent Educational Services, IES
Independent Research Library Association, IRLA
Index Medicus, IM
Index of Achievement Values, IAV
Indian Education Committee, IEC
Indian Rights Association, IRA
Indian Self-Identified Certified Staff, ISICS
Indiana Computer Educators, ICE
Indiana Higher Education Telecommunications System, IHETS
Individual Reading Instruction System, IRIS
Individualized Bilingual Instruction, IBI
Individualized Career Education Planning, ICEP
Individualized Classroom Environment Questionnaire, ICEQ
Individualized Computer Literacy Education Plan, ICLEP
Individualized Education Program, IEP
Individualized Instructional Planning, IIP
Individualized Science Instructional System, ISIS
Individualized Study by Telecommunications (Alaska), IST
Individualized Transition Plans, ITP
Individualized Vocational Program, IVP
Individually Guided Education, IGE
Individually Prescribed (or Planned) Instruction, IPI
Indochina Curriculum Group, ICG
Induced Course Load Matrix, ICLM
Industrial Arts Association of Alabama, IAAA
Industrial Arts Curriculum Project, IACP
Industrial Cooperative Association, ICA
Industrial Model Vocational Training Systems, IMVTS
Industry Education Council, IEC
Informal Reading Inventory, IRI
Informal Word Recognition Inventory, IWRI
Information Analysis Product (Educational Resources Information Center), IAP
Information Exchange System for Minority Personnel, IESMP
Information Industry Association, IIA
Information Retrieval Center on the Disadvantaged, IRCD
Information Science and Automation Division (American Library Association), ISAD
Information-Based Education, IBE
Inquiry and Assistance Project, IAP
Institute for Advanced Studies of World Religions, IASWR
Institute for Certification in Engineering Technologies, ICET
Institute for Certification of Computer Professionals, ICCP
Institute for Childhood Resources, INICR
Institute for Computers in Jewish Life, ICJL
Institute for Development of Education Activities, I/D/E/A
Institute for Educational Leadership, IEL
Institute for Environmental Education, IEE
Institute for Global Conflict and Cooperation, IGCC

Institute for Manpower Program Analysis, Consultation and Training, Inc., IMPACT
Institute for Native American Development, INAD
Institute for Personality and Ability Testing, IPAT
Institute for Political/Legal Education, IPLE
Institute for Responsive Education, IRE
Institute for Social Research, ISR
Institute for Studies in American Music, ISAM
Institute for Study of Regulation, ISR
Institute for the Advancement of Philosophy for Children, IAPC
Institute for the Study of Educational Policy, ISEP
Institute of American Indian Arts, IAIA
Institute of Black Studies, IBS
Institute of Educational Research, IER
Institute of Electrical and Electronics Engineers, IEEE
Institute of European Studies, IES
Institute of International Education, IIE
Institute of Laboratory Animal Resources, ILAR
Institute of Lifetime Learning, ILL
Institutional Child Protection Project (Ohio State University), ICPP
Institutional Goals Inventory, IGI
Institutional Research, IR
Instructional Affairs Committee (National Council of Teachers of Mathematics), IAC
Instructional Dimensions Study, IDS
Instructional Management and Presentation System, IMPS
Instructional Resources Center, IRC
Instructional Scientific Equipment Program (National Science Foundation), ISEP
Instructional System in Mathematics Program, ISM
Instructional Technologist, IT
Instructional Telecommunications Consortium (American Association of Community and Junior Colleges), ITC
Instructional Television, ITV
Instructional Television Fixed Service, ITFS
Instructor and Course Evaluation System, ICES
Instrument for the Analysis of Science Teaching, IAST
Instrumental Enrichment Program, IE
Insulin-Dependent Diabetes Mellitus, IDDM
Integrated Library Information Systems, ILIS
Integrated Sentence-Modeling Curriculum, ISMC
Intellectual Achievement Responsibility Questionnaire, IARQ
Intellectual Freedom Roundtable (American Library Association), IFRT
Intelligence Quotient, IQ
Intelligent Authoring Systems, IAS
Intelligent Computer-Assisted Instruction, I-CAI
Interaction Involvement Scale, IIS
Interaction Place Map, IPM
Interaction Process Analysis, IPA
Interactive Financial Planning System (EDUCOM), IFPS
Interactive Instructional Systems—Presentation and Authoring Special Interest Group (Association for the Development of Computer-Based Instructional Systems), IISPA

Interactive Language Instruction Assistance for the Deaf, ILIAD
Interactive Research and Development, IR&D
Interactive Video/Audio Special Interest Group (Association for the Development of Computer-Based Instructional Systems), SIG IVA
Interactive Videodisc, IVD
Interactive Videodisc for Special Education Technology, IVSET
Interagency Collaborative Boards (Michigan), ICB
Interagency Group for Computer-Based Training, IGCBT
Interagency Language Rountables (U.S. Government), ILR
Interagency Research Information System, IRIS
Inter-American College Association, IACA
Interassociational Presidents' Committee on Collegiate Athletics, IPCCA
Intercollegiate Association for Women Students, IAWS
Intercollegiate Broadcasting System, IBS
Intercultural Development Research Association, IDRA
Interfuture, IF
Interior Design Educators Council, IDEC
Interlibrary Loan, ILL
Intermediate Service Agency, ISA
Internal-External Locus of Control, IE
International Association for Educational Assessment, IAEA
International Association for Learning Laboratories, IALL
International Association for Mass Communication Research, IAMCR
International Association for the Evaluation of Educational Achievement, IEA
International Association for the Study of Cooperation in Education, IASCE
International Association of Agricultural Librarians and Documentalists, IAALD
International Association of Buddhist Students, IABS
International Association of Business Communicators, IABC
International Association of Campus Law Enforcement Administrators, IACLEA
International Association of Cooking Schools, IACS
International Association of Counseling Services, IACS
International Association of Educators for World Peace, IAEWP
International Association of Law Libraries, IALL
International Association of Master Penmen and Teachers of Handwriting, IAMPTH
International Association of Music Libraries, IAML
International Association Of Organ Teachers, IAOT
International Association Of Orientalist Librarians, IAOL
International Association of Parents of the Deaf, IAPD
International Association of Physical Education and Sports for Girls and Women, IAPESGW
International Association of Pupil Personnel Workers, IAPPW
International Association of School Librarianship, IASL

International Association of Schools of Social Work, IASSW

International Association of Sound Archives, IASA

International Association of Teachers of English as a Foreign Language, IATEFL

International Association of Technological University Libraries, IATUL

International Association of Universities, IAU

International Association of University Professors of English, IAUPE

International Baccalaureate, IB

International Board on Books for Young People, IBBY

International Bureau of Education, IBE

International Camp Counselor Program, ICCP

International Center of Photography, ICP

International Centre for Parliamentary Documentation, CIDP

International Christian Youth Exchange, ICYE

International Communication Association, ICA

International Conference on Cataloging Principles, ICCP

International Congress for Individualized Instruction, ICII

International Council for Adult Education, ICAE

International Council for Computers in Education, ICCE

International Council for Educational Development, ICED

International Council of Educators of Blind Youth, ICEBY

International Council of Scientific Unions, ICSU

International Council of Scientific Unions/Abstracting Board, ICSU/AB

International Council on Archives, ICA

International Council on Education for Teaching, ICET

International Council on Health, Physical Education and Recreation, ICHPER

International Council on the Future of the University, ICFU

International Development Research Centre (Canada), IDRC

International Environmental Education Programme (UNESCO), IEEP

International Federation of Catholic Alumnae, IFCA

International Federation of Library Associations, IFLA

International Federation of Training and Development Organizations, IFTDO

International Fellowship of Evangelical Students, IFES

International Graphic Arts Education Association, IGAEA

International Group for Psychology and Mathematics Education, IGPME

International Horn Society, IHS

International Institute for Advanced Studies, IIAS

International Institute for Educational Planning (UNESCO), IIEP

International Institutional Services, IIS

International Library Information Center, ILIC

International Organization for the Education of the Hearing Impaired, IOEHI

International Organization for the Study of Human Development, IOSHD

International Phonetic Alphabet, IPA

International Phonetic Association, IPA

International Programme for the Development of Communication (UNESCO), IPDC

International Reading Association, IRA

International Relations Committee (American Library Association), IRC

International Relations Round Table (American Library Association), IRRT

International Research and Exchanges Board, IREX

International Schools Services, ISS

International Simulation and Gaming Association, ISAGA

International Society for Business Education, ISBE

International Society for Education through Art, INSEA

International Society for Educational Planning, ISEP

International Society for Intercultural Education, Training And Research, SIETAR/INTL

International Society for Music Education, ISME

International Society for Prevention of Child Abuse and Neglect, ISPCAN

International Society of Phonetic Sciences, ISPhS

International Standard Bibliographic Description, ISBD

International Standard Book Number, ISBN

International Standard Program Number, ISPN

International Standard Serial Number, ISSN

International Student Service, ISS

International Study of Educational Achievement, IEA

International Survey Library Association, ISLA

International Teaching Alphabet, ITA

International Television Association, ITVA

International Thespian Society, ITS

International University Consortium for Telecommunications in Learning, IUC

International Visual Literacy Association, IVLA

International Year for Disabled Persons, IYDP

International Year of the Child, IYC

Interparental Conflict Scales, IPC

Interpersonal Cognitive Problem-Solving Program, ICPS

Interpersonal Communication Inventory, ICI

Interpersonal Relationship Scale, IRS

Interpretive Structural Modeling, ISM

Inter-Sound Interval, ISI

Interstate Distributive Education Curriculum Consortium, IDECC

Interstimulus Interval, ISI

Inter-university Consortium for Educational Computing, ICEC

Inter-University Consortium for Political and Social Research, ICPSR

Inventory of Learning Processes, ILP

Invitation To Bid, ITB

Iowa Silent Reading Test, ISRT

Iowa Test of Basic Skills, ITBS

Iowa Tests of Educational Development, ITED

Iranian Students Counseling Center, ISCC

Irrational Beliefs Test, IBT

ISBD (Monographs), ISBD(M)

ISBD (Serials), ISBD(S)

Item Response Theory, IRT

ITPA-Auditory Reception Subtest, ITPA-AR
Japan-America Student Conference, JASC
Japanese American Curriculum Project, JACP
Jesuit Association of Student Personnel Administrators, JASPA
Jesuit Secondary Education Association, JSEA
Jewish Education Service of North America, JESNA
Jewish Educators Assembly, JEA
Jewish Music Educators Association, JMEA
Job Description Index, JDI
Job Training Partnership Act, JTPA
Job-Oriented Basic Skills Program (U.S. Navy), JOBS
Jobs for America's Graduates, Inc., JAG
Johnson Informal Reading Inventory, JIRI
Joint Commission on Accreditation of Hospitals, JCAH
Joint Committee on Contemporary China, JCCC
Joint Council on Economic Education, JCEE
Joint Council on Educational Telecommunications, JCET
Joint Dissemination Review Panel (U.S. Department of Education), JDRP
Joint National Committee for Languages, JNCL
Journal of the American Society of Information Science, JASIS
Journalism Association of Community Colleges, JACC
Journalism Education Association, JEA
Junior Achievement, JA
Junior Engineering Technical Society, JETS
Junior High School Network Project, JHSN
Junior Members Round Table (American Library Association), JMRT
Junior Statesmen Foundation, JSF
Junior Statesmen of America, JSA
Junior Varsity, JV
Juris Doctor, J.D.
Kahn Test of Symbol Arrangement, KTSA
Kamehameha Early Education Program (Hawaii), KEEP
Kanata High Technology Training Association (Canada), KHTTA
Kansas Advisory Council on Environmental Education, KACEE
Kansas Committee for Prevention of Child Abuse, KCPCA
Kansas Education Dissemination/Diffusion System, KEDDS
Kansas Individualized Curriculum Sequencing, KICS
Kaufman Assessment Battery for Children, K-ABC
Kent Infant Development Scale, KID
Kentucky Allied Health Project, KAHP
Kentucky Environmental Education Program, KEEP
Kentucky's Individualized Kindergartens, KIK
Key Math Diagnostic Arithmetic Test, KMDAT
Key Word In Context, KWIC
Key Word In Title, KWIT
Key Word Out of Context, KWOC
Kindergarten Evaluation of Learning Potential, KELP
Kindergarten Language Screening Test, KLST
Kindling Individual Development Systems Project, KIDS
Kinetic Family Drawing Method, KFD

Kinetic School Drawing Method, KSD
Knowledge Network of Washington, KNOW-NET
Kuder Preference Record, KPR
Kuder Preference Record—Vocational, KPR-V
Labor Agreement Information Retrieval System (Civil Service Commission), LAIRS
Labor Management Relations Act, LMRA
Labor Management Relations Service, LMRS
Labor Statistics Database, LABSTAT
Laboratory Animal Data Bank, LADB
LAMA Buildings and Equipment Section, LAMA BES
LAMA Circulation Services Section, LAMA CSS
LAMA Library Organization and Management Section, LAMA LOMS
LAMA Public Relations Section, LAMA PRS
LAMA Statistics Section, LAMA SS
Language Acquisition Device, LAD
Language Across the Curriculum, LATC
Language and Language Behavior Abstracts, LLBA
Language Assessment Battery, LAB
Language Assessment Scales, LAS
Language Experience Approach, LEA
Language Information Network and Clearinghouse System, LINCS
Language Instruction for Recent Immigrants through Computer Technology, LIRIC
Language Inventory Test, LIT
Language Measurement and Assessment Inventory, LM&AI
Language Proficiency Test (National Security Agency), LPT
Large Type, LT
Latin America Scholarship Program of American Universities, LASPAU
Latin American Studies Association, LASA
Law Enforcement Assistance Act, LEAA
Law Enforcement Education Program, LEEP
Law School Admission Council, LSAC
Law School Admission Services, LSAS
Law School Admission Test, LSAT
Law School Computer Group, LSCG
Law-Related Education, LRE
Lawson's Classroom Test of Formal Reasoning, CTFR
Leader Authenticity Scale, LAS
Leaderless Group Discussion, LGD
Leadership and Management Education and Training, LMET
Leadership Behavior Description Questionnaire, LBDQ
Leadership, Education, and Development Project, LEAD
Leadership Institute, LI
League for Innovation in the Community College, LICC
Learning Activity Package, LAP
Learning and Language Impaired, LLI
Learning and/or Behavior Disordered, LBD
Learning, Assessment, Retention Consortium (California), LARC
Learning Disabilities Research Institute (University of Virginia), LDRI
Learning Disabled, LD
Learning Environment Inventory, LEI

The Learning Exchange, TLE
Learning Experience Approach, LEA
Learning Methods Test, LMT
Learning Potential Assessment Device, LPAD
Learning Research and Development Center, LRDC
Learning Resources Center, LRC
Learning Resources Network, LERN
Learning Styles Inventory, LSI
Learning Styles Inventory—Primary Version, LSI-P
Learning Systems Model, LSM
Legislative Audit Council (South Carolina), LAC
Leisure Diagnostic Battery, LDB
Lesson Design System, LDS
Leveling/Sharpening Aggressions Test, LSAT
Leveling/Sharpening House Test, LSHT
Levenson's Internal, Powerful Others, and Chance
    Scales, LIPC
Library Administration and Management Association,
    LAMA
Library and Information Science Abstracts, LISA
Library and Information Technology Association, LITA
Library Bill of Rights, LBR
Library General Information Survey, LIBGIS
Library History Round Table (American Library
    Association), LHRT
Library Information Bibliographic System, LIBS
Library Information Retrieval System, LIRS
Library Instruction Round Table (American Library
    Association), LIRT
Library of Congress, LC
Library of Congress Card Number, LCCN
Library of Congress Subject Headings, LCSH
Library Personnel Administration Section, LAMA PAS
Library Public Relations Council, LPRC
Library Research Round Table (American Library
    Association), LRRT
Library Resources and Technical Services, LRTS
Library Services and Construction Act, LSCA
Library-College Associates, LCA
Licensed Practical Nurse, LPN
Life Events Questionnaire, LEQ
Life Expectancy Inventory, LEI
Life Experiences Survey, LES
Life Role Expectations Inventory, LREI
Limited English Proficiency, LEP
Limited English Speaking, LES
Lincoln Educational Foundation, LEF
Linear Structural Relations, LISREL
Linguistic Association of the Southwest, LASSO
Linguistic Awareness Reading Test, LARR
Linguistic Society of America, LSA
LITA Audiovisual Section, LITA AVS
LITA Information Science and Automation Section,
    LITA ISAS
LITA Video and Cable Communications Section, LITA
    VCCS
Lloyd Shaw Foundation, LSF
Local Course Improvement (National Science
    Foundation), LOCI
Local Education Agency, LEA
Local Information Sources for Teachers, LIST

Locus Of Control, LOC
Locus Of Responsibility Inventory, LORI
Loevinger Sentence Completion Test, LSCT
Long-Range Planning for School Improvement
    (Pennsylvania), LRPSI
Louisiana Association of Business Educators, LABE
Louisiana Council on Economic Education, LCEE
Low-Power Television, LPTV
Luria-Nebraska Neuropsychological Test Battery,
    LNNB
Lutheran Education Association, LEA
Lutheran Educational Conference of North America,
    LECNA
MacAndrew Alcoholism Scale, MAC
Machine Assisted Reference Section (American Library
    Association), MARS
Machine Readable Cataloging, MARC
The Madison Project, TMP
Magnetic Information Technology, MINT
Mainstreamed Special Educator Model, MSEM
Maintenance and Operations, M&O
Major Urban Resource Libraries, MURL
Man: A Course Of Study, MACOS
Man in the Biosphere Programme (Canada), MAB
Man Zeichen Test, MZT
Management Behavior Questionnaire, MBQ
Management By Objectives, MBO
Management Information System, MIS
Manifest Needs Questionnaire, MNQ
Manitoba Association for Educational Data Systems,
    MAN-AEDS
Manpower Assessment and Placement System, MAPS
Manpower Consortium for the Information Professions,
    MCIP
Manpower Development Higher Education System,
    MDHES
Map and Geography Round Table (American Library
    Association), MAGERT
Marine Librarians Association, MLA
Marketing and Distribution Education Association,
    MDEA
Martinek-Zaichkowsky Self-Concept Scale, MZSCS
Maryland Committee for Children, MCC
Maryland Cooperative Extension Service, MCES
Maryland Functional Mathematics Test, MFMT
Maryland Functional Reading Test, MFRT
Maryland Functional Writing Program, MFWP
Maryland Preschool Self-Concept Scale, MPSS
Maslach Burnout Inventory, MBI
Master of Architecture, M.Arch.
Master of Arts, M.A.
Master of Arts in Education, M.A. in Ed.
Master of Arts in Library Science, M.A.L.S.
Master of Business Administration, M.B.A.
Master of Divinity, M.Div.
Master of Education, M.Ed.
Master of Fine Arts, M.F.A.
Master of Laws, LL.M.
Master of Library Science, M.L.S.
Master of Music, M.M.
Master of Music, M.Mus.

Master of Music Education, M.M.E.
Master of Public Health, M.P.H.
Master of Science, M.S.
Master of Science, M.Sc.
Master of Science in Chemical Engineering, M.S.C.E.
Master of Science in Education, M.S.in Ed.
Master of Science in Electrical Engineering, M.S.E.E.
Master of Science in Journalism, MSJ
Master of Science in Library Science, M.S.L.S.
Master of Science in Nursing, M.S.N.
Master of Social Work, M.S.W.
Master of Theology, Th.M.
Masters of Arts in Teaching, M.A.T.
Matching Familiar Figures Test, MFFT
Math Anxiety Scales, MAS
Math Network Curriculum Project, MNCP
Mathematical Association of America, MAA
Mathematics Anxiety Rating Scale, MARS
Mathematics Applied to Novel Situations Test, MANS
Mathematics Attitude Scales, MAS
Mathematics Attribution Scale, MAS
Mathematics Diagnostic/Prescriptive Inventory, MDPI
Mathematics Disabled, MD
Mathematics Education for Gifted Secondary School
    Students Project, MEGSSS
Mathematics Functional Literacy Test, MFLT
Mathematics Olympiads for Elementary Schools,
    MOES
Mathematics-Methods Program, MMP
Matter-Relation-Matter Semantic Units, MRM
McCarthy Scales of Children's Abilities, MSCA
McCarthy Screening Test, MST
Mean Length of Utterance, MLU
Mean Square Fit, MSF
Means-Ends Problem Solving Measure, MEPS
Measure of Adult English Proficiency, MAEP
Measure of Elementary Communication Apprehension,
    MECA
Measure of Intellectual Development, MID
Measure of Language Proficiency, MELP
Measure of Sampling Adequacy Index, MSA
Media Evaluation Services (North Carolina), MES
Median, MDN
Medical College Admission Test, MCAT
Medical College Admissions Assessment Program,
    MCAAP
Medical College of Pennsylvania Pharmaceutical
    Education Programs, MCPPEP
Medical Library Association, MLA
Medical Literature Analysis Retrieval System (National
    Library of Medicine), MEDLARS
Medical Technologist, M.T.
Meeting Street School Screening Test, MSSST
Melodic Dictation Computerized Instruction, MEDICI
Memory for Sequence Subtest of the Goldman-
    Fristoe-Woodcock Auditory Skills Test Battery, MS-
    GFW
Memory Quotient, MQ
Memory-For-Designs Test, MFD
Mental Age, MA
Mental Development Index, MDI

Mental Health Research Project, MHRP
Mental Health Values Questionnaire, MHVQ
Mental Measurement Yearbook, MMY
Mental Retardation, MR
Mentally Gifted Minor, MGM
Metrolina Educational Consortium (North Carolina),
    MEC
Metropolitan Achievement Tests, MAT
Metropolitan Council for Educational Opportunity
    (Massachusetts), METCO
Metropolitan Reading Test, MRT
Mexican-American Legal Defense and Educational
    Fund, MALDEF
Mexican-American Women's National Association,
    MANA
Michigan Association for Computer Users in Learning,
    MACUL
Michigan Business Education Association, MBEA
Michigan Community College Community Services
    Association, MCCCSA
Michigan Community College Occupational Education
    Evaluation System, MCCOEES
Michigan Council of Teachers of Mathematics, MCTM
Michigan Educational Assessment Program, MEAP
Michigan Educational Research Association, MERA
Michigan Educational Resource Information Center,
    MERIC
Michigan English Proficiency Examination, MEPE
Michigan Interorganizational Committee on Continuing
    Library Education, MICCLE
Michigan Picture Language Inventory, MPLI
Michigan Student Information System, MiSIS
Michigan Test of English Language Proficiency, MTELP
Microcomputer Assisted Instruction, MCAI
Microcomputer Education Application Network,
    MEAN
Microcomputer Program Oriented Budgeting System,
    MICROCOMP POB
Microcomputer Software and Information For Teachers,
    MicroSIFT
Microcomputer Vocational Education Reporting
    System, MICRO-VERS
Microelectronics Education Program, MEP
Microfiche, MF
Microfilm, MF
Microwave Multipoint Distribution Systems, MDS
Mid-America State Universities Association, MASUA
Mid-Continent Regional Educational Laboratory,
    MCREL
Middle Atlantic Planetarium Society, MAPS
Middle East Librarians' Association, MELA
Middle Grades Assessment Program, MGAP
Middle Income Student Assistance Act, MISAA
Middle States Association of Colleges and Schools, MSA
Midwest Modern Language Association, MMLA
Midwestern Regional Library Network, MIDLNET
Migrant Student Record Transfer System, MSRTS
Military Applicant Profile (U.S. Army), MAP
Miller Analogies Test, MAT
Miniature Situations Test, MST

Minicomputer User Special Interest Group (Association for the Development of Computer-Based Instructional Systems), MINI-MICRO

Minimal Brain Dysfunction, MBD

Minimum Competency Testing, MCT

Minimum Enrollment and Reasonable Progress, MERP

Minnesota Adaptive Instructional System, MAIS

Minnesota Business Educators, Inc., MBEI

Minnesota Child Development Inventory, MCDI

Minnesota Computer Literacy and Awareness Assessment, MCLAA

Minnesota Council on the Teaching of Foreign Languages, MCTFL

Minnesota Educational Computing Consortium, MECC

Minnesota Educational Media Organization, MEMO

Minnesota Interlibrary Telecommunications Exchange, MINITEX

Minnesota Multi-Phasic Personality Inventory, MMPI

Minnesota Satisfaction Questionnaire, MSQ

Minnesota Scholastic Aptitude Test, MSAT

Minnesota State Drafting Advisory Committee, MSDAC

Minnesota Teacher Attitude Inventory, MTAI

Mississippi Student Information System, MISSIS

Missouri Business Education Association, MBEA

Missouri Mathematics Effectiveness Project, MMEP

MMPI-Depression Scale, MMPI-D

Model Adoption Exchange Payment System, MAEPS

Model for Articulated Vocational Education, MAVE

Model Secondary School for the Deaf (Gallaudet College), MSSD

Modeling Association of America, International, MAAI

Modern Language Aptitude Test, MLAT

Modern Language Association of America, MLA

Modern Rythmic Gymnastics, MRG

Modified-Adopted-Fernald Technique, M-A-F-T

Modular Counseling Curriculum, MCC

Montana Council for Computers in Education, MCCE

Mood Adjective Checklist, MACL

Moody Institute of Science, MIS

Mooney Problem Checklist, MPCL

Moral Action Choice Test, MACT

Mother Language, ML

Motor-Free Visual Perception Test, MVPT

Mountain West Desegregation Assistance Centers, MWDAC

Mountain-Plains Business Education Association, M-PBEA

Movement Shorthand Society, MSS

Multidimensional Attitude Scale on Mental Retardation, MASMR

Multidimensional Scaling, MDS

Multidimensional-Multiattributional Causality Scale, MMCS

Multiethnic/Multicultural Christian Education Resources Center, MMCERC

Multihandicapped Hearing-Impaired, MHHI

Multi-International Teacher Education Cooperatives, MITECS

Multiple Affect Adjective Checklist, MAACL

Multiple Classification Analysis, MCA

Multiple Linear Regression, MLR

Multi-Purpose Occupational Information System (North Carolina), MPOIS

Multistate Bar Examination, MBE

Multivariate Analysis Of Variance, MANOVA

Music Educators National Conference, MENC

Music Library Association, MLA

Music Teachers National Association, MTNA

Musical Aptitude Profile, MAP

Mutual Assistance Associations, MAA

Myers-Briggs Type Indicator, MBTI

Narcissistic Personality Inventory, NPI

Narrower Term, NT

National Academy of Arbitrators, NAA

National Academy of Education, NAEd

National Academy of Sciences, NAS

National Accrediting Agency for Clinical Laboratory Sciences, NAACLS

National Accrediting Commission of Cosmetology Arts and Sciences, NACCAS

National Action Committee on the Status of Women (Canada), NAC

National Action Council for Minorities in Engineering, NACME

National Adult Vocational Education Association, NAVEA

National Advisory Committee On Mathematics Education, NACOME

National Advisory Council for Bilingual Education, NACBE

National Advisory Council on Adult Education, NACAE

National Advisory Council on Equality of Educational Opportunity, NACEEO

National Advisory Council on Indian Education, NACIE

National Advisory Council on Vocational Education, NACVE

National Aeronautics and Space Administration, NASA

National Agricultural Library, NAL

National Alliance of Black School Educators, NABSE

National Alliance of Business, NAB

National Alliance of Voluntary Learning, NAVL

National Architectural Accrediting Board, NAAB

National Archives and Records Service, NARS

National Art Education Association, NAEA

National Assessment of Educational Progress, NAEP

National Assessment of Reading and Literature, NARL

National Assocation of College Wind and Percussion Instructors, NACWPI

National Association for Asian and Pacific American Education, NAAPAE

National Association for Bilingual Education, NABE

National Association for Business Teacher Education, NABTE

National Association for Campus Activities, NACA

National Association for Community Development, NACD

National Association for Core Curriculum, NACC

National Association for Creative Children and Adults, NACCA

National Association for Education Computing, NAEC

National Association for Equal Educational Opportunities, NAEEO

National Association For Equal Opportunity in Higher Education, NAFEO

National Association for Foreign Student Affairs, NAFSA

National Association for Gifted Children, NAGC

National Association for Girls and Women in Sport (American Alliance for Health, Physical Education, Recreation, and Dance), NAGWS

National Association for Humanities Education, NAHE

National Association for Industry-Education Cooperation, NAIEC

National Association for Intercollegiate Athletics, NAIA

National Association for Legal Support of Alternative Schools, NALSAS

National Association for Physical Education in Higher Education, NAPEHE

National Association for Real Estate License Law Officials, NARELLO

National Association for Remedial/Developmental Studies in Postsecondary Education, NARDSPE

National Association for Research in Science Teaching, NARST

National Association for Sport and Physical Education, NASPE

National Association for the Accreditation of Colleges and Secondary Schools, NAACSS

National Association for the Advancement of Black Americans in Vocational Education, NAABAVE

National Association for the Advancement of Colored People, NAACP

National Association for the Education of Young Children, NAEYC

National Association for the Exchange of Industrial Resources, NAEIR

National Association for the Visually Handicapped, NAVH

National Association for Trade and Industrial Education, NATIE

National Association for Vietnamese-American Education, NAVAE

National Association for Women Deans, Administrators, and Counselors, NAWDAC

National Association of Academic Athletic Advisors, N4A

National Association of Academies of Science, NAAS

National Association of Administrators of State and Federal Education Programs, NAASFEP

National Association of Baptist Professors of Religion, NABPR

National Association of Barber Schools, NABS

National Association of Biology Teachers, NABT

National Association of Black Professors, NABP

National Association of Blind Teachers, NABT

National Association of Boards of Education, NABE

National Association of Business Education State Supervisors, NABESS

National Association of Classroom Educators in Business Education, NACEBE

National Association of College Admissions Counselors, NACAC

National Association of College and University Attorneys, NACUA

National Association of College and University Business Officers, NACUBO

National Association of College and University Food Services, NACUFS

National Association of College and University Residence Halls, NACURH

National Association of College Deans, Registrars, and Admissions Officers, NACDRAO

National Association of College Stores, NACS

National Association of Colleges and Teachers of Agriculture, NACTA

National Association of Cosmetology Schools, NACS

National Association of Educational Buyers, NAEB

National Association of Educational Negotiators, NAEN

National Association of Educational Office Personnel, NAEOP

National Association of Elementary School Principals, NAESP

National Association of Episcopal Schools, NAES

National Association of Federal Program Administration, NAFPA

National Association of Federally Impacted Schools, NAFIS

National Association of Geology Teachers, NAGT

National Association of Homes for Children, NAHC

National Association of Independent Colleges and Universities, NAICU

National Association of Independent Schools, NAIS

National Association of Industrial and Technical Teacher Educators, NAITTE

National Association of Industrial Technology, NAIT

National Association of Interdisciplinary Ethnic Studies, NAIES

National Association of Jazz Educators, NAJE

National Association of Management/Marketing Educators, NAME

National Association of Manufacturers, NAM

National Association of Minority Engineering Program Administrators, NAMEPA

National Association of Minority Students and Educators in Higher Education, NAMSE

National Association of Music Executives in State Universities, NAMESU

National Association of Pastoral Musicians, NPM

National Association of Postsecondary and Adult Vocational Home Economics Educators, NAPAVHEE

National Association of Principals of Schools for Girls, NAPSG

National Association of Private, Nontraditional Schools and Colleges, NAPNSC

National Association of Private Schools for Exceptional Children, NAPSEC

National Association of Professional Educators, NAPE

National Association of Professors of Christian Education, NAPCE

National Association of Professors of Hebrew, NAPH

National Association of Pupil Personnel Administrators, NAPPA

National Association of Regional Councils, NARC

National Association of Reporter Training Schools, NARTS

National Association of School Nurses, NASN

National Association of School Psychologists, NASP

National Association of School Security Directors, NASSD

National Association of Schools and Colleges of the United Methodist Church, NASCUMC

National Association of Schools of Art and Design, NASAD

National Association of Schools of Dance, NASD

National Association of Schools of Music, NASM

National Association of Schools of Public Affairs and Administration, NASPAA

National Association of Schools of Theatre, NAST

National Association of Secondary School Principals, NASSP

National Association of Self-Instructional Language Programs, NASILP

National Association of Social Workers, NASW

National Association of State Administrators and Supervisors of Private Schools, NASASPS

National Association of State Approved Colleges and Universities, NASACU

National Association of State Boards of Education, NASBE

National Association of State Directors of Special Education, NASDSE

National Association of State Directors of Teacher Education Certification, NASDTEC

National Association of State Directors of Vocational Education, NASDVE

National Association of State Education Department Information Officers, NASEDIO

National Association of State Supervisors and Directors of Secondary Education, NASSDSE

National Association of State Supervisors of Music, NASSM

National Association of State Supervisors of Trade and Industrial Education, NASSTIE

National Association of State Supervisors of Vocational Home Economics, NASSVHE

National Association of State Text Book Administrators, NASTA

National Association of State Universities and Land-Grant Colleges, NASULGC

National Association of Student Activity Advisers, NASAA

National Association of Student Councils, NASC

National Association of Student Employment Administrators, NASEA

National Association of Student Financial Aid Administrators, NASFAA

National Association of Student Personnel Administrators, NASPA

National Association of Supervisors of Agricultural Education, NASAE

National Association of Supervisors of Business Education, NASBE

National Association of Teacher Educators for Business Education, NATEBE

National Association of Teacher Educators for Vocational Home Economics, NATEVHE

National Association of Teachers' Agencies, NATA

National Association of Teachers of Singing, NATS

National Association of the Deaf, NAD

National Association of Trade and Technical Schools, NATTS

National Association of University Women, NAUW

National Association of Vocational Education Special Needs Personnel, NAVESNP

National Association of Vocational Home Economics Teachers, NAVHET

National Athletic Trainers Association, NATA

National Audio-Visual Association, NAVA

National Black Child Development Act, NBCDA

National Black Child Development Institute, NBCDI

National Board Dental Hygiene Examination, NBDHE

National Board of Medical Examiners, NBME

National Business Consortium for the Gifted and Talented, NBCGT

National Business Education Association, NBEA

National Business Law Council, NBLC

National Cable Television Association, NCTA

National Campus Ministry Association, NCMA

National Captioning Institute, NCI

National Case Study Questionnaire, NCSQ

National Catholic Business Education Association, NCBEA

National Catholic Educational Association, NCEA

National Catholic Forensic League, NCFL

National Center for a Barrier Free Environment, NCBFE

National Center for Adult, Continuing and Manpower Education, NCACME

National Center for American Indian Education, NCAIE

National Center for Atmospheric Research (National Science Foundation), NCAR

National Center for Audiotape, NCAT

National Center for Bilingual Research, NCBR

National Center for Business and Economic Communication, NCBEC

National Center for Community Education, NCCE

National Center for Education Brokering, NCEB

National Center for Education Statistics, NCES

National Center for Educational Communication, NCEC

National Center for Educational Research and Development, NCERD

National Center for Health Statistics, NCHS

National Center for Higher Education Management Systems, NCHEMS

National Center for Research in Vocational Education, NCRVE

National Center for Service-Learning, NCSL

National Center for the Improvement of Educational Systems, NCIES

National Center for the Improvement of Learning (American Association of School Administrators), NCIL

National Center for the Study of Collective Bargaining in Higher Education, NCSCBHE

National Center for the Study of Corporal Punishment and Alternatives in the Schools, NCSCPAS

National Center on Educational Media and Materials for the Handicapped, NCEMMH

National Character Laboratory, NCL

National Chicano Council on Higher Education, NCCHE

National Clearinghouse for Commuter Programs, NCCP

National Coaches Council, NCC

National Coalition for Democracy in Education, NCDE

National Coalition for Public Education and Religious Liberty, NCPERL

National Coalition for Quality Integrated Education, NCQIE

National Coalition for Women and Girls in Education, NCWGE

National Coalition of Alternative Community Schools, NCACS

National Coalition of Independent College and University Students, COPUS

National Coalition of Title 1/Chapter 1 Parents, NCTCP

National Collegiate Association for Secretaries, NCAS

National Collegiate Athletic Association, NCAA

National Commission for Cooperative Education, NCCE

National Commission on Certification of Physician's Assistants, Inc., NCCPA

National Commission on Excellence in Education, NCEE

National Commission on Libraries and Information Science, NCLIS

National Commission on New Technological Uses of Copyrighted Text, CONTU

National Commission on Resources for Youth, NCRY

National Committee, Arts for the Handicapped, NCAH

National Committee for Citizens in Education, NCCE

National Committee for Russian Language Study (American Association for the Advancement of Slavic Studies), NCRLS

National Committee for the Furtherance of Jewish Education, NCFJE

National Committee on the Education of Migrant Children, NCEMC

National Committee on the Emeriti, NCE

National Community Education Association, NCEA

National Conference of Bar Examiners, NCBE

National Conference of State Legislatures, NCSL

National Conference of Yeshiva Principals, NCYP

National Conference on Parent Involvement, NCPI

National Conference on Research in English, NCRE

National Congress for Educational Excellence, NCEE

National Congress of American Indians, NCAI

National Congress of Church-Related Colleges and Universities, NCCRCU

National Consortium for Black Professional Development, NCBPD

National Consortium for Computer-Based Music Instruction (Association for the Development of Computer-Based Instructional Systems), NCCBMI

National Coordinating Council of Educational Opportunities Associations, NCCEOA

National Council for Black Family and Child Development, NCBFCD

National Council for Black Studies, NCBS

National Council for Geographic Education, NCGE

National Council for Research and Planning, NCRP

National Council for Resource Development, NCRD

National Council for Textile Education, NCTE

National Council for the Accreditation of Teacher Education, NCATE

National Council for the Social Studies, NCSS

National Council of Administrative Women in Education, NCAWE

National Council of Administrators of Adult Education, NCAAE

National Council of Architectural Registration Boards, NCARB

National Council of Bureau of Indian Affairs Educators, NCBIAE

National Council of Community College Business Officials, NCCBO

National Council of Dance Teacher Organizations, NCDTO

National Council of Educational Opportunity Associations, NCEOA

National Council of Engineering Examiners, NCEE

National Council of Higher Education Loan Programs, NCHELP

National Council of Instructional Administrators, NCIA

National Council of Local Administrators of Vocational Education and Practical Arts, NCLA

National Council of Secondary School Athletic Directors, NCSSAD

National Council of State Consultants in Elementary Education, NCSCEE

National Council of State Directors of Community and Junior Colleges, NCSDCJC

National Council of State Education Associations, NCSEA

National Council of State Supervisors of Foreign Languages, NCSSFL

National Council of Supervisors of Mathematics, NCSM

National Council of Teachers of English, NCTE

National Council of Teachers of Mathematics, NCTM

National Council of University Research Administrators, NCURA

National Council of Urban Education Associations, NCUEA

National Council on Communication Disorders, NCCD

National Council on Educational Research, NCER

National Council on Foreign Languages and International Studies, NCFLIS

National Council on Governmental Accounting, NCGA

National Council on Measurement in Education, NCME

National Council on Religion and Public Education, NCRPE

National Council on Teacher Retirement, NCTR

National Council On the Aging, NCOA

National Council on the Evaluation of Foreign, CEC

National Council on Year-Round Education, NCYRE

National Crisis Center for the Deaf, NCCD

National Curriculum Study Institute (Association for Supervision and Curriculum Development), NCSI

National Data Base on Aging, NDBA

National Defense Education Act, NDEA

National Development Program in Computer Assisted Learning (Great Britain), NDPCAL

National Diffusion Network, NDN

National Direct Student Loans, NDSL

National Education Association, NEA

National Education Association Political Action Committee, NEA-PAC

National Educational Computing Conference, NECC

National Employment Counselors Association (American Personnel and Guidance Association), NECA

National Endowment for the Arts (National Foundation on the Arts and the Humanities), NEA

National Endowment for the Humanities (National Foundation on the Arts and the Humanities), NEH

National Energy Conservation Policy Act, NECPA

National Environmental Data Referral Service, NEDRES

National Environmental Policy Act, NEPA

National Extension Homemakers Council, NEHC

National Federation of Abstracting and Indexing Services, NFAIS

National Federation of Local Cable Programmers, NFLCP

National Federation of Modern Language Teachers Associations, NFMLTA

National Forensic League, NFL

National Forensics Association, NFA

National Forum of Catholic Parent Organizations, NFCPO

National Foundation for the Improvement of Education, NFIE

National Foundation of Dentistry for the Handicapped, NFDH

National Foundation on the Arts and the Humanities, NFAH

National Fraternal Society of the Deaf, NFSD

National Fraternity of Student Musicians, NFSM

National Gay Task Force, NGTF

National Guild of Community Schools of the Arts, NGCSA

National Guild of Piano Teachers, NGPT

National Head Start Association, NHSA

National Health Insurance, NHI

National Heart, Lung, and Blood Institute, NHLBI

National Highway Traffic Safety Administration, NHTAS

National History Day, NHD

National Home Study Council, NHSC

National Honor Society, NHS

National Humanities Faculty, NHF

National Identification Program for the Advancement of Women in Higher Education Administration, NIP

National Incidence Study, NI

National Indian Council On Aging, NICOA

National Indian Counselors Association, NICA

National Indian Education Association, NIEA

National Indian Youth Council, NIYC

National Information Center for Educational Media, NICEM

National Information Center for Special Education Material/National Instructional Material Information System, NICSEM/NIMIS

National Inservice Network, NIN

National Institute for Architectural Education, NIAE

National Institute for Microcomputer Based Learning, NIMBL

National Institute for Multicultural Education, NIME

National Institute for Occupational Safety and Health, NIOSH

National Institute for Work and Learning, NIWL

National Institute of Allergy and Infectious Diseases (National Institutes of Health), NIAID

National Institute of Child Health and Human Development (National Institutes of Health), NICHHD

National Institute of Dental Research (National Institutes of Health), NIDR

National Institute of Education (Department of Education), NIE

National Institute of Environmental Health Sciences (National Institutes of Health), NIEHS

National Institute of Governmental Purchasing, NIGP

National Institute of Handicapped Research (U.S. Department of Education), NIHR

National Institute of Independent Colleges and Universities, NIICU

National Institute of Mental Health, NIMH

National Institute of Neurological and Communicative Disorders and Stroke (National Institutes of Health), NINCDS

National Institute of Science, NIS

National Institute on Aging, NIA

National Institute on Alcohol Abuse and Alcoholism, NIAAA

National Institute on Drug Abuse, NIDA

National Institutes of Health, NIH

National Interscholastic Athletic Administrators Association, NIAAA

National Joint Committee for Learning Disabilities, NJCLD

National Junior College Athletic Association, NJCAA

National Junior Honor Society, NJHS

National Junior Horticultural Association, NJHA

National Labor Relations Board, NLRB

National Laboratory for the Advancement of Education, NLAE

National League of Nursing, NLN

National Librarians Association, NLA

National Library of Canada, NLC

National Library of Medicine, NLM

National Library Service for the Blind and Physically
    Handicapped (Library of Congress), NLS
National Library Week, NLW
National Longitudinal Study of Mathematical Ability,
    NLSMA
National Longitudinal Study of the Class of '72, NLS
National Lutheran Parent-Teacher League, NLPTL
National Marine Education Association, NMEA
National Merit Scholarship Corporation, NMSC
National Merit Scholarship Qualifying Test, NMSQT
National Micrographics Association, NMA
National Middle School Association, NMSA
National Middle School Resource Center, NMSRC
National Network for Curriculum Coordination in
    Vocational and Technical Education, NNCCVTE
National Network of Bilingual Centers, NNBC
National Network of Graduate Business School Women,
    NNGBSW
National Occupational Information Coordinating
    Committee, NOICC
National Operating Committee on Standards for
    Athletic Equipment, NOCSAE
National Opinion Research Center (University of
    Chicago), NORC
National Organization for the Continuing Education of
    Roman Catholic Clergy, NOCERCC
National Organization for Women, NOW
National Organization on Legal Problems in Education,
    NOLPE
National Orientation Directors Association, NODA
National Origin Minority Education (New Hampshire
    Department of Education), NOME
National Park Service, NPS
National Periodicals Center, NPC
National Piano Foundation, NPF
National Project on Career Education, NPCE
National Public Radio, NPR
National Reading Conference, NRC
National Referral Center (Library of Congress), NRC
National Rehabilitation Information Center, NARIC
National Research Council, NRC
National Retired Teachers Association (American
    Association of Retired Persons), NRTA
National Rifle Association of America, NRA
National Scholarship Service and Fund for Negro
    Students, NSSFNS
National Scholastic Press Association, NSPA
National School Boards Association, NSBA
National School Development Council, NSDC
National School Orchestra Association, NSOA
National School Public Relations Association, NSPRA
National School Supply and Equipment Association,
    NSSEA
National School Transportation Association, NSTA
National School Volunteer Programs, Inc., NSVP
National Schools Committee for Economic Education,
    NSCEE
National Science Board of the National Science
    Foundation, NSB
National Science Foundation, NSF
National Science Supervisors Association, NSSA

National Science Teachers Association, NSTA
National Self-Government Committee, NSGC
National Serials Data Program, NSDP
National Sex Equity Demonstration Project, NSEDP
National Sex Forum, NSF
National Shorthand Reporters Association, NSRA
National Small Business Training Network, NSBTN
National Society for Internships and Experiential
    Education, NSIEE
National Society for Medical Research, NSMR
National Society for Performance and Instruction, NSPI
National Society for the Study of Education, NSSE
National Society of Professional Engineers, NSPE
National/State Leadership Training Institute on Gifted
    and Talented, N/S-LTI-G/T
National Student Aid Coalition, NSAC
National Student Educational Fund, NSEF
National Student Exchange, NSE
National Student Speech Language Hearing Association,
    NSSLHA
National Student Volunteer Program, NSVP
National Study of School Evaluation, NSSE
National Teachers Examination, NTE
National Technical Information Service (U.S.
    Department of Commerce), NTIS
National Technical Institute for the Deaf, NTID
National Theatre Institute, NTI
National Training Laboratories, NTL
National Union Catalog, NUC
National University Consortium, NUC
National University Continuing Education Association,
    NUCEA
National University Teleconference Network, NUTN
National Vocational Agricultural Teachers' Association,
    NVATA
National Vocational Educational Professional
    Development Consortium, NVEPDC
National Vocational Guidance Association (American
    Personnel and Guidance Association), NVGA
National Wildlife Federation, NWF
National Women's Education Fund, NWEF
National Women's Studies Association, NWSA
National Writing Project, NWP
National Youth Practitioners Network, NYPN
Native American Research Institute, NARI
Native American Rights Fund, NARF
Native American Studies, NAS
Native Speaker, NS
Natural Language Processing Program, NLPP
Nature of Scientific Knowledge Scale, NSKS
Naval Education and Training Command, NAVEDTRA
Naval Reserve Officer Training Corps, NROTC
Navy Integrated Training Resources and Administration
    System, NITRAS
Navy Verbal Skills Curriculum, VSC
Near East College Association, NECA
Nebraska Reading Retrieval System, NRRS
Needs-Based Goal Attainment Scale, NGAS
Neighborhood Info Centers Project, NIC
Neighborhood Youth Corps, NYC
Nelson-Denny Reading Test, NDRT

Neonatal Behavioral Assessment Scale, NBAS
Neonatal Behavioral Assessment Scale—Kansas Revision, NBAS-K
Nepal Studies Association, NSA
Network of Education Libraries (Australia), NEL
Network Technical Architecture Group (Library of Congress), NTAG
Neurolinguistic Programming, NLP
Neurological Impress Method, NIM
New Directions in Creativity Program, NDC
New England Association of Schools and Colleges, NEASC
New England Business Educators Association, NEBEA
New England Information Center, NEIC
New England Library Information Network, NELINET
New England School Development Council, NESDEC
New Hampshire Association for Computer Education Statewide, NH ACES
New Jersey College Basic Skills Placement Test, NJCBSPT
New Jersey Developmental Disabilities Council, NJDDC
New Mexico High School Proficiency Examination, NMHSPE
New Reading System, NRS
New School for Democratic Management, NSDM
New World Foundation, NWF
New York Association of Child Care Workers, ACCW
New York City Urban Corps, NYCUC
New York State Association of Foreign Language Teachers, NYSAFLT
New York State Industrial Arts Association, NYSIAA
New York State Interlibrary Loan Network, NYSILL
New York State Longitudinal Study, NYLS
Newspaper Fund, NF
Nieman Foundation, NF
Night Vision Aid, NVA
Noise Subtest of the Goldman-Fristoe-Woodcock Auditory Skills Test Battery, NS-GFW
Non-English Speaking, NES
Non-Formal Education, NFE
Non-Governmental Organizations, NGO
Nonlinear Iterative Partial Least Squares, NIPALS
Non-native Speakers, NNS
Nonverbal, NV
Nordic Documentation Center for Mass Communication Research (Denmark), NORDICOM
Normal Curve Equivalent, NCE
Normal Curve Equivalent Scores, NCES
Norm-Referenced, NR
Norm-Referenced Testing, NRT
North American Association for Environmental Education, NAAEE
North American Association of Summer Sessions, NAASS
North American Indian Women's Association, NAIWA
North American Jewish Students' Network, NAJSN
North American Professional Driver Education Association, NAPDEA
North American Simulation And Gaming Association, NASAGA

North American Society for the Psychology of Sport and Physical Activity, NASPSPA
North American Students of Cooperation, NASCO
North Carolina Association for Institutional Research, NCAIR
North Carolina State Occupational Information Coordinating Committee, NC SOICC
North Central Association of Colleges and Schools, NCA
North Central Conference on Summer Schools, NCCSS
North-Central Business Education Association, N-CBEA
Northeast Conference on the Teaching of Foreign Languages, NEC
Northeast Document Conservation Center, NEDCC
Northeast Modern Language Association, NEMLA
Northeast Regional Exchange, NEREX
Northwest Arctic Inupiat Corporation (Alaska), NANA
Northwest Association of Schools and Colleges, NASC
Northwest Council for Computer Education, NCCE
Northwest Educators of the Hearing Impaired, NEHI
Northwest Forensics Conference, NFC
Northwest Regional Educational Laboratory, NWREL
Northwest Regional Exchange, NWRx
Northwestern Syntax Screening Test, NSST
Not an acronym: A bibliographic data service, OCLC
Not an acronym: A catalog of library holdings on computer output microfilm, COMcat
Not an acronym: A computer-aided diagnostic consultation system, MYCIN
Not an acronym: A computer-based career guidance and counselor support system, DISCOVER
Not an acronym: A computer-based guidance system, ENCORE
Not an acronym: A computer-based reading and study skills curriculum developed for Navy recruits, PREST
Not an acronym: A computer-managed instruction and testing program for basic mathematics skills in grades 1 through 8, IPASS
Not an acronym: A computing language for teaching programming and for computer-assisted instruction, LEPUS
Not an acronym: A computing network for higher education and other nonprofit organizations, EDUNET
Not an acronym: A consortium of five regional computer centers, CONDUIT
Not an acronym: A professional association for the development, management and use of information systems in higher education, CAUSE
Not an acronym: A prototype on-line library catalog at the University of California, MELVYL
Not an acronym: An Indiana network that promotes microcomputer use in the public schools, MICRONET
Not an acronym: An information retrieval system developed by the IDRC, IDRC/MINISIS
Not an acronym: Bilingual, multicultural, English/Spanish curriculum, SOCMATICAS
Not an acronym: Canada's national telecommunications network, DATAPAC

Not an acronym: Computer-based writing program, QUILL

Not an acronym: Intelligent computer-aided diagnostic consultation system, CENTAUR

Not an acronym: Intelligent computer-aided diagnostic consultation system, NEOMYCIN

Not an acronym: Kentucky's capacity building project, SEARCH

Not an acronym: Medical computer bibliographic service of the National Library of Medicine, MEDLINE

Not an acronym: Name for the National Consortium on Uses of Computers in Mathematical Sciences Education (Affiliated with the Association for the Development of Computer-Based Instructional Systems), MATH

Not an acronym: Name of a software program for the management of school purchasing systems, PURCHASE

Not an acronym: Name of a software program that monitors funds generated through extracurricular activities, BURSAR

Not an acronym: Name of the Electronic Mail and Information Network of the American Library Association, ALANET

Not an acronym: On-line catalog at the University of California, Los Angeles, ORION

Not an acronym: On-line search program of Lockheed Information Systems, DIALOG

Not an acronym: On-line search service of System Development Corporation, ORBIT

Not an acronym: Programming Language, NATAL

Not an acronym: Simulation game focusing on parent-child relations, SIMPAR

Not an acronym: The on-line system developed by QL Systems Ltd., Ontario, QL/SEARCH

Not Applicable, NA

Nowicki-Strickland Internal-External Control Scale for Adults, ANS-IE

NSST-Receptive Portion, NSST-R

Number of Variables, NV

Nurse Practitioner, N.P.

Nursing Curriculum Project (Southern Regional Education Board), NCP

Observation Schedule And Records, OSCAR

Observational System for Instructional Analysis, OSIA

Observe Rating Form, ORF

Obsessive Compulsive Scale, OCS

Occupational Education Project, OEP

Occupational Information Access System, OIAS

Occupational Interest Inventory, OII

Occupational Outlook Handbook, OOH

Occupational Safety and Health Act of 1970, OSHA

Occupational Therapy, OT

Off Reservation Boarding School, ORBS

Offer Self-Image Questionnaire for Adolescents, OSIQA

Office Education Association, OEA

Office for Intellectual Freedom (American Library Association), OIF

Office for Library Outreach Services (American Library Association), OLOS

Office for Library Personnel Resources (American Library Association), OLPR

Office for the Gifted and Talented (U.S. Department of Education), OGT

Office of Bilingual Education and Minority Languages Affairs (Department of Education), OBEMLA

Office of Civil Rights (U.S. Department of Education), OCR

Office of Drug Abuse Policy, ODAP

Office of Economic Opportunity, OEO

Office of Federal Contract Compliance Programs (U.S. Department of Labor), OFCCP

Office of Indian Education Programs (Bureau of Indian Affairs), OIEP

Office of Juvenile Justice and Delinquency Prevention, OJJDP

Office of Management and Budget, OMB

Office of Management Studies (Association of Research Libraries), OMS

Office of Mental Retardation and Developmental Disabilities (New York), OMRDD

Office of Special Education and Rehabilitation Services (Department of Education), OSERS

Office of Special Education (U.S. Department of Education), OSE

Office of Talented Identification and Development (Johns Hopkins University), OTID

Office of Technology Assessment (U.S. Congress), OTA

Office on Educational Credit and Credentials (American Council on Education), OECC

Ohio Educational Library Media Association, OELMA

Ohio Modern Language Teachers Association, OMLTA

Ohio Music Education Association, OMEA

Ohio Program of Intensive English, OPIE

Ohio State University Psychological Exam, OSUPE

Ohio Vocational Education Achievement Test Program, OVEATP

Ohio Vocational Interest Survey, OVIS

Oklahoma Citizen's Commission on Education, OCCE

Oklahoma Educational Computer User's Group, OECUP

Older Americans Act of 1965, OAA

Older Americans Resources and Services, OARS

Omaha Reading Instruction System, ORIS

Omnibus Personality Inventory, OPI

O'Neill Educational Ideologies Inventory, OEII

On-line Database Information Network (Pennsylvania), ODIN

Online Public Access Catalog, OPAC

Ontario Educational Research Council, OERC

Ontario Educational Research Information System, ONTERIS

Ontario Institute for Studies in Education, OISE

Ontario Library Association, OLA

Ontario Society for Training and Development, OSTD

On-the-Job Training, OJT

Open Access Satellite Education Services, OASES

Open Court Language Development Program: Kindergarten, OCLDP-K

Open Door Student Exchange, ODSE

Open Systems Interconnection, OSI

Operating System, OS
Operation Enterprise, OE
Optical Character Recognition, OCR
Optimism-Pessimism Test Instrument, OPTI
Optional Educational Programs, OEP
Oral Deaf Adults Section (Alexander Graham Bell
   Association for the Deaf), ODAS
Oral Directions Test, ODT
Oral Langauge Sentence Imitation Diagnostic Inventory,
   OLSIDI
Ordinary Least Squares, OLS
Oregon Business Education Association, OBEA
Oregon Educational Computing Consortium, OECC
Organisation Mondiale pour l'Education Prescolaire
   (World Organization for Early Childhood Education),
   OMEP
Organization for Economic Cooperation and
   Development (France), OECD
Organization for Equal Education of the Sexes, OEES
Organization for Rehabilitation through Training, ORT
Organization of American Historians, OAH
Organization of American Kodaly Educators, OAKE
Organization of American States, OAS
Organization of Athletic Administrators, OAA
Organization of Professional Acting Coaches and
   Teachers, OPACT
Organizational Climate Description Questionnaire,
   OCDQ
Organizational Climate Index, OCI
Organizational Communication Conflict Instrument,
   OCCI
Organizational Development, OD
Orleans-Hanna Algebra Prognosis Test, OHAPT
Otis Lennon Mental Ability Test, OLMAT
Out of Print, OP
Outdoor Education, OE
Outdoor Education Association, OEA
Outward Bound, OB
Overseas Education Association, OEA
Overseas Education Fund, OEF
Overseas Liaison Committee (American Council on
   Education), OLC
Pacific and Asian Linguistics Institute, PALI
Pacific Northwest Council on Foreign Languages and
   Literatures, PNCFL
Pacific Northwest Indian Reading and Language
   Development Program, IRLDP
Packaging Education Foundation, PEF
Paired Comparisons, PC
Paired Hands Test, PHT
Palmar Sweat Index, PSI
Pan-Pacific Education and Communications
   Experiments Using Satellites (National Aeronautics
   and Space Administration), PEACESAT
Paper Copy, PC
Paragraph Completion Method, PCM
Parallel Alternate Curriculum, PAC
Parent Advisory Council, PAC
Parent Advocacy Coalition for Educational Rights
   (Minnesota), PACER
Parent As A Teacher Inventory, PAAT

Parent Attitude toward Child Expressiveness Scale,
   PACES
Parent Cooperative Preschools International, PCPI
Parent Daily Telephone Reports, PDR
Parent Education Follow Through Program, PEFTP
Parent Effectiveness Training, PET
Parent Loans for Undergraduate Students, PLUS
Parent Needs Inventory, PNI
Parent Problem-Solving Instrument, PPSI
Parent Teacher Association, PTA
Parent-Child Activity Rating Scale, PCAR
Parent-Child Interaction Scale, PCI
Parenting Stress Index, PSI
Parents and Teachers Against Violence in Education,
   PTAVE
Parent's Confidential Statement, PCS
Parents Without Partners, PWP
Parisi Spanish Proficiency Test, PSPT
Partial Least Squares, PLS
Partnership for Rural Improvement (Washington), PRI
Part-Time, P-T
Passage Reading Test, PRT
Patriotic Education, Inc., PEI
Peabody Individual Achievement Test, PIAT
Peabody Language Development Kit: Preschool,
   PLDK-P
Peabody Picture Vocabulary Test, PPVT
Pediatric Nurse Practitioner, PNP
Peer Attitudes Toward the Handicapped Scale, PATH
Peer Intervention Network, PIN
Peer Nomination Inventory of Depression, PNID
Peer Role-Taking Questionnaire, PRTQ
Pennsylvania Association for Retarded Children, PARC
Pennsylvania Comprehensive Mathematics Plan,
   PCMP
Pennsylvania Comprehensive Reading Program, PCRP
Pennsylvania Higher Education Assistance Agency,
   PHEAA
Pennsylvania Learning Resources Association, PLRA
Pennsylvania Resources and Information Center for
   Special Education, PRISE
People of America Responding to Educational Needs of
   Today's Society, P.A.R.E.N.T.S.
Perceptions Of Developmental Skills Profile, PODS
Perceptual-Communicative Disorders, PCD
Perez Self-Concept Inventory, PSCI
Performance Intelligence Quotient, PIQ
Performance Scales Intelligence Quotient, PSIQ
Performance-based Adult Vocational Education, PAVE
Performance-Based Evaluation Instrument, PBEI
Performance-Based Teacher Education, PBTE
Performance-Self-Esteem Scale, PSES
Person Perception Questionnaire, PPQ
Personal Attitude Survey, PAS
Personal Attribute Inventory for Children, PAIC
Personal Attributes Questionnaire, PAQ
Personal Orientation Inventory, POI
Personal Record Of School Experiences, PROSE
Personal Report of Public Speaking Apprehension,
   PRPSA
Personality Inventory for Children, PIC

Personalized System of Instruction, PSI
Personnel Data System, PDS
Persons In Need of Supervision, PINS
Phencyclidine, PCP
Philological Association of the Pacific Coast, PAPC
Philosophic Society for the Study of Sport, PSSS
Philosophy of Education Society, PES
Photographic Art and Science Foundation, PASF
Physical Education, PE
Physical Science Study Committee, PSSC
Physically Disabled, PD
Piagetian Logical Operations Test, PLOT
Pictorial Test of Intelligence, PTI
Pier-Harris Self-Concept Scale, PHSCS
Pirchei Agudath Israel, PAI
Pittsburgh's Research-based Instructional Supervising
    Model, PRISM
Plan of Action for Challenging Times, PACT
Planning, Evaluation, and Resource Management
    Model (Connecticut), PERM
Planning, Management, and Evaluation, PME
Planning, Monitoring, and Implementing Model, PMI
Plastics Education Foundation, PEF
Plastics Institute of America, PIA
PLATO Users Group (Association for the Development
    of Computer-Based Instructional Systems), PUG
Play Schools Association, PSA
Play Units for Severely Handicapped, P.U.S.H.
Polish-American Librarians Association, PALA
Porch Index of Communicative Ability, PICA
Portable Assisted Study Sequence Program (California),
    PASS
Portable Rod-and-Frame Test, PRFT
Porter Need Satisfaction Questionnaire, PNSQ
Portland Problem Behavior Checklist, PPBC
Positive Action Through Holistic Evaluation Program,
    PATHE
Post-Evaluative Conference Rating Scale, PECRS
Post-Traumatic Stress Disorder, PTSD
Practical Research into Organizational Behavior and
    Effectiveness, PROBE
Pre-conscious Activity Scale, PAS
Predischarge Remedial Education Program, PREPS
Preliminary Scholastic Aptitude Test, PSAT
Pre-Medical Student Assessment Test, PMSAT
Pre-Professional Skill Test, P-PST
Pre-Reading Assessment Inventory, PRAI
Preschool and Primary Nowicki-Strickland Internal-
    External Control Scale, PPNS-IE
Preschool Embedded Figures Test, PEFT
Preschool Interpersonal Problem Solving, PIPS
Preschool Inventory, PSI
Preschool Language Scale, PLS
Preserved Context Indexing System, PRECIS
A Presidential Classroom for Young Americans,
    APCYA
President's Environmental Merit Awards Program,
    PEMAP
Pre-Speech Assessment Scale, PSAS
Preventive Intervention Research Centers (National
    Institutes of Mental Health), PIRC

Primary Representational System, PRS
Primary Self-Concept Inventory, PSCI
Primary Trait System, PTS
Prime Time School Television, PTST
Principal Problem Strategy Questionnaire, PPSQ
Principal-Teacher Interaction Study, PTI
Principles of Adult Learning Scale, PALS
Priorities In School Mathematics Project, PRISM
Privacy Protection Study Commission, PPSC
Private Child Care Providers, PCCP
Private Industry Council, PIC
Private Libraries Association, PLA
Proactive Interference, PI
Probe Ministries International, PMI
Problem Solving Inventory, PSI
Processes Of Science Test, POST
Professional and Organizational Development Network
    in Higher Education, POD
Professional and Scholarly Publishing Division
    (Association of American Publishers), PSP
Professional Development Program Improvement
    Center, PDPIC
Professional Education and Training for Research
    Librarianship Program, PETREL
Professional Improvement Points Program (Louisiana),
    PIPS
Professional Qualification Examination (National
    Security Agency), PQE
Professional Student Exchange Program (Western
    Interstate Commission on Higher Education), PSEP
Profile Of Mood States Inventory, POMS
Profile Of Nonverbal Sensitivity, PONS
Profoundly Mentally Retarded, PMR
Program Analysis and Review System, PARS
Program Development Branch (Division of Innovation
    and Development, U.S. Department of Education),
    PDB
Program Evaluation and Review Technique, PERT
Program for Acquiring Competence in
    Entrepreneurship, PACE
Program for Assessing Youth Employment Skills,
    PAYES
Program for Hearing-Handicapped Infants Providing
    Medical, Academic, and Psychological Services, HI-
    MAPS
Program of Research and Evaluation for Public Schools,
    PREPS
Program On Noncollegiate Sponsored Instruction
    (American Council on Education), PONSI
Program with Developing Institutions, PDI
Programmed Instruction Learning On Teaching (A
    simplified programming language for computer-
    assisted instruction), PILOT
Programmed Logic for Automated Teaching Operations,
    PLATO
Programmer Aptitude Test, PAT
Programming In The Arts (National Endowment for the
    Arts), PITA
Programming Language for Interactive Teaching,
    PLANIT
Programming Language/Version One, PL/1

Programs in the Arts for Special Education Project,
    PASE
Progressive Utilization Theory, PROUT
Project Developmental Continuity (Head Start), PDC
Project for an Energy-Enriched Curriculum, PEEC
Project: Individualized Reading And Mathematics
    Inter-District, PIRAMID
Project on Equal Education Rights (National
    Organization for Women), PEER
Project On National Vocational Education Resources,
    PONVER
Project on the Status and Education of Women, PSEW
Projects With Industry Program, PWI
Promoting Intellectual Adaptation Given Experiential
    Transforming Project, P.I.A.G.E.T.
Protocol Data Unit, PDU
Providing Professional Developmemt, Assessment, and
    Coordination of Competency-based Education
    Project (Illinois), PACCE
Provincial Intermediate Teachers Association (Canada),
    PITA
Prueba de Admisión para Estudios Graduados
    (Educational Testing Service), PAEG
Psychological Abstracts, PA
Psychological Distress Inventory, PDI
Psychomotor Development Index, PDI
Public Action Coalition on Toys, PACT
Public Affairs Information Service, PAIS
Public Broadcasting Service, PBS
Public Choice Society, PCS
Public Education Religious Studies Center, PERSC
Public Employment Relations Board, PERB
Public Employment Relations Commission, PERC
Public Health Service, PHS
Public Interest Research Group, PIRG
Public Law, PL
Public Library Association, PLA
Public Library Association Alternative Education
    Program Section, PLA AEPS
Public Library Association Armed Forces Library
    Section, PLA AFLS
Public Library Association Community Information
    Section, PLA CIS
Public Library Association Metropolitan Libraries
    Section, PLA MLS
Public Library Association Public Library Systems
    Section, PLA PLSS
Public Library Association Small and Medium-Sized
    Libraries Section, PLA SMLS
Public Relations Student Society of America, PRSSA
Public Service Satellite Consortium, PSSC
Public Understanding Of Science Program, PUOS
Pupil Control Ideology Form, PCI
Pupil Evaluation Inventory, PEI
Pupil-Perceived Needs Assessment, PPNA
Quality Circles, QC
Quality of School Life Scale, QSL
Quality of Working Life, QWL
Quality Response Rating Scale, QRRS
Quebec Association of Computer Users in Education,
    QACUE

Question-Answer Relations Technique, QAR
Questionnaire for Students, Teachers, and
    Administrators, QUESTA
Quick Assessment Test, QAT
Quick Test, QT
Quick Word Test, QWT
Random Access Memory, RAM
RASD History Section, RASD HS
RASD Machine-Assisted Reference Service Section,
    RASD MARS
Rathus Assertiveness Scale, RAS
Rational Emotive Therapy, RET
Raven's Progressive Matrices Test, RPM
Read Only Memory, ROM
Readiness-Instruction-Maintenance Model, RIM
Reading And Mathematics Observation System,
    RAMOS
Reading Attitude Imagination Technique, RAIT
Reading Comprehension Interview, RCI
Reading Is Fundamental, RIF
Reading Reform Foundation, RRF
Reading Resource Teacher, RRT
Reading, Writing and Arithmetic Development System,
    REWARD
Reading-Disabled, RD
Reading-Free Vocational Interest Inventory, RFVII
Real World Reading Test, RWRT
Really Outstanding Color Television About Practically
    Unlimited Subjects (Australia), ROCTAPUS
Record of Oral Language, ROL
Recording For the Blind, Inc., RFB
Records and Archives Management Programme
    (UNESCO), RAMP
Reduction In Force, RIF
Reference and Adult Services Division (American
    Library Association), RASD
Regents External Degree Examinations (New York),
    REDE
Regional Early Childhood Direction Centers, RECDC
Regional Educational Laboratory for the Carolinas,
    RELC
Regional Educational Service Agencies, RESA
Regional Educational Service Areas, RESA
Regional Educational Service Centers, RESC
Regional Occupation Planning and Evaluation System,
    ROPES
Regional Resource Centers, RRC
Register for International Service in Education (Institute
    of International Education), RISE
Registered Dietitian, R.D.
Registered Nurse, RN
Registered Physical Therapist, R.P.T.
Registry of Interpreters for the Deaf, RID
Regular Education Teachers and Principals Project,
    RETAP
Regular Educator Expectancy Scale, REES
Rehabilitation Engineering Society of North America,
    RESNA
Rehabilitation Services Administration, RSA
Related Term, RT
Religious Education Association, REA

Religious Speech Communication Association, RSCA
Remote Associations Test, RAT
Renzulli/Smith Learning Style Inventory, RSLSI
Request For Proposals, RFP
Research Advisory Committee (National Council of Teachers of Mathematics), RAC
Research and Demonstration Center for the Education of Handicapped Children and Youth, RDCEHCY
Research and Development Center for Teacher Education (University of Texas, Austin), RDCTE
Research and Information Services for Education, RISE
Research Association of Minority Professors, RAMP
Research Center for Group Dynamics (Institute for Social Research), RCGD
Research & Development, R&D
Research in Accrediting Efforts Project (Illinois), REA
Research In Science Education (National Science Foundation), RISE
Research in Undergraduate Institutions (National Science Foundation), RUI
The Research Instruments Project, TRIP
Research Libraries Group, RLG
Research Libraries Information Network, RLIN
Research on the Early Abilities of Children with Handicaps Project, REACH
Reserve Officers Training Corps, ROTC
Resident Advisor, RA
Resident Assistant, RA
Resource Access Projects (Administration for Children, Youth, and Families), RAP
Resource Allocation and Management Program, RAMP
Resource Centers for Science Education (National Science Foundation), RCSE
Resource Cost Model, RCM
Resource Requirement Prediction Model, RRPM
Resource Specialist Program (California), RSP
Resources and Technical Services Division (American Library Association), RTSD
Resources In Computer Education, RICE
Resources In Education, RIE
Resources on Educational Equity for the Disabled Project, REED
Response System with Variable Prescriptions, RSVP
Response-sensitive Sequencing Strategy, RSS
Responsibility for Student Achievement Scale, RSA
Responsive Multicultural Basic Skills Approach, RMBS
Retinitis Pigmentosa, RP
Retired Operating Staff Employment Services (University of New Hampshire), ROSES
Retired Senior Volunteer Program, RSVP
Retrieval and Acceleration of Promising Young Handicapped and Talented Program, RAPYHT
Retrospective Conversion of Cataloging Records (Library of Congress), RECON
Revised Bogardus Social Distance Scale, RBSDS
Revised Token Test, RTT
Revolving Door Identification Model, RDIM
Rhode Island Business Educators Association, RIBEA
Road Builders Training Association, RBTA
Rocky Mountain Modern Language Association, RMMLA

Role Category Questionnaire, RCQ
Role Construct Repertory Test, REP
Rorschach Prognostic Rating Scale, RPRS
Ross Educational Philosophical Inventory, REPI
Round Table, RT
Round Table of National Organizations for Better Education, RTNOBE
RTSD Cataloging and Classification Section, RTSD CCS
RTSD Reproduction of Library Materials Section, RTSD RLMS
RTSD Resources Section, RTSD RS
RTSD Serials Section, RTSD SS
Rucker-Gable Educational Programming Scale, RGEPS
Rural Education Association, REA
Rural Student Vocational Program (Washington), RSVP
Rural Texas Domestic Violence Health Professionals Education Program, RTDVHPEP
Sample Size, SS
San Mateo Educational Resources Center (California), SMERC
Saskatchewan Association for Computers in Education, SACE
Satellite Instructional Television Experiment, SITE
Scale for the Evaluation of Group Counseling Experiences, SEGCE
Scandinavian Summer, SS
Schedule for Affective Disorders and Schizophrenia, SADS
Schedule for Classroom Activity Norms, SCAN
Schedule Of Social Functioning, SOSF
Schilling Body Coordination Test, SBCT
Scholarly Activities Rating Scale, SARS
Scholastic Aptitude Test, SAT
Scholastic Aptitude Test-Mathematical, SAT-M
Scholastic Aptitude Test-Verbal, SAT-V
School and College Ability Tests, SCAT
School Attendance Review Board, SARB
School Employment Procedures Act of 1977, SEPA
School Finance Equalization Management System, SFEMS
School Heads Advisory Commitee (National Association of Independent Schools), SHAC
School Improvement Model, SIM
School Improvement Program, SIP
School Improvement Through Instructional Process (Maryland), SITIP
School Information and Research Service, SIRS
School Library Manpower Project, SLMP
School Management Study Group, SMSG
School Mathematics Study Group, SMSG
School Nurse Practitioner, SNP
School Practices Information File, SPIF
School Projectionist Club of America, SPCA
School Retrofit Design Analysis System, SRDAS
School-Aged Maternity, SAM
Schoolhouse Energy Efficiency Demonstration Project, SEED
Schools, Colleges, and Departments of Education, SCDEs
Science—A Process Approach, S-APA

Science and Self-Determination Project (Upward Bound), SSD
Science Citation Index, SCI
Science Classroom Behavior Q-Sort, SCBQ
Science College Ability Test, SCAT
Science Curriculum Improvement Study, SCIS
Science Education Development and Research Division (National Science Foundation), SEDR
Science Fiction Research Association, SFRA
Science Participation Scales, SPS
Science Process Competency Test, SPCT
Science Talent Search, STS
Science Teacher Inventory of Need, STIN
Science Teaching Observational Instrument, STOI
Scientific and Technical Aerospace Reports (National Aeronautics and Space Administration), STAR
Scientific Communications And Technology Transfer System (National Science Foundation), SCATT
Scope Note, SN
Scott, Foresman Achievement Test, SFAT
Screening Test of Adolescent Language, STAL
Screening Test of Spanish Grammar, STSG
Screenwriting Coalition for Industry Professionals and Teachers, SCRIPT
Sea Education Association, SEA
Search for Excellence in Science Education (National Science Teacher Association), SESE
Second International Science Study, SISS
Second Language, L2
Second Language Acquisition, SLA
Secondary Education Review Project, SERP
Secondary Level English Proficiency Test, SLEP
Secondary School Admission Test, SSAT
Secondary School Admission Test Board, SSATB
Secondary School Theatre Association, SSTA
Secondary Training for Alaskan Rural Students, STARS
Seeing Essential English, SEE
Seeing-Eye Elephant Network (a computer-assisted instruction program), SEEN
Selective Dissemination of Information, SDI
Selective Service College Qualification Test, SSCQT
Self Paced Instruction for Competency Education, SPICE
Self-Directed Search, SDS
Self-Estimate Questionnaire, SEQ
Self-Evaluation Maintenance Model, SEM
Self-Feeling Awareness Scale, SFAS
Self-Injurious Behavior, SIB
Self-Monitoring Negative Checklist, SMNC
Self-Monitoring Scale, SMS
Self-Observational Scales, SOS
Self-Rating Depression Scale, SDS
Self-Reported Delinquency, SRD
Self-Righteousness Questionnaire, SRQ
Self-Testimony Scale, STS
Semantic Differential, SD
Semantic Feature Analysis, SFA
Seminar on the Acquisition of Latin American Library Materials, SALALM
Semiotic Society of America, SSA

Sensible Policy for Information Resources and Information Technology Group, SPIRIT
Sentence Combining Exercise, SCE
Sentence Completion Test, SCT
Sequenced Inventory of Communication Development, SICD
Sequential Test of Educational Progress—Writing Test, STEP-W
Sequential Tests of Educational Progress, STEP
Service Corps Of Retired Executives, SCORE
Servicemembers Opportunity College Program, SOCP
Servicemembers Opportunity Colleges, SOC
Servicemembers Opportunity Colleges Associate Degree, SOCAD
Severely and Profoundly Handicapped, SPH
Sex Equity in Educational Leadership Project (Oregon), SEEL
Sex Information and Education Council of the United States, SIECUS
Sharing Business Success Program (Association of School Business Officials of the United States and Canada), SBS
Short Form Test of Academic Aptitude, SFTAA
Short Michigan Alcoholism Screening Test, SMAST
Short Portable Mental Status Questionnaire, SPMSQ
Short-Term Memory, STM
Simple Mail Transfer Protocol, SMTP
Simulated Interpersonal Problem Situation, SIPS
Simulation Language, SIMULA
Single-concept User-adaptable Microcomputer-based Instructional Technique, SUMIT
Situational Attitude Scale—Women, SASW
Skill Qualifications Test, SQT
Sleep-Learning Association, SLA
Slosson Intelligence Test, SIT
Slosson Oral Reading Test, SORT
Small Business Administration, SBA
Small Business Management Training, SBMT
Smithsonian Institute Traveling Exhibition Service, SITES
Social Behavior Assessment, SBA
Social Competence Intervention Package for Preschool Youngsters, SCIPPY
Social Desirability Scale, SDS
Social Mapping Matrix Assessment, SMMA
Social Problem-Solving Test, SPST
Social Readjustment Rating Scale, SRRS
Social Responsibilities Round Table (American Library Association), SRRT
Social Science Citation Index, SSCI
Social Science Education Consortium, SSEC
Social Science Research Council, SSRC
Social Security Disability Insurance, SSDI
Social Studies Priorities, Practices, And Needs, SPAN
Social-Emotional Inventory, SEI
Société Canadienne d'Orientation et de Consultation, SCOC
Société Canadienne pour l'Étude de l'Éducation, SCEE
Société des Professeurs Français et Francophones en Amerique, SPFA

Société Internationale pour l'Enseignement Commercial, SIEC
Sociedad Honoraria Hispanica, SHH
Society for Academic Achievement, SAA
Society for Applied Learning Technology, SALT
Society for Business Ethics, SBE
Society for College and University Planning, SCUP
Society for College Science Teachers, SCST
Society for Educational Reconstruction, SER
Society for French-American Cultural Services and Educational Aid, FACSEA
Society for History Education, SHE
Society for Industrial and Applied Mathematics, SIAM
Society for Management Information Systems, SMIS
Society for Microcomputers In Life and Education, SMILE
Society for Nutrition Education, SNE
Society for Philosophy of Religion, SPR
Society for Photographic Education, SPE
Society for Public Health Education, SOPHE
Society for Research in Child Development, SRCD
Society for Research into Higher Education (Great Britain), SRHE
Society for Slovene Studies, SSS
Society for South India Studies, SSIS
Society for Technical Communication, STC
Society for the Advancement of Chicanos and Native Americans in Science, SACNAS
Society for the Advancement of Education, SAE
Society for the Advancement of Good English, SAGE
Society for the Advancement of Scandinavian Study, SASS
Society for the Study of Early China, SSEC
Society of American Achivists, SAA
Society of American Law Teachers, SALT
Society of Christian Ethics, SCE
Society of Data Educators, SDE
Society of Ethnic and Special Studies, SESS
Society of Federal Labor Relations Professionals, SFLRP
Society of Park and Recreation Educators, SPRE
Society of Professionals In Dispute Resolution, SPIDR
Society of Professors of Education, SPE
Society of State Directors of Health, Physical Education and Recreation, SSDHPER
Society of Wine Educators, SWE
Socioeconomic Status, SES
Sociolinguistic Test, SLT
Sociometric Status, SMS
Sociomoral Reflection Maturity Score, SRMS
Sociomoral Reflection Measures, SRM
Sociomoral Relfection Objective Measure, SROM
Soil Conservation Society of America, SCSA
Solving Problems of Access to Careers in Engineering and Science, SPACES
Some Essential Learner Outcomes (Minnesota), SELO
Something About Myself Inventory, SAM
Sooner Exchange for Educational Knowledge (Oklahoma), SEEK
Sound Pressure Level, SPL

Sources to Upgrade the Career Counseling and Employment of Special Students (Florida), SUCCESS
South Atlantic Modern Language Association, SAMLA
South Carolina Association of Biology Teachers, SCABT
South Carolina Handicapped Services Information System, SCHSIS
South Central Modern Language Association, SCMLA
South Dakota Medical Information Exchange, SDMIX
Southeast Asian Ministers of Education Organization, SEAMEO
Southeast Florida Educational Consortium, SFEC
Southeast Library Network, SOLINET
Southeast Louisiana Library Network Cooperative, SEALLING
Southeastern Association of Community College Researchers, SACCR
Southeastern Education Laboratory, SEL
Southeastern Library Association, SELA
Southern Association for Children Under Six, SACUS
Southern Association for Institutional Research, SAIR
Southern Association of Agricultural Scientists, SAAS
Southern Association of Colleges and Schools, SACS
Southern Business Administration Association, SBAA
Southern Business Education Association, SBEA
Southern Center for Studies in Public Policy, SCSPP
Southern Central Kansas Environmental Education Center, SKEEC
Southern Conference On Language Teaching, Inc., SCOLT
Southern Education Foundation, SEF
Southern Educational Communications Association, SECA
Southern Regional Education Board, SREB
Southern Speech Communication Association, SSCA
Southwest Educational Development Laboratory, SEDL
Southwestern Cooperative Educational Laboratory, SWCEL
Spache's Diagnostic Reading Scales, SDRS
Spacial Appreciation Test, SPA
Spanish/English Language Performance Screening, S/ELPS
Spanish Oral Reading Text, SORT
Spaulding Teacher Activity Rating Schedule, STARS
Special Education in the Regular Classroom Project (U.S. Office of Special Education and Rehabilitation Services), SERC
Special Education Local Planning Agency, SELPA
Special Interest Group, SIG
Special Interest Group for Computer Science Education (Association for Computing Machinery), SIG CSE
Special Interest Group for Computer Uses in Education, SIG CUE
Special Interest Group for University and College Computing Sciences, SIGUCCS
Special Libraries Association, SLA
Special Student Access to Vocational Education Project, SSAVE
Specific Aptitude Test Battery, SATB
Speech Communication Association, SCA
Speech Handicapped, SH

Speech Sounds Perception Test, SSPT
Speilberger's Trait-Anxiety Inventory, STAI
Spiral-Ecological Approach to Supervision, SEAS
Spreading Activation Processor for Information
    Encoded in Network Structures, SAPIENS
Staff Development for School Improvement Program,
    SDSI
Staff Organizations Round Table (American Library
    Association), SORT
Stages of Concern Questionnaire, SoCQ
Standard Book Number, SBN
Standard English, SE
Standard Error of the Mean, SEM
Standard Metropolitan Statistical Areas, SMSA
Standard Occupational Classification, SOC
Standard Progressive Matrices, SPM
Standardized Curriculum Oriented Pupil Evaluation,
    SCOPE
Standardized Proficiency Entry Level 2 Test (National
    Security Agency), SPEL-2
Standardized Test of Essential Writing Skills, STEWS
Standardized Test Of Reading Effectiveness, STORE
Stanford Achievement Test, SAT
Stanford Achievement Test, Special Edition for Hearing
    Impaired Students, SAT-HI
Stanford Diagnostic Reading Test, SDRT
Stanford Early School Achievement Test, SESAT
Stanford Preschool Internality-Externality Scale, SPIES
Stanford Program on International and Cross Cultural
    Education, SPICE
Stanford Public Information Retrieval System, SPIRES
Stanford Test of Academic Skills, TASK
Stanford-Binet Intelligence Scale, SBIS
Stanford-Binet Intelligence Test, SBIT
State Advisory Councils for Vocational Education,
    SACVE
State Capacity Building, SCB
State Compensatory Education, SCE
State Computer Committee (North Dakota), SCC
State Department of Education, SDE
State Department of Education—Information System
    (Minnesota), SDE-IS
State Education Agency, SEA
State Education Department, SED
State Education Research Clearinghouse (California),
    SERCH
State Environmental Education Coordinators
    Association, SEECA
State Higher Education Executive Officers Association,
    SHEEO
State Job Training Coordinating Councils, SJTCC
State Leadership Assistance for Technology in Education
    (U.S. Department of Education), SLATE
State Occupational Information Coordinating
    Committee, SOICC
State Student Assessment Test (Florida), SSAT
State Student Incentive Grants, SSIG
State Teachers Retirement System (Ohio), STRS
State-Trait Anxiety Inventory, STAI
State-Trait Anxiety Inventory for Children, STAIC
Statewide Course Numbering System (Florida), SCNS

Statistical Analysis Group in Education, SAGE
Statistical Analysis System, SAS
Statistical Package for the Social Sciences, SPSS
Stimulus Onset Asynchrony, SOA
Storage and Information Retrieval System, STAIRS
Storage and Retrieval of Bibliographic References
    Program, SRBR
Strengthening Developing Institutions Program, SDIP
Strong Vocational Interest Blank, SVIB
Strong-Campbell Interest Inventory, SCII
Structure of Instruction Rating Scale, SIRS
Structure Of Intellect-Learning Abilities Test, SOI-LA
Structured Environment for the Emotionally Disturbed
    Project, SEED
Structured Pediatric Psychosocial Interview, SPPI
Structured Photographic Language Test, SPLT
Student Accountability Model (California), SAM
Student Census-date Report File, STUCENFL
Student Contact Hours, SCH
Student Credit Hours, SCH
Student Descriptive Questionnaire, SDQ
Student Developmental Task Inventory, SDTI
Student Eligibility Report, SER
Student Guidance Information Service (Ontario), SGIS
Student Loan Insurance Fund, SLIF
Student Loan Marketing Association, SLMA
Student Loan Marketing Association, Sallie Mae
Student National Medical Association, SNMA
Student Needs Assessment Survey, SNAS
Student Organization Development, SOD
Student Press Law Center, SPLC
Student Product Assessment Form, SPAF
Student Science Training Program, SSTP
Student Semester Hours, SSH
Student Teacher Concerns Instrument, STC
Student Teams-Achievement Divisions, STAD
Students' Evaluations of Educational Quality, SEEQ
Student's Perception of Ability Scale, SPAS
Students Taking Action with Recognition (Kentucky),
    STAR
Study Behavior Inventory, SBI
Study of Children's Learning Styles, SCLS
Study of Mathematically Precocious Youth, SMPY
A Study Of Schooling, ASOS
Study Of Values Test, SOV
Study With A Teacher Program (Ohio), SWAT
Subscription Television, STV
Subsidiary Communications Authorization, SCA
Sudden Infant Death Syndrome, SIDS
Suggestive-Accelerative Learning and Teaching, SALT
Suinn Test Anxiety Behavior Scale, STABS
Summer Food Service Program, SFSP
Supervised Occupational Experience, SOE
Supervising Teacher Behavior Description
    Questionnaire, STBDQ
Supervision Through Educational Management By
    Objectives and Results, STEMBOR
Supervisory Behavior Description Questionnaire, SBDQ
Supplemental Educational Opportunity Grants, SEOG
Supplemental Security Income, SSI

Supplemental Tuition Assistance Program (New York), STAP

Survey of Interpersonal Value, SIV

Survey of Pupil Opinion, SURPO

Survey of Student Personnel Objectives, SSPO

Survey of Study Habits and Attitudes, SSHA

Survey, Question, Read, Recite, and Review Method of Reading Instruction, SQ3R

Survey Research Center (Institute for Social Research), SRC

Surveying, Questioning, Reading, Recording, Reciting, and Reflecting Method, SQ4R

Survival Education Association, SEA

Surviving Today's Experiences and Problems Successfully Curriculum (West Virginia), STEPS

Sustained Silent Reading, SSR

Suzuki Association of the Americas, SAA

Sverige-Amerika Stiftelsen (Sweden-America Foundation), SAS

Symmetric Tonic Neck, STN

Symptom Evaluation Survey, SES

Syntactic Density Score, SDS

Syracuse University Resources for Educators of Adults, SUREA

System Development Corporation, SDC

System for Pupil and Program Evaluation and Development, SPPED

System of Interactive Guidance and Information, SIGI

System Of Multicultural, Pluarlistic Assessment, SOMPA

Systematic Training for Effective Parenting, STEP

Systeme de projections des professions au Canada, SPPC

Systems and Procedures Exchange Center (Association of Research Libraries), SPEC

Systems Information Processing Analysis, SIPA

Talented And Gifted, TAG

Talking Screen Textwriting Program, TSTP

Tapping Achievement Potential Project, TAP

Targeted Jobs Demonstration Program, TJDP

Targeted Jobs Tax Credit, TJTC

Task Attribution Questionnaire, TAQ

Task Force on Computers in Chemical Education (American Chemical Society), TFCCE

Tax Equity and Fiscal Responsibility Act, TEFRA

Tax Sheltered Annuity, TSA

Teacher Assessment of Leverage, TAL

Teacher Authoring System, TAS

Teacher Certification Test, TCT

Teacher Concerns Questionnaire, TCQ

Teacher Education and Computer Centers (California), TECC

Teacher Education And Mathematics Project, TEAM

Teacher Education Centers, TEC

Teacher Effectiveness Training, TET

Teacher Occupational Stress Factor Questionnaire, TOSFQ

Teacher Organized Training for the Acquisition of Language, TOTAL

Teacher Participation Project, TPP

Teacher Performance Assessment Instruments, TPAI

Teacher Performance Evaluation, TPE

Teacher Rating Form, TRF

Teacher Recruitment for Educational Excellence, TREE

Teacher Stress Scale, TSS

Teacher-Based Instruction, TBI

Teachers Insurance and Annuity Association, TIAA

Teachers of English as an Additional Language (British Columbia), TEAL

Teachers of English to Speakers of Other Languages, TESOL

Teacher's Questionnaire Inventory, TQI

Teacher's Report Form of the Child Behavior Checklist, TRF

Teaching Analysis By Students, TABS

Teaching Appraisal for Instructional Improvement Instrument, TA III

Teaching English as a Foreign Language, TEFL

Teaching English as a Second Language, TESL

Teaching Events Stress Inventory, TESI

Teaching, Learning and Curriculum Model, TLC

Team-Assisted Individualization, TAI

Technical And Further Education (Australia), TAFE

Technical Assistance Centers, TAC

Technical Assistance Development System (Handicapped Children's Early Education Program), TADS

Technical Assistance Project, TAP

Technical Education Research Center, Inc., TERC

Technical Information Center (U.S. Department of Energy), TIC

Technician Education Council (Great Britain), TEC

Telecommunications Device for the Deaf, TDD

Television Computer Assisted Instruction, TVCAI

"Tell-Me-A-Story" Thematic Appreciation Test, TEMAS

Templin-Darley Test of Articulation, TDTA

Tendency to Seek Help Questionnaire, TSH

Tennessee Business Education Association, TBEA

Tennessee Self-Concept Scale, TSCS

Test Anxiety Inventory, TAI

Test Anxiety Scale for Children, TASC

Test of Auditory Comprehension of Language, TACL

Test Of Basic Experiences, TOBE

Test of Early Language Development, TELD

Test of Ecology Comprehension, TEC

Test of Engery Concepts and Values, TECV

Test of English as a Foreign Language, TEFL

Test Of English as a Foreign Language, TOEFL

Test Of English for International Communication, TOEIC

Test of General Information, TGI

Test of Integrated Process Skills, TIPS

Test Of Language Development, TOLD

Test Of Logical Thinking, TOLT

Test Of Reading Comprehension, TORC

Test of Spoken English, TSE

Test of Standard Written English, TSWE

Test of Syntactic Abilities, TSA

Test Of Written Language, TOWL

Tests of Achievement and Proficiency, TAP

Tests of Adult Basic Education, TABE

Tetreau-Trahan Visual Interest Test, TTVIT

Texas Assessment Modeling Systems, TAMS

Texas Assessment of Basic Skills, TABS
Texas Association for Bilingual Education, TABE
Texas Association for Community Service and Continuing Education, TACSCE
Texas Association for Educational Data Systems, TAEDS
Texas Computer Education Association, TCEA
Texas Council of Industrial Arts Supervisors, TCIAS
Texas Council on Industrial Arts Teacher Education, TCIATE
Texas Data Base System, TDBS
Texas Foreign Language Association, TFLA
Texas Part-Time Work Experience Program, PT-WEX
Texas Preschool Screening Inventory, TPSI
Texas Social Behavior Inventory, TSBI
Texas State Library Communications Network, TSLNC
Texas Student Information System, TEXSIS
Theatre Library Association, TLA
Thematic Appreciation Test, TAT
Theory and Research Special Interest Group (Association for the Development of Computer-Based Instructional Systems), SIG/TAR
Thinking Creatively in Action and Movement Test, TCAM
TIAA-College Retirement Equities Fund, TIAA-CREF
Time-Shared, Interactive, Computer-Controlled Information Television, TICCIT
Title I Evaluation and Reporting System, TIERS
Token Test, TT
Torrance Test of Creative Thinking, TTCT
Toxicology Information Online (National Library of Medicine), TOXLINE
Trades Education (Great Britain), TRADEC
Traditionally Black Institutions, TBI
Trainable Mentally Handicapped, TMH
Trainable Mentally Retarded, TMR
Training Access (British Columbia), TRAC
Training Analysis and Evaluation Group (Department of the Navy), TAEG
Training Program Evaluation, TPE
Training, Research and Assistance Cooperative Extension Service, TRACES
Transactional Analysis, TA
Transborder Data Flow, TDF
Transportation Officer Basic Course (U.S. Army), TOBC
Transportation Research Information Service, TRIS
Traveling Scholar Program, TSP
Trilanguage Education Learning Environment Program (New York City), TELE
Tripoli Science Association, TSA
Tri-State Parenting Collaborative Project (Minnesota, North Dakota, South Dakota), TSPC
Tuition Assistance Program (New York), TAP
Tuition Exchange, TE
Tuition Tax Credit, TTC
Tukey's Honestly Significant Difference Test, HSD
Tune-in, Question, Listen, Review Technique, TQLR
Tutoring Adults through Literacy Councils, TALC
Type-Token Ratio, TTR
Ukranian Library Association of America, ULAA

Ukranian Political Science Association in the United States, UPSA
Undergraduate Pre-Service Science Teacher Education Program (Iowa), UPSTEP
Unified School District, USD
Unified Sciences and Mathematics for Elementary Schools, USMES
Uniform Child Custody Jurisdiction Act, UCCJA
Uniform Performance Assessment System, UPAS
Uninterrupted Sustained Silent Reading, USSR
Union for Experimenting Colleges and Universities, UECU
Union List of Selected Serials of Michigan, ULOSSOM
Unisex Edition of the American College Testing Program Interest Inventory, UNIACT
United Campuses to Prevent Nuclear War, UCPNW
United Federation of College Teachers, UFCT
United Federation of Teachers, UFT
United Indians of All Tribes Foundation, UIATF
United Nations Children's Fund, UNICEF
United Nations Education Project, UNEP
United Nations Educational, Scientific, and Cultural Organization, UNESCO
United Negro College Fund, UNCF
United Parent-Teachers Association of Jewish Schools, UPTA
United States Information Agency, USIA
United States Institute for Theatre Technology, USITT
United States Student Association, USSA
United States Student Travel Service, USSTS
United States Youth Soccer Association, USYSA
United Student Aid Funds, USA Funds
United Students and Techers for Educational Development, USTED
United Synagogue Commission on Jewish Education, USCJE
Universal Bibliographic Control, UBC
Universal Decimal Classification, UDC
Universal Library System Ltd., ULISYS
Universal Primary Education, UPE
Universal Proutist Student Federation, UPSF
Universal Serials and Book Exchange, USBE
University Affiliated Facility, UAF
University and College Designers Association, UCDA
University and College Theatre Association, UCTA
University Aviation Association, UAA
University Consortium for Instructional Development and Technology, UCIDT
University Council for Educational Administration, UCEA
University Field Staff International, UFSI
University Field Staff International—Institute of World Affairs, UFSI-IWA
University Film and Video Association, UFVA
University Film and Video Foundation, UFVF
University Microfilms International, UMI
University Photographers Association of America, UPAA
University Professors for Academic Order, UPAO
University Risk Management and Insurance Association, URMIA

Up With People, UWP
Upper Midwest Regional Educational Laboratory, UMREL
Upward Bound, UB
Urban Affairs Association, UAA
Urban Crime Prevention Program, UCPP
Urban Development Action Grant, UDAG
Urban Libraries Council, ULC
Urban Mass Transportation Administration (U.S. Department of Transportation), UMTA
U.S. Office of Personnel Management, OPM
Used For, UF
Utah Council for Computers in Education, UCCE
Validation, Verification, and Testing (of Software), VVT
Validity Network Schema, VNS
Value-Added Tax, VAT
Venereal Disease, VD
Ventures in Community Improvement Demonstration Project, VICI
Verbal Scale Intelligence Quotient, VSIQ
Vermont Business Teachers Association, VBTA
Vernacular Black English, VBE
Veterans Administration, VA
Veterans' Educational Assistance Program, VEAP
Veterinary Aptitude Test, VAT
Video Long Play, VLP
Videocassette Recorder, VCR
Videodisc Authoring and Production Systems, VAPS
Videodisc Player, VDP
Videodisc Training Delivery System, VTDS
Videodiscs Interactive with Microcomputers Project (U.S. Department of Education), VIM
Video-Documentary Clearinghouse, VDC
Videotape Recorder, VTR
Vineland Adaptive Behavior Scale, VABS
Vineland Social Maturity Scale, VSMS
Virginia Association for Institutional Research, VAIR
Visualizer-Verbalizer Questionnaire, VVQ
Vital Information on Education and Work, VIEW
Vocabulary Review Group (Educational Resources Information Center), VRG
Vocational Adult Secondary Training (British Columbia), VAST
Vocational and Occupational Information Center for Educators (California), VOICE
Vocational Decision-Making Difficulty Scale, VDMD
Vocational Development Checklist, VDC
Vocational Development Inventory, VDI
Vocational Education Act, VEA
Vocational Education Curriculum Materials, VECM
Vocational Education Data System, VEDS
Vocational Education Evaluation and Assessment Process (Pennsylvania), VEEAP
Vocational Education for the Handicapped, VEH
Vocational English as a Second Langauge, VESL
Vocational Industrial Clubs of America, VICA
Vocational Preference Inventory, VPI
Vocational Rehabilitation, VR
Vocational Rehabilitation Program Standards Evaluation System, VRPSES
Vocational Technical and Adult Education, VTAE

Vocational-Technical, V-T
Vocational-Technical Education Consortium of States, V-TECS
Voice-Based Learning System, VBLS
Volunteers in Service to America, VISTA
Volunteers in Technical Assistance, VITA
Vowel Matching Test, VMT
Walker Problem Behavior Identification Checklist, WPBIC
Wallace Self-Concept Scale, WSCS
Warrent Officer Candidate Military Development Course (U.S. Army), WOCMDC
Washington Center for Learning Alternatives, WCLA
Washington Child Development Council (District of Columbia), WCDC
Washington Library Network, WLN
Washington Pre-College Test, WPC
Washington Public Employees Retirement System, WPERS
Washington State Teachers Retirement System, WSTRS
Washington Workshop Foundation, WWF
Water Quality Instructional Resources Information System, IRIS
Watson-Glaser Critical Thinking Appraisal, WGCTA
Ways to Improve Education in Desegregated Schools Project (Southwest Educational Development Laboratory), WIEDS
Wechsler Adult Intelligence Scale, WAIS
Wechsler Intelligence Scale for Children, WISC
Wechsler Intelligence Scale for Children—Revised, WISC-R
Wechsler Memory Scale, WMS
Wechsler Preschool and Primary Scale of Intelligence, WPPSI
Weighted Common Examination Total, WCET
Wepman Auditory Discrimination Test, ADT
West Virginia Assessment And Tracking System, WVAATS
West Virginia Business Education Association, WVBEA
Western Association of Schools and Colleges, WASC
Western College Association, WCA
Western College Reading and Learning Association, WCRLA
Western College Reading Association, WCRA
Western Curriculum Coordination Center, WCCC
Western Educational Society for Telecommunications, WEST
Western Interpreters Association, WIA
Western Interstate Commission for Higher Education, WICHE
Western Interstate Library Coordinating Organization, WILCO
Western Ohio Regional Library Development System, WORLDS
Western Psychological Association, WPA
What I Think and Feel, WITF
Wide Angle Mobility Light, WAML
Wide-Area Telecommunications Service, WATS
Widening Occupational Roles Kit, WORK
Wide-Range Achievement Test, WRAT
Wiig-Semel Test of Linguistic Concepts, WST

Wilderness Education Association, WEA
Wilderness Leadership International, WLI
Wildlife Management Institute, WMI
Willingness to Risk Questionnaire, WRQ
Winston Churchill Foundation, WCF
Wisconsin Card Sorting Test, WCST
Wisconsin Career Information System, WCIS
Wisconsin Competency Based Occupational
  Curriculum Data System, WisCom
Wisconsin Design for Reading Skill Development,
  WDRSD
Wisconsin Elementary and Secondary School
  Accounting System, WESSAS
Wisconsin Information Resources for Education, WIRE
Wisconsin Instructional Computing Consortium, WICC
Wisconsin Procedure for Appraisal of Clinical
  Competence, W-PACC
Wisconsin Program for the Renewal and Improvement
  of Secondary Education, WRISE
Wisconsin System for Instructional Management, WIS-
  SIM
Woman Library Workers, WLW
Women As Manager Scales, WAMS
Women Band Directors National Association, WBNA
Women Educators, WE
Women in Mathematics Education, WME
Women In Scholarly Publishing, WISP
Women in Science Scale, WiSS
Women On Words and Images, WOWI
Women's Caucus for Political Science, WCPS
Women's Caucus for the Modern Languages, WCML
Women's Caucus: Religious Studies, WC:RS
Women's College Coalition, WCC
Women's Computer Literacy Project, WCLP
Women's Education Equity Act, WEEA
Women's Education Equity Act Program, WEEAP
Women's Equity Action League, WEAL
Women's Role Questionnaire Scale, WRQ
Woodcock Reading Mastery Test, WRMT
Woodcock-Johnson Psycho-Educational Battery,
  WJPEB
Woodcock-Johnson Tests of Cognitive Ability, WJTCA
Woodrow Wilson National Fellowship Foundation,
  WWNFF
Word Processing, WP
Work and Family Orientation Scale, WFOS
Work Experience Career Exploration Program, WECEP
Work Experience Liberal Arts Program, WELAP
Work Experience Program, WEP
Work Performance Survey System, WPSS
Working at Student Time-Saving in Education Project
  (Illinois), WASTE
Working Memory, WM
World Administration Radio Conference, WARC
World Confederation of Organizations of the Teaching
  Profession, WCOTP
World Conference on Computers in Education, WCCE
World Council for Curriculum and Instruction, WCCI
World Council for Gifted and Talented Children,
  WCGTC
World Education, WE

World Education Fellowship, WEF
World Event/Interaction Survey, WEIS
World Federation of the Deaf, WFD
World Health Organization, WHO
World Modeling Association, WMA
World Science Information System (UNESCO),
  UNISIST
Writing Skills Assessment Test, WSAT
Writing-Aid And Author's Helper, WANDAH
Wyoming Educational Computing Council, WECC
Wyoming Infant Stimulation Program, WISP
Year Round Education, YRE
Young Adult Services Division (American Library
  Association), YASD
Young Adults, YA
Young Children's Social Desirability Scale, YCSDS
Young People's LOGO Association, YPLA
Your Style Of Learning And Thinking Inventory,
  SOLAT
Youth Career Information Project (Northwest Regional
  Educational Laboratory), YCIP
Youth Community Conservation and Community
  Improvement Programs, YCCIP
Youth Effectiveness Training, YET
Youth Employment and Demonstration Project Act,
  YEDPA
Youth Employment and Training Program, YETP
Youth Entitlement Incentive Pilot Projects, YIEPP
Youth For Understanding, YFU
Youth Resources, YR